Law and Society
Recent Scholarship

Edited by Melvin I. Urofsky

A Series from LFB Scholarly

The Press and Rights to Privacy

First Amendment Freedoms vs. Invasion of Privacy Claims

Erin K. Coyle

LFB Scholarly Publishing LLC
El Paso 2012

Library of Congress Cataloging-in-Publication Data

Coyle, Erin K., 1977-
The press and rights to privacy : First Amendment freedoms vs. invasion of privacy claims / Erin K. Coyle.
p. cm. -- (Law and society)
Includes bibliographical references and index.
ISBN 978-1-59332-493-3 (hardcover : alk. paper)
1. Freedom of the press--United States. 2. Privacy, Right of--United States. 3. Press law--United States. I. Title.
KF4774.C69 2012
342.7308'53--dc23

2012001981

ISBN 978-1-59332-493-3

Printed on acid-free 250-year-life paper.

Manufactured in the United States of America.

Table of Contents

Acknowledgments

I owe many people thanks for the guidance and support that they have contributed to numerous projects integral to the development of this book. I am especially thankful for the thoughtful comments that Ruth Walden, R. Michael Hoefges, Donald Shaw, Anne Klinefelter, Tom Hodson, and Louis Day provided on projects related to this book and earlier drafts of this book. I am grateful to each of them and to my colleagues at the Manship School for asking probing questions and engaging in numerous discussions that have helped expand the scope my research.

I am indebted to the Manship School for the generous research support provided for this book through the William K. "Bill" Carville Professorship and the J. Patrick Gebhhart Professorship.

Finally, I would like to thank Michael James, Kathryn Mary, David Weibel, Elise Bernard, Tom Vizcarrando, Jeremy Padgett, and Joanna Zimmerman for proofreading chapters.

CHAPTER 1

The Right to Publish and Rights to Privacy

In October 1983, a woman told a representative of the Duval County Sheriff's Department in Florida that she was robbed and raped at knife-point. The department placed that incident report, which included the full name of the woman, B.J.F., in the pressroom, where journalists copied reports for publication.[1] After a reporter-trainee for The *Florida Star* found the incident report, the weekly newspaper published B.J.F.'s full name, identifying her as a female who reported she was robbed and sexually assaulted, "violat[ing] its internal policy of not publishing the names of sexual offense victims."[2] B.J.F. subsequently testified that she learned from co-workers and acquaintances that the weekly newspaper had published details from her incident report. Her mother received phone calls from a man who threatened to rape B.J.F. again. Distressed by the embarrassing disclosure and resulting threats, B.J.F. changed her phone number and residence and sought police protection and mental health counseling.[3]

Almost two years later, in 1985, B.J.F. sued the sheriff's department and The Florida Star for invading her privacy by publishing her full name in their descriptions of crimes reported to the Duval County Sheriff's Department.[4] She sought damages for the department's and newspaper's violation of a Florida statute that stated, ""'No person shall print, publish, or broadcast, or cause or allow to be printed, published, or broadcast, in any instrument of mass communication the name, address, or other identifying fact or information of the victim of any sexual offense.'""[5] Before the claims were tried, the sheriff's department settled with B.J.F. for $2,500. The newspaper, however, argued at trial that sanctioning the press was unconstitutional because its trainee-reporter had found B.J.F.'s name in an incident report available for public viewing in the sheriff's department. A jury found the newspaper was liable for $75,000 in compensatory and $25,000 in punitive damages, and in a 1986 per curiam opinion, the First District Court of Appeals upheld that verdict.[6] Almost a year later, the Florida Supreme Court declined to review the case.[7]

A Landmark Ruling

In June 1989, however, the U.S. Supreme Court reversed the lower courts' findings in a landmark 6-3 ruling that some legal experts have criticized for favoring the right to publish over the right to privacy.[8] Writing for the majority in *Florida Star v. B.J.F.*, Justice Thurgood Marshall acknowledged that there is "tension between the right which the First Amendment accords to a free press, on the one hand, and the protections which various statutes and common-law doctrines accord to personal privacy against the publication of truthful information, on the other. . . ."[9] Reasoning that "press freedom and privacy rights are both 'plainly rooted in the traditions and significant concerns of our society,'" Justice Marshall described privacy and free expression interests as sufficiently sensitive and significant to "counsel relying on limited principles that sweep no more broadly than the appropriate context of the instant case."[10] Thus, the Court refrained from determining whether truthful publication "is automatically constitutionally protected" or whether there is a "zone of personal privacy within which the State may protect the individual from intrusion by the press."[11]

<u>Favoring a right to publish</u>

Justice Marshall noted that the Court had "without exception upheld the press' (sic) right to publish" by focusing on the conflict "only as it arose in a discrete factual context" when ruling on clashes between press freedom and privacy.[12] Reasoning that the reporter truthfully reported lawfully obtained information relevant to a matter of public significance, the majority found that imposing damages on The Florida Star for publishing B.J.F.'s name violated the First Amendment.

The Court noted that neither party contended the newspaper had reported inaccurate information, nor did the reporter-trainee violate the law by finding information erroneously made available to the public by the government. Moreover the reported information pertained to a matter of public significance, "a matter of paramount public import: the commission, and investigation, of a violent crime which had been reported to authorities."[13] Finally, the Court found that imposing liability for violating the Florida statute was not essential to furthering three highly significant interests—protecting the privacy of sexual assault victims, protecting the safety of victims, and encouraging the reporting of sexual assault–which might be considered interests of the highest order in some cases. Justice Marshall indicated that the state law failed to serve the asserted interests because it was underinclusive, targeting only instruments of mass communication. The court held, "[W]here a newspaper publishes truthful information which it has lawfully obtained, punishment may lawfully be imposed, if at all, only when narrowly tailored to a state interest of the highest order."[14] *Florida Star*, thus, established a qualified constitutional privilege for mass media disclosures of matters of public significance.[15]

Criticizing the majority

In a dissenting opinion in which Chief Justice Rehnquist and Justice O'Connor joined, Justice White asserted that the majority's holding in *Florida Star* accepted "the appellant's invitation to obliterate one of the most noteworthy legal inventions of the 20th century: the tort of the publication of private facts."[16] At that time in many states, common law or statutory law allowed individuals to file suit for an invasion of privacy under a disclosure of private facts theory. That allowed individuals to seek legal redress for harm resulting from the widespread disclosure of such sensitive truthful information that a reasonable person would find the disclosure highly objectionable. Justice White faulted the Court for failing to attempt to balance the right to privacy and "the public's right to know about matters of general concern."[17]

The Evolution of a Contemporary Conflict

Attempts to balance the constitutional right to publish and tort-based rights to privacy are relatively new. Privacy law is only a little more than 100 years old and still evolving.[18] Most states have recognized at least one of the four types of privacy tort actions during that time. As state and federal appellate courts have considered what legal standards should be applied in their jurisdictions, they have examined the relatively short history of common law privacy torts as well as a short list of U.S. Supreme Court cases involving privacy tort conflicts with the First Amendment.

Seeking protection against controversial journalistic practices

Legal commentators generally recognize an 1890 *Harvard Law Review* article as the origin of laws that protect individuals from media invasions of privacy in the United States.[19] In that article, "The Right to Privacy," Samuel D. Warren and Louis D. Brandeis called on judges to extend the common law to protect the "inviolate personality," or inner person, from unwanted public exposure likely to result from keyhole journalism.[20] The tendency for journalists to report details about individuals' personal lives led some people to equate reporting with peering through keyholes to pry into private realms. Warren and Brandeis, attorneys in Boston at that time, argued that judges should develop common law to protect individuals from the emotional distress resulting from unwanted public disclosures of personal information "as part of a more general right to immunity of the person."[21] In their article, the attorneys observed that newspaper reporters and amateur photographers were intruding on private affairs to collect personal information and powerful images that would lure readers to purchase newspapers.[22] They wrote:

> Instantaneous photographs and newspaper enterprises have invaded the sacred precincts of private and domestic life. Gossip is no longer the resource of the idle and of the vicious, but has become a trade, which is pursued with industry as well as effrontery. To occupy the indolent, column upon column is filled with idle gossip, which can only be procured by intrusion upon the domestic circle.[23]

Hundreds of law review articles subsequently cited the Warren and Brandeis article as a foundation for common law and statutory remedies addressing invasions of privacy.[24] Warren and Brandeis were reacting to technological and cultural changes that affected many Americans. Some legal experts have theorized that the young attorneys also were responding to personal concerns about newspaper coverage of the Warren family. A landmark article published in the California Law Review in 1960 suggests that Warren and Brandeis wrote "The

Right to Privacy" because Warren was upset by newspaper coverage of a Warren family member's wedding,[25] and an article published in the Michigan State Law Review in 2008 argues that Warren was upset by multiple newspapers' coverage of his marriage to a Senator's daughter who was part of a prominent political family "in the public eye."[26] Warren and Brandeis's arguments for a common law right to privacy were published when the yellow press, which one journalism historian described as "a product of a lusty, fiercely competitive, and intolerant time," published sensational details about individuals.[27]

<u>Seeking protection against instantaneous photography</u>

Many Americans desired respite, reserve, and secrecy as surges in urban populations and newspaper circulations challenged the physical and social boundaries that traditionally allowed individuals to protect their intimate lives from public scrutiny during the final decades of the nineteenth century.[28] Some feared how they would be portrayed in photographs captured by the "snap camera," an affordable and portable camera that "enabled people to take candid pictures and created a 'craze' for amateur photography."[29] At that time, Americans' conception of privacy related to a desire for protection against emotional distress caused by individuals' losses of control over their personal information and public image.[30] Those concerns initially were addressed by appropriation, the first privacy tort recognized by state statute in New York in 1903[31] and under common law in Georgia in 1905,[32] the tort that addressed harms resulting from the unauthorized use of individuals' photographs for commercial purposes, such as advertisements, which were not protected by the First Amendment at that time. By 1911, nine states had recognized a statutory or common law right to privacy, or right to be let alone.[33]

<u>Expanding recognition of privacy torts by states</u>

Privacy laws developed slowly during the first quarter of the twentieth century before the U.S. Supreme Court announced that the First Amendment applied to the states via the Fourteenth Amendment in 1925 in *Gitlow v. New York*.[34] The Court's ruling in that case, which involved the constitutionality of a conviction under a state criminal anarchy statute, provided the foundation for constitutional defenses to limit common law and statutory claims.[35] Despite the potential for press freedom and state statutes to clash as a result of *Gitlow*, courts and legislatures continued to recognize the right to privacy.[36]

In 1939, members of the American Law Institute — attorneys and legal scholars responsible for drafting and approving official reports on trends in American law[37] — recognized the right of privacy in the *Restatement of Torts*.[38] The original *Restatement* section declared, "[A] person who unreasonably and seriously interferes with another's interest in not having his affairs known to others or his likeness exhibited to the public is liable to the other."[39] By 1960, William Prosser, the great twentieth century American tort scholar,[40] found more than 300 court rulings had recognized a legal right to privacy. He categorized those rulings as four distinct privacy torts:

1) Intrusion upon the plaintiff's seclusion or solitude, or into his private affairs.
2) Public disclosure of embarrassing private facts about the plaintiff.
3) Publicity which places the plaintiff in a false light in the public eye.
4) Appropriation, for the defendant's advantage, of the plaintiff's name or likeness.[41]

In that article, Prosser also acknowledged that the right of privacy already "came into head-on collision with the constitutional guaranty of freedom of the press. The result was the slow evolution of a compromise between the two."[42] Prosser explained that limited privileges had evolved to recognize "the rights of the press." One prevented plaintiffs from prevailing in cases involving publicity given to public figures. The second prevented plaintiffs from prevailing in cases focusing on the publicizing of newsworthy information, or matters of public interest.[43]

Professor Edward Bloustein, a philosopher and expert on tort law, criticized Prosser's reduction of the common law invasion of privacy into torts that "involve violations of 'four different interests,' none of which, it turns out, is a distinctive interest in privacy."[44] Bloustein suggested that an individual's sense of human dignity and one's liberty to act according to her personal will are both distinctive interests that privacy laws ought to protect. Other scholars subsequently have argued that Prosser's categorization has stunted the development of privacy law and influenced the tendency for courts to "consider privacy and free speech to be always in direct conflict."[45]

Deciding tort actions may limit First Amendment freedoms

Courts referred to conflicts between state free press and privacy rights during the first half of the twentieth century. Reported privacy cases, however, did not invoke the First Amendment until the mid-1960s.[46] The U.S. Supreme Court set the foundation for common law tort actions to trigger First Amendment protection in 1964 in *New York Times v. Sullivan*, a defamation case filed by a Montgomery, Alabama, commissioner. The Court held that the First Amendment forbids a state from awarding damages to a public official plaintiff unless a media defendant published the information with actual malice, meaning knowledge of falsity or reckless disregard for the truth of the information.[47] Three years later, in *Time, Inc. v. Hill*, the Court handed down its first ruling on First Amendment press rights and state privacy torts, extending the actual malice rule created in *Sullivan* to false light invasion of privacy cases involving discussion of matters of public concern.[48]

Clarifying the threat privacy torts pose for the press

Five years after *Time Inc. v. Hill,* Don R. Pember provided one of the most significant analyses of privacy law for professional journalists.[49] Pember's 1972 book, *Privacy and the Press: The Law, The Mass Media, and The First Amendment*, traced the evolution of the legal right to privacy through invasion of privacy suits filed against media defendants in the United States. He identified three types of media actions that led to privacy suits: "1) The use of an individual's name or photograph in an advertisement without his consent; 2) the publication of private information about an individual; and 3) the publication of nondefamatory falsehoods about a person."[50]

Pember's book provided an important foundation for scholarship examining how state and federal courts had reconciled common law invasion of privacy rights with the First Amendment right of freedom of the press. His study suggested that state courts had recognized the inevitable conflict between press and privacy rights for decades although the U.S. Supreme Court had ruled on only one tort-based invasion of privacy case that involved a media defendant.[51] Since then, the Supreme Court, federal appellate courts, and many state high courts have handed down scores of rulings involving the press and privacy torts—often citing *Florida Star* and the trilogy of cases on which that ruling relied.

Florida Star and Its Progeny

In 1989, a 6-3 U.S. Supreme Court ruling established a constitutional privilege that shielded the truthful reporting of lawfully obtained information relevant to a matter of public significance against sanction by a state law, unless that law served a state interest of the highest order and was narrowly tailored to serve that interest.[52] That constitutional principle combined key principles from three of the Court's previous rulings involving press freedom and privacy rights: *Cox Broadcasting Corp. v. Cohn,*[53] *Oklahoma Publishing Co. v. District Court,*[54] and *Smith v. Daily Mail Publishing Co.*[55]

Cox Broadcasting Corp. v. Cohn

In 1975 in *Cox Broadcasting*, the Court ruled that a broadcast station could not constitutionally be sanctioned for publishing the name of a deceased 17-year-old rape victim when the name was obtained from court records open to public inspection.[56] In that ruling, Justice Byron White recognized the potential for press freedom and privacy to conflict in a disclosure of private facts case. He wrote:

> Because the gravamen of the claimed injury is the publication of information, whether true or not, the dissemination of which is embarrassing or otherwise painful to an individual, it is here that claims of privacy most directly confront the constitutional freedoms of speech and press.[57]

White continued, "In this sphere of collision between claims of privacy and those of the free press, the interests on both sides are plainly rooted in the traditions and significant concerns of our society."[58] The Court was limited to focusing on the narrow question raised by the controversy at issue in the case—whether a state may sanction a news outlet for accurately broadcasting the name of a rape victim when that name was obtained from judicial records open to public inspection. It held that the First and Fourteenth Amendments forbid a state from sanctioning the press for "truthfully publishing information released to the public in official court records."[59] Justice White reasoned that judicial proceedings resulting from the commission of crime "are without question events of legitimate concern to the public and consequently fall within the responsibility of the press to report the operations of government."[60]

Although *Cox Broadcasting* and *Florida Star* both involved the disclosure of rape victims' names, Justice Marshall indicated in the latter ruling that the facts at issue in those cases were sufficiently distinct to prevent *Cox Broadcasting* from being read as controlling in *Florida Star.*[61] *Cox Broadcasting* involved the broadcast of a deceased rape victim's name when that information was available from judicial records.[62] The information in *Florida Star* was obtained from a law enforcement record reporting the occurrence of a crime.[63] Because B.J.F.'s name was obtained and published before judicial proceedings commenced, Justice Marshall asserted that the rationale for *Cox Broadcasting* that recognized the press served an important function by exposing judicial proceedings to public scrutiny was not applicable to *Florida Star.*[64]

Oklahoma Publishing Co. v. District Court

Two years after *Cox Broadcasting*, the Court relied on that ruling when considering in *Oklahoma Publishing Co. v. District Court* whether the First and Fourteenth Amendments prevented a state court from prohibiting "the publication of widely disseminated information obtained at court proceedings which were in fact open to the public."[65] That case arose after an Oklahoma District Court enjoined members of the news media from publishing or disseminating the name or picture of a minor in connection with a juvenile court proceeding, although an 11-year-old boy accused of killing a railroad switchman appeared in a detention hearing journalists were allowed to attend.[66] The Court held that a state court could not constitutionally enjoin members of the news media from publishing the name or photograph of a juvenile when the information was lawfully obtained and publicly available.[67]

Smith v. Daily Mail Publishing Co.

Cox Broadcasting and *Oklahoma Publishing* both shaped the First Amendment principle established in 1979 in *Smith v. Daily Mail Publishing Co.*,[68] the principle that Justice Marshall used to analyze

Florida Star. In *Daily Mail*, the Supreme Court considered whether a West Virginia statute violated the First and Fourteenth Amendments by allowing the state to impose criminal sanctions on any newspaper that published the name of a youth charged as a juvenile offender, unless the newspaper had obtained the prior written approval of the juvenile court. That case arose after two newspapers published the name of a 14-year-old student accused of shooting and killing a 15-year-old at a junior high school. As was true in *Cox Broadcasting* and *Oklahoma Publishing Co.*, the government had made the identity available to the public prior to the news media's disclosure. In *Daily Mail*, the Court reasoned, "[I]f a newspaper lawfully obtains truthful information about a matter of public significance then state officials may not constitutionally punish publication of the information, absent a need to further a state interest of the highest order."[69] Thus, the First and Fourteenth Amendments did not allow the government to impose liability for the newspapers' publication of the juvenile defendant's identity.

Florida Star v. B.J.F.

Justice Marshall later asserted in *Florida Star* that the *Daily Mail* principle required the Court to reverse the lower courts' rulings for B.J.F.[70] In a dissenting opinion, Justice White disagreed, asserting that neither *Cox Broadcasting*, *Oklahoma Publishing*, nor *Daily Mail* required "the harsh outcome" reached by the majority in *Florida Star*.[71] Justice White argued that *Florida Star* involved the disclosure of a rape victim's name erroneously released in an incident report,[72] but *Cox Broadcasting* involved the publication of a victim's name released in judicial proceedings that were open to the public, which "made public disclosure of the victim's name almost inevitable."[73] Second, Justice White argued that *Daily Mail* involved the disclosure of the name of a person accused of committing a crime, which does not raise the same privacy concerns involved when a crime victim's name is released.[74] He asserted that the *Daily Mail* ruling states that "*there is no issue here of privacy*," thus the privacy issue in *Florida Star* places that case "outside of *Daily Mail's* 'rule.'"[75] He argued that the Florida statute did precisely what the Court required in *Cox Broadcasting*—it required the state to avoid releasing sensitive information to the public rather than sanction news media for publishing information the state made available to the public.[76]

In the dissenting opinion, Justice White wrote that he would have "protect[ed] B.J.F.'s desire for privacy and peace-of-mind" and found "no public interest in immunizing the press from liability in the rare cases where a State's efforts to protect a victim's privacy have failed."[77] He argued that releasing the name of a rape victim did not serve a public interest, and thus he would not suggest the First Amendment shielded the Florida Star from liability for publishing that sensitive information. Justice White reasoned, "[I]t is not too much to ask the press, in instances such as this, to respect simple standards of decency and refrain from publishing a victim's name, address, and/or phone number."[78] That suggests the First Amendment should not automatically protect insensitive disclosures of details that are more likely to satisfy individuals' curiosity than they are to serve the public's right to know about public safety or public officials performance of public duties.

Bartnicki v. Vopper

More than a decade later, a narrow majority of the U.S. Supreme Court cited *Florida Star* to support a narrow, fact-tied holding in a 2001 ruling involving a First Amendment right to disclose matters of public importance and privacy-related torts. In that case, *Bartnicki v. Vopper*, the Court indicated that "'the sensitivity and the significance of interests presented in clashes between First Amendment and privacy rights'" require case-by-case analysis of those interests.[79] That 5-4 ruling indicates that important interests may be found "on both sides of the constitutional calculus."[80] Nonetheless, the Court refrained from seriously discussing the privacy interests at issue in the case. In that case, which was filed after a radio station broadcast a recording of an illegally-intercepted telephone conversation between two public school union members discussing ongoing collective bargaining negotiationswith the school board, the Court limited its focus to the First Amendment protections for the disclosure of truthful information of public concern. The majority held that a radio talk show host could not be held liable constitutionally for invasion of privacy because he had broadcast truthful and lawfully-obtained information on a matter of public concern. The Court asserted, "In these cases, privacy concerns give way when balanced against the interest in publishing matters of public importance."[81]

The Court concluded that the specific recording in question involved a matter of public concern – "months of negotiations over the proper level of compensation for teachers" – and that a "stranger's illegal conduct" in intercepting the call and leaking it to the media did "not suffice to remove the First Amendment shield" applied in the case.[82] Imposing sanctions on "the publication of truthful information of public concern," according to the Supreme Court, "implicates the core purposes of the First Amendment."[83] The majority found that the public's interest in learning about a matter of public debate must supersede the privacy interests at issue when information was lawfully obtained and truthfully reported.

In the dissenting opinion, Chief Justice Rehnquist argued that "the Court's decision diminishes, rather than enhances, the purposes of the First Amendment," in a time when "millions of Americans" communicate via electronic technology, heightening concerns about threats to privacy. Rehnquist focused on individuals' willingness to communicate freely when they expect technology may help them control who may receive specific information. "The chilling effect of the Court's decisions upon these conversations will surely be great."[84]

Thus, the U.S. Supreme Court has declared that freedom of expression and privacy both serve important societal interests.[85] Recent majority rulings, however, have indicated that free expression interests should trump tort-based privacy interests when disclosed information pertains to matters of public significance, or public importance.[86] While that approach appears to favor free expression interests, many questions remain unanswered about what details could be considered matters of public importance. Given that resulting lack of certainty, the constitutional exception for disclosures of matters of public significance ultimately could be less speech-protective than the common law principle that exempts disclosures of matters of public interest from liability for invasion of privacy.

Post-*Florida Star* Tensions for Press Freedom and Privacy

Since the Court published *Florida Star*, legal experts have suggested the Court's failure to create clear guidelines has a potentially chilling effect on the press's freedom to publish. In 1991, Jane Kirtley, then head of the Reporters Committee for Freedom of the Press, claimed "concern for personal privacy" posed one of the greatest threats to the First Amendment.[87] Kirtley suggested courts' approaches to the conflict had allowed privacy values to limit press rights. She warned that the common law right to privacy had "helped to create exceptions to and carve-outs of constitutional principles that threaten to erode both press freedom and the public's right to know."[88] More than a decade later, David Anderson, a scholar of tort and First Amendment law, warned that uncertainty about the constitutional limitations on torts, in general, threatened to chill press freedom and that the lack of precision in defining restrictions on expression could cause "excessive deterrence," dissuading the media from publishing non-tortious, as well as tortious, content.[89]

Calls for greater clarity

Bruce Sanford, author of a leading treatise on privacy and libel law, summarized the case law as "laden with fact-intensive cases in which results are of limited precedential value."[90] In *Libel and Privacy Law*, published in 1999, Sanford suggested those rulings implied that "slight alterations in material or in newsgathering" could convert "provocative, enterprising journalism" into a tortious invasion of privacy.[91] He described editors as tending to be "fearful" of invasion of privacy lawsuits during the twentieth century.[92] And in 2009, Amy Gajda, a media law scholar, noted, "[S]ome courts have grown distinctly less deferential to journalism in privacy cases."[93] She argued that courts' willingness to allow judges and juries to define "the legitimate scope of news coverage marks a potentially significant shift in the relationship between the courts and the media."[94]

On the other hand, a few legal scholars have suggested the Supreme Court's narrow, fact-tied rulings have favored free expression and provided little clarity on privacy rights.[95] In 1992, Ken Gormley, a scholar of constitutional law, claimed that the Court's rulings on privacy torts resulted in "state privacy tort actions [being] effectively squashed in nearly every instance when they have come into conflict with the constitutional guarantee of free press."[96] Some legal scholars have challenged the adequacy of tort-based privacy law in the twenty-first century, calling the torts "ineffective,"[97] "disappointing,"[98] and "ill-suited" to address harms in our digital media age,[99] with a track record of "function[ing] inadequately and far[ing] poorly in the courts,"[100] as well as challenging modern interpretations of speech and press freedom.[101] In 2007, privacy scholar Daniel Solove argued that

American law "must expand its recognition of privacy interests and reach a more careful balance between privacy and free speech, one that doesn't give free speech an undue advantage."[102] Three years later, Solove and privacy scholar Neil M. Richards called on courts to "develop a better understanding of the relationship between free speech and tort-based privacy remedies."[103]

Significant legal questions remain unanswered

Courts and commentators are still sorting out how to reconcile the privacy and free press values that clash in such cases. A 2007 publication by the Reporters Committee for Freedom of the Press described the right to privacy as an evolving area of law in which "many legal questions remain unsettled" in most jurisdictions and advised journalists that they need to know "how the law in their jurisdiction balances" individuals' interests in privacy against the interests of the press and public.[104] The uncertainty, of course, cuts both ways, making it difficult for individuals to know when they have legitimate privacy invasion claims against the media and for media to know when they have strong First Amendment defenses.

The potential ramifications from the lack of clarity in this area are widespread. Most states have recognized at least one of the four privacy torts: appropriation of another's name or likeness to one's own benefit,[105] disclosure of private facts,[106] placing another in a false light,[107] and intrusion upon seclusion.[108] The disclosure and appropriation torts address emotional harms resulting from publication of true information and thus most directly conflict with the First Amendment right to publish information.[109] The false light tort poses less of a First Amendment challenge because it targets false and misleading publications. Courts generally do not view claims that media defendants intruded on individuals' seclusion as directly conflicting with First Amendment rights because the intrusion tort addresses harms to one's solitude that result from an invasive action rather than from publication or publicity.[110]

This study aims to identify if and how federal appellate courts and state high courts, without much guidance from the Supreme Court, have reconciled free press and privacy values in cases involving one or both of those widely accepted common law privacy torts involving publication or publicity. Specifically, this book examines cases involving disclosure of private facts or appropriation in an effort to identify how courts have attempted to reconcile these two sets of values considered fundamental in our democratic society.[111] Chapter two explicates those values.

Chapter 1 Notes

[1] 491 U.S. 524, 527-30 (1989).
[2] *Id.* at 528.
[3] *Id.*
[4] *Id.*
[5] Florida Star v. B.J.F., 499 So.2d 883, 84 n.2 (1098) (quoting Fla. Stat. § 794.03 (1974)).
[6] Florida Star v. B.J.F., 499 So.2d 883, 884 (Fla. Dist. Ct. App. 1986).
[7] Florida Star v. B.J.F., 509 So.2d 1117 (Fla. 1987).
[8] 491 U.S. 524, 529-30 (1989). *See, e.g.*, Peter B. Edelman, *Free Press v. Privacy: Haunted by the Ghost of Justice Black*, 68 TEX. L. REV. 1195, 1207 (1989) ("The Court in Florida Star made a choice. It decided that when the violation of privacy involves publication of private information about an individual, free speech wins; everything is newsworthy, and nothing is private."); Ken Gormley, *One Hundred Years of Privacy*, 1992 WIS. L. REV. 1335, 1387-88 ("[S]tate privacy tort actions have been effectively squashed in nearly every instance when they have come into conflict with the constitutional guarantee of free press.").
[9] 491 U.S. 524, 530 (1989).
[10] *Id.* at 533 (quoting Cox Broad. Corp. v. Cohn, 420 U.S. 469, 491 (1975).
[11] *Id.* at 541.
[12] *Id.* at 530-33 (citing Smith v. Daily Mail, 443 U.S. 97 (1979); Oklahoma Publ'g Co. v. Dist. Court, 430 U.S. 308 (1977); Cox Broad. v. Cohn, 420 U.S. 469 (1975)).
[13] *Id.* at 536-37.
[14] *Id.* at 541.
[15] *Id.* at 526.
[16] *Id.* at 550.
[17] *Id.* at 551.
[18] *See* Edelman, *supra* note 8, at 1195 (1990) (stating Warren and Brandeis called for recognition of a legal right to privacy "in their classic article"); Diane L. Zimmerman, *False Light Invasion of Privacy: The Light That Failed*, 64 N.Y.U. L. REV. 363, 365 (1989) ("The common law right of privacy was conceived in the late nineteenth century by the fertile intellects of Samuel Warren and Louis Brandeis").
[19] *See, e.g.*, C. Edwin Baker, *Autonomy and Informational Privacy, or Gossip: The Central Meaning of The First Amendment*, 21 SOC. PHIL. & POL'Y 215, 215 (2004) (describing the legal right of informational privacy as "the great modern achievement often attributed to the classic Samuel Warren and Louis Brandeis article); John H. Fuson, Comment, *Has The Promise Of The Free Press Failed?*, 148 U. PA. L. REV. 629, 646 (1999) (calling the article "history's most influential law review article"); Daniel Solove, *The Virtues of Knowing Less: Justifying Privacy Protections Against Disclosure*, 53

DUKE L.J. 966, 970 (2003) ("The tort of public disclosure originates from an 1890 article by Samuel Warren and Louis Brandeis.").

[20] Samuel D. Warren and Louis D. Brandeis, *The Right to Privacy*, 4 HARV. L. REV. 193, 194-96 (1890).

[21] *Id.*

[22] *Id.* at 195.

[23] *Id.*

[24] *See, e.g.*, Elbridge L. Adams, *The Right of Privacy, And Its Relation to the Law of Libel*, 39 AM. L. REV. 37, 37 (1905) (describing the article as "one of the most brilliant excursions in the field of theoretical jurisprudence"); Randall P. Bezanson, *The Right to Privacy Revisited: Privacy, News, and Social Change, 1890-1990*, 80 CALIF. L. REV. 1133, 1134 (1992) (explaining that the attorneys' article "presented the idea of privacy as it should be understood); Edward J. Bloustein, *Privacy as an Aspect of Human Dignity: An Answer to Dean Prosser*, 39 N.Y.U.L. REV. 962, 963-64 (1964); Edward J. Bloustein, *Privacy, Tort Law, and the Constitution: Is Warren and Brandeis' Tort Petty and Unconstitutional as Well?*, 46 TEX. L. REV. 611, 611 (1968); Ruth Gavison, *Too Early for a Requiem*, 43 S. CAROLINA L. REV. 437, 438-39 (1992) (stating that "the article is supposed to be the most influential law review article ever written, an essay that single-handedly created a tort and an awareness of the need for legal remedies for invasion of privacy. It is a classic, a pearl of common-law reasoning. . . ."); Alfred Hill, *Defamation and Privacy Under the First Amendment*, 76 COLUM. L. REV. 1204, 1254 (1976); Irwin R. Kramer, *The Birth of Privacy Law: A Century Since Warren and Brandeis*, 39 CATH. U. L. REV. 703, 703-04 (1990); Richard S. Murphy, *Property Rights in Personal Information: An Economic Defense of Privacy*, 84 GEO. L.J. 2381 (1995); Louis F. Nizer, *The Right of Privacy: A Half Century's Developments* 39 MICH. L. REV. 526, 528-29 (1941); Robert C. Post, *Rereading Warren and Brandeis*, 41 CASE W. RES. L. REV. 647, 649-53 (1990); William L. Prosser, *Privacy*, 48 CAL. L. REV. 383 (1960); Fred R. Shapiro, *The Most Cited Law Review Articles*, 73 CALIF. L. REV. 1540, 1545 (1985); Diane L. Zimmerman, *Requiem For a Heavyweight: Farewell to Warren and Brandeis's Privacy Tort*, 68 CORNELL L. REV. 292, 293 (1982).

[25] Prosser, *supra* note 24.

[26] Amy Gajda, *What If Samuel D. Warren Hadn't Married a Senator's Daughter?: Uncovering the Press Coverage that Led to "The Right To Privacy,"* 2008 MICH. ST. L.REV. 35, 35-37.

[27] W. JOSEPH CAMPBELL, YELLOW JOURNALISM 8 (2003).

[28] *E.g.*, MICHAEL SCHUDSON, DISCOVERING THE NEWS 88-106 (1978); Louis F. Nizer, *The Right of Privacy: A Half Century's Developments* 39 MICH. L. REV. 526, 528-29 (1941).

[29] Neil M. Richards & Daniel J. Solove, *Privacy's Other Path: Recovering the Law of Confidentiality*, 96 GEO L.J. 123, 128 (2007).

[30] *E.g.*, Hyman Gross, *The Concept of Privacy*, 42 N.Y.U.L. Rev. 33, 36 (1967); Jonathan Kahn, *Privacy as a Legal Principle of Identity Maintenance*, 33 SETON HALL L. REV. 371, 376-78 (2003).

[31] N.Y. CIV. RIGHTS LAW §§ 50-51 (LEXIS 2010).

[32] Pavesich v. New England Life Ins. Co., 50 S.E. 68, 69-70 (Ga. 1905).

[33] DON R. PEMBER, PRIVACY AND THE PRESS: THE LAW, THE MASS MEDIA, AND THE FIRST AMENDMENT 76 (1972).

[34] The Supreme Court first applied the First Amendment to the states in *Gitlow v. New York*, 268 U.S. 652 (1925). The earliest recorded privacy case was *Roberson v. Rochester Folding Box Co.*, 64 N.E. 442 (N.Y. 1902), in which the New York Court of Appeals refused to recognize a common law right of privacy. That case led to enactment of the New York Civil Rights Law, making appropriation of an individual's likeness for commercial purposes a misdemeanor and allowing civil suits for damages and injunctions. N.Y. CIVIL RIGHTS LAW §§ 50, 51 (1909). In 1905, the Georgia Supreme Court became the first state high court to recognize a common law right of privacy in *Pavesich v. New England Life Ins. Co.*, 50 S.E. 68 (1905).

[35] G. Edward White, *The First Amendment Comes of Age: Emergence of Free Speech in Twentieth-Century America*, 95 MICH. L. REV. 299, 332 (1997).

[36] Kramer, *supra* note 24, at 718.

[37] The American Law Institute was formed after a committee of attorneys, legal scholars, and judges found that the complexity and uncertainty of American law were its primary flaws. The Institute asked lawyers and scholars to synthesize legal judgments to provide specific rules in a series of texts called *Restatements of the Law*. One commentator proposed that the *Restatements* have become "the pinnacle of this process of deliberative synthesis, so much so that they themselves take on the weight of binding authority, displacing the earlier material from which they have drawn their conclusions." Oliver R. Goodenough, *Go Fish: Evaluating the Restatement's Formulation of the Law of Publicity*, 47 S.C.L. REV. 709, 713 (1996). *See also* MORRIS L. COHEN & KENT C. OLSON, LEGAL RESEARCH IN A NUTSHELL 52-53 (2003) (asserting the work published in the *Restatements* "is perhaps more persuasive in the courts than any other secondary material. Courts may sometimes even adopt Restatement provisions as correct statements of each law").

[38] Kramer, *supra* note 24, at 718.

[39] RESTATEMENT OF TORTS § 867 (1939).

[40] Bloustein, *supra* note 24, at 962 (observing that "Dean Prosser is by far the most influential contemporary exponent of the tort").

[41] Prosser, *supra* note 24, at 389.

[42] *Id.* at 410.

[43] *Id.*

[44] Bloustein, *supra* note 24, at 965 & n.14 (suggesting that the four torts proposed by Prosser involve "the interest in freedom from mental distress," "the interest in reputation," and "the proprietary interest in name and likeness").

[45] Neil M. Richards & Daniel J. Solove, *Prosser's Privacy Law: A Mixed Legacy*, 98 CAL. L. REV. 1887, 1923 (2010).

[46] PEMBER, *supra* note 33, at 76-77.

[47] 376 U.S. 254 (1964).

[48] 285 U.S. 372 (1967).

[49] PEMBER, *supra* note 33, at 76-77.

[50] *Id.* at 233.

[51] Time, Inc. v. Hill, 385 U.S. 374 (1967).

[52] *Florida Star*, 491 U.S. at 541.

[53] 420 U.S. 469 (1975).

[54] 430 U.S. 308 (1977).

[55] 443 U.S. 97 (1979).

[56] *Cox Broad.*, 420 U.S. at 471-72.

[57] *Id.* at 489.

[58] *Id.* at 491.

[59] *Id.* at 496.

[60] *Id.* at 492.

[61] 491 U.S. 524, 532 (1989) (citing *Cox Broad.*, 420 U.S. at 494-95).

[62] 420 U.S. at 494-95.

[63] 491 U.S. at 532.

[64] *Id.* (citing 420 U.S. at 494-95).

[65] 430 U.S. 308, 309-10 (1977) (citing *Cox Broad.*, 420 U.S. 469, 496 (1975)).

[66] *Id.* at 308-09.

[67] *Id.* at 311-12.

[68] 443 U.S. 97, 102-03 (1979) (citing *Cox Broad.*, 420 U.S. at 495 and *Oklahoma Publ'g*, 430 U.S. 380 (1977)).

[69] *Id.* at 103.

[70] 491 U.S. 524, 531-32 (1989) (citing Smith v. Daily Mail Publ'g Co., 443 U.S. at 103).

[71] *Id.* at 543 (White, J., dissenting) (citing *Cox Broad.*, 420 U.S. 496 (1975); *Oklahoma Publ'g*, 430 U.S. 308 (1977); and *Smith*, 443 U.S. at 97.

[72] *Id.* at 546-47.

[73] *Id.* at 543-44.

[74] *Id.* at 545-47.

[75] *Id.* at 546-47.

[76] *Id.* (citing Fla. Stat. § 794.03 (1983); *Cox Broad.*, 420 U.S. at 496).

[77] *Id.* at 553.

[78] *Id.* at 547 (White, J., dissenting).

[79] Bartnicki v. Vopper, 532 U.S. 514, 529 (2001) (quoting *Florida Star*, 491 U.S. at 532-33).

[80] *Id.* at 532.

[81] *Id.* at 534.

[82] *Id.* at 535.

[83] *Id.* at 533-34.

[84] Id. at 554 (Rehnquist, C.J., dissenting).

[85] Florida Star v. B.J.F., 491 U.S. 524, 533 (1989).

[86] *See, e.g.*, Snyder v. Phelps, 131 S. Ct. 1207, 1220 (2011); *Bartnicki*, 532 U.S. at 534; *Florida Star*, 491 U.S. at 533-34.

[87] Jane Kirtley, *Freedom of the Press: The Most Serious Threat Is . . . The Cloak of Privacy*, 30 COLUM. JOURNALISM REV. 46 (1991).

[88] *Id.*

[89] David A. Anderson, *First Amendment Limitations on Tort Law*, 69 BROOK. L. REV. 755, 761-65 (2004). Anderson also commented that the Supreme Court's approach for identifying the constitutional limitations for privacy torts that target the content of publications "does not yet appear to be solidified." *Id.* at 758.

[90] BRUCE W. SANFORD, LIBEL AND PRIVACY § 11.1 (rev. 2d ed. Supp. 2004)(1999).

[91] *Id.*

[92] *Id.*

[93] Amy Gajda, *Judging Journalism: The Turn Toward Privacy and Judicial Regulation of the Press*, 97 CALIF. L. REV. 1039, 1042 (2009).

[94] *Id.*

[95] *See, e.g.*, Edelman, *supra* note 8, at 1207 ("The Court in Florida Star made a choice. It decided that when the violation of privacy involves publication of private information about an individual, free speech wins; everything is newsworthy, and nothing is private."); Thomas I. Emerson, *The Right of Privacy and Freedom of The Press,* 14 HARV. C.R.-C.L. L. REV. 328, 336 (1979) ("The constitutional basis for the privacy tort thus remains largely an open question."); Ken Gormley, *supra* note 8, at 1387-88 ("[S]tate privacy tort actions have been effectively squashed in nearly every instance when they have come into conflict with the constitutional guarantee of free press.").

[96] Gormley, *supra* note 8, at 1387-90 (1992) (citing Time, Inc., 385 U.S. at 374; Cantrell v. Forest City Publ'g Co. 419 U.S. 254 (1975); Cox Broad., 420 U.S. at 469).

[97] Neil M. Richards & Daniel J. Solove, *Prosser's Privacy Law: A Mixed Legacy*, 98 CALIF. L. REV. 1887, 1889 (2010).

[98] *Id.* at 1918.

---

[99] Danielle Keats Citron, *Mainstreaming Privacy Torts*, 98 CALIF. L. REV. 1805, (2010).

[100] Andrew J. McClurg, *Kiss and Tell: Protecting Intimate Relationship Privacy Through Implied Contracts of Confidentiality*, 74 U. CIN. L. REV. 887, 907 (2006).

[101] *Id.* at 888.

[102] DANIEL J. SOLOVE, THE FUTURE OF REPUTATION: GOSSIP, RUMOR, AND PRIVACY ON THE INTERNET, 190 (2007).

[103] Richards & Solove, *supra* note 97, at 1923.

[104] *A primer on Invasion of Privacy*, 31 NEWS MEDIA & L. 2, 2 (Fall 2007).

[105] The RESTATEMENT (SECOND) OF TORTS § 652C (1977) declares, "One who appropriates to his own use or benefit the name or likeness of another is subject to liability to the other for invasion of his privacy." Neither the highest state courts nor the legislatures in Iowa, North Dakota, Oregon, Rhode Island, South Dakota, and Wyoming have recognized this tort in a reported opinion. MEDIA LAW RESOURCE CENTER, MEDIA PRIVACY & RELATED LAW 1555 (2010).

[106] The RESTATEMENT (SECOND) OF TORTS § 652D (1977) states, "One who gives publicity to a matter concerning the private life of another is subject to liability to the other for invasion of his privacy, if the matter publicized is of a kind that (a) would be highly offensive to a reasonable person, and (b) is not of legitimate concern to the public." Most jurisdictions have recognized the publication of private facts tort via common law. Only Montana, Nebraska, New York, North Carolina, North Dakota, and Virginia have not. MEDIA LAW RESOURCE CENTER, MEDIA PRIVACY, *supra* note 105, at 1549-52.

[107] The RESTATEMENT (SECOND) OF TORTS § 652E (1977) states, "One who gives publicity to a matter concerning another that places the other before the public in a false light is subject to liability to the other for invasion of his privacy, if (a) the false light in which the other was placed would be highly offensive to a reasonable person, and (b) the actor had knowledge of or acted in reckless disregard as to the falsity of the publicized matter and the false light in which the other would be placed." False light invasion of privacy claims are not recognized in Colorado, Massachusetts, Minnesota, Missouri, North Carolina, North Dakota, South Carolina, Texas, Virginia, Washington, and Wisconsin. MEDIA LAW RESOURCE CENTER, MEDIA PRIVACY, *supra* note 105, at 1549-1552.

[108] The RESTATEMENT (SECOND) OF TORTS § 652B (1977) states, "One who intentionally intrudes, physically or otherwise, upon the solitude or seclusion of another or his private affairs or concerns, is subject to liability to the other for invasion of his privacy, if the intrusion would be highly offensive to a reasonable person." Bruce Sanford explained that intrusion is similar to

trespass, but intrusion addresses a "highly offensive invasion of personal privacy" that "need not be a physical trespass." SANFORD, *supra* note 90, at §11.2.

[109] *See, e.g.*, Neil M. Richards, *The Puzzle of Brandeis, Privacy, and Speech*, 63 VAND. L. REV. 1295, 1346 (2010); Emerson, *supra* note 95, at 331-32 ("At most points the law of privacy and the law sustaining a free press do not contradict each other. . . . There, are, however, two major areas where an accommodation must be developed. One concerns the privacy tort, where the privacy right comes into sharp contrast with the right to publish. The other involves the right of the press to obtain information from the government"); Diane L. Zimmerman, *Information as Speech, Information as Goods: Some Thoughts on Marketplaces and the Bill of Rights*, 33 WM. & MARY L. REV. 665, 722-24 (1992) (suggesting that making the appropriation of a name or likeness for a commercial use actionable challenges the First Amendment right to publish information); Diane L. Zimmerman, *False Light, supra* note 18, at 364; Diane L. Zimmerman, *Requiem, supra* note 24, at 293 (asserting that no matter how courts or legislatures formulate a tort that addresses the disclosure of true information, as a disclosure tort or appropriation tort, such a law "cannot coexist with constitutional protections for freedom of speech and press").

[110] Melville B. Nimmer, *The Right to Speak from* Times *to* Time*: First Amendment Theory Applied to Libel and Misapplied to Privacy*, 56 CAL. L. REV. 935, 957 (1968). Intrusion is considered a "law of general applicability" that does not conflict with the press's First Amendment right to publish news.

[111] Rodney A. Smolla, *Privacy and the First Amendment Right to Gather News*, 67 GEO. WASH. L. REV. 1097, 1126-28 (1999).

CHAPTER 2

Fundamental Democratic Values

Press freedom and privacy both serve values considered fundamental for American democratic society.[1] Free expression and privacy rights even serve some of the same values, such as autonomy.[2] Despite those underlying similarities, the press's First Amendment rights occasionally conflict with privacy rights recognized by state common law and statutory torts[3] that protect individuals' privacy interests against invasions by individuals or private entities.[4] In order to analyze if and how state high courts and federal appellate courts have weighed free press values and privacy values when those sets of values conflict in privacy tort cases, it is necessary to identify and explicate the key values served by press and privacy rights.

Free Expression Values: The Liberty Model

The liberty model is based on an individual's right to communicate, which includes the right to publish information, and is associated with key overlapping values often identified as autonomy, self-fulfillment, and self-realization. The model also serves other values—allowing individuals to participate in the search for and discovery of truth and the social and political decision-making process. While the liberty model firmly emphasizes the individual's right to communicate, it recognizes this individual right can also have societal benefits—helping all of society find truth, facilitating communal decision-making and promoting change with stability. Unlike the audience model, which will be discussed in the next part, the liberty model sees social benefits as corollaries to the individual values that result from protecting the liberty to communicate free of impediments from government and society. The liberty model holds that freedom of expression serves the ultimate good of society by promoting values that primarily benefit individuals.[5] Free expression theory relevant to this model recognizes a broad right for individuals to communicate.

Individual autonomy and self-realization

In "Scope of the First Amendment Freedom of Speech," published in the *UCLA Law Review* in 1977, C. Edwin Baker contended that a broad "liberty model" would provide "the most coherent theory" of freedom of expression, grounding First Amendment rights in the autonomy value recognized by social contract doctrines.[6] Baker asserted that those doctrines require the community to respect "the dignity and equal worth" of individual members for the community "legitimately to expect individuals to respect collective decisions."[7] His liberty model emphasizes the importance of protecting individuals' free expression rights against governmental or societal restrictions that limit individual autonomy.[8] Under that model, the First Amendment requires that a speaker have the freedom to choose the content of his or her speech.[9] That aspect of personal agency, or control over one's decisions and actions, is essential for the liberty model to serve its key values—self-fulfillment and individual participation in change.[10] The scope of protection tied to those values is limited to nonviolent, noncoercive activity that "fosters individual self-realization and self-determination without improperly interfering with the legitimate claims of others."[11] That freedom of expression model, then, would allow governors to limit only expression that harms other individuals, thereby violating the social contract. Baker supported that limitation by quoting the nineteenth century philosopher John Stuart Mill's argument that "'[t]he only purpose for which power can be rightfully exercised over any member of a civilized community, against his will, is to prevent *harm to others*.'"[12]

In 1972, Thomas Scanlon, a legal philosopher, had also drawn on what he termed the "Millian principle" to propose an individual liberty model of freedom of expression, which he said was grounded in the Kantian notion of autonomy: "[A] legitimate government is one whose authority citizens can recognize while still regarding themselves as equal, autonomous, rational agents."[13] Scanlon identified two types of harms to individuals that, under an autonomy principle, could not justify restricting expression.

> There are certain harms which, although they would not occur but for certain acts of expression, nonetheless cannot be taken as part of a justification for legal restrictions on these acts. These harms are: (a) harms to certain individuals which consist in their coming to have false beliefs as a result of those acts of expression; (b) harmful consequences of acts performed as a result of those acts of expression, where the connection between the acts of expression and the subsequent harmful acts consist merely in the fact that the act of expression led the agents to believe (or increased their tendency to believe) these acts to be worth performing.[14]

Both types assign some degree of agency for the resulting harms to the injured individuals themselves—not solely to the communicator. Both involve individuals' formation of beliefs, a process that must remain within the control of any individual who values autonomy and self-realization.[15]

Individual autonomy and democracy

Thomas I. Emerson, a major First Amendment scholar, also connected the underlying values of freedom of expression to the development of personal autonomy, which he asserted was essential for the development and maintenance of a well-functioning democratic society.[16]

Emerson's book, *The System of Freedom of Expression*, published in 1969, linked four key functions, or values, of freedom of expression, to serving both individual and communal interests.[17] He described the first function of freedom of expression as encouraging self-fulfillment or self-realization.[18] Emerson proposed that the ability to express ideas, without fear of censorship or unwarranted punishment, is essential to develop one's personal dignity and to affirm one's sense of self, personal autonomy, and independence—all of which are essential for self-fulfillment.[19]

Emerson's other functions of freedom of expression serve both individual and social interests. The second function, the attainment of truth, suggests individuals' ability to discover truth through discussion and debate is essential to the ultimate good of society.[20] Emerson's third function recognizes freedom of expression as necessary for individuals to participate in social and political decision-making.[21] As Baker recognized, that function depends on individuals' ability to assert opinions as autonomous individuals and as members of society.[22]

Emerson also contended that freedom of expression is essential to promoting orderly change within a society.[23] That function envisions freedom of expression as somewhat of a safety valve, a mechanism through which individuals can discuss matters that might foster anger, violence, or other antisocial behavior if left unaddressed. Emerson considered each of those functions integral parts of a well-functioning system of freedom of expression, which includes the right to speak, to publish, and to receive information.[24]

Liberty for the press

The autonomy value, which assigns each communicator the agency to determine the content of his or her communications, has been applied to press freedom as well as speech freedom. In several law review articles, Randall Bezanson, a prominent First Amendment scholar, has tied the First Amendment freedom of the press to editorial autonomy—the right of the press to publish information free from laws that impose government suppression or result in self-censorship.[25]

Editorial autonomy and self-realization

Although the self-fulfillment and self-realization values of freedom of expression may seem inapplicable to the institutional press, even the earliest free expression theorists, John Milton and John Stuart Mill, associated those values with freedom to publish. Milton's *Areopagatica*, published in 1644, provided a foundation for the model that emphasizes personal liberty and freedom from censorship.[26] The English poet and philosopher suggested that censorship and licensing, which at that time were required prior to publication, threatened individuals' abilities to discover the religious truth necessary for personal salvation, an aspect of self-realization and self-fulfillment.[27]

Just over two centuries later, in 1859, Mill's *On Liberty* specifically addressed liberty of the press. Mill contended that government actions that suppress expression, whether by individuals or the press, undermined the ultimate development of humanity by hindering individuals from debating the merits of opposing opinions, a process that can benefit both the individual and society.[28] Emphasizing the benefit to individuals, Mill said liberty of expression is intricately connected to that sphere of life in which "society, as distinguished from the individual, has, if any, only an indirect interest."[29] That sphere comprises 1) "the inward domain of consciousness," 2) "liberty of conscience, in the most comprehensive sense," 3) "liberty of thought and feeling," and 4) "absolute freedom of opinion and sentiment on all subjects."[30] Although freedom to speak and publish can affect others and society in general, Mill described those liberties as "being of almost as much importance as the liberty of thought itself, and resting in great part on the same reasons, is practically inseparable from it."[31] Mill's concept of free expression provides individuals with freedom "without impediment from our fellow-creatures, so long as what we do does not harm them."[32] For Mill those liberties, based on individual autonomy and its reciprocal values of self-realization and self-fulfillment, were necessary for any society to remain free from tyranny by governors or society at large.[33]

<u>Editorial autonomy and democracy</u>

Professor Bezanson identified two principles necessary for the press to serve its key functions.[34] The first principle means that government regulations cannot provide the press with "special treatment."[35] As an example Bezanson discussed *Cox Broadcasting v. Cohn*, in which he said the U.S. Supreme Court applied the neutrality principle when it struck down a Georgia statute that sanctioned the press for publishing the name of a rape victim that was first reported in court documents.[36] Bezanson noted the statute did not prevent individuals from discussing or publishing that information; thus "the statute effectively singled out the press for regulation."[37] Bezanson declared, "[W]e may surmise that the statute would not have offended the first amendment if it had also prohibited public, as well as press," from revealing the identity of rape victims in order to protect the victim's privacy.[38]

Under Bezanson's second principle, the principle of independence, the First Amendment prevents the government from influencing the content of the press.[39] For instance, Bezanson wrote that in *Miami Herald Publishing Co. v. Tornillo*, the Court struck down a Florida statute that required newspapers to provide political candidates with space to respond to opponents' criticism.[40] The Court held that it was "unconstitutional for the state to compel a newspaper publisher to print replies by candidates for public office who have been assailed in the press."[41] That ruling declared the First Amendment protects the press's right to editorial autonomy "with regard to public issues or matters pertaining to public officials."[42] Thus, Bezanson connected the scope of press freedom to the institutional press's agency, or autonomy, its editorial freedom to determine the content of what it communicates.

Summary

Scholars have recognized several key liberty values served by freedom of expression. In a democratic society grounded in social contract theory, freedom of speech and press serves the individual's needs for autonomy, self-fulfillment and self-realization, as well as enabling the individual to discover truth and participate in social and political decision-making. While the focus of the liberty value is on the individual, proponents also recognize that freedom of speech and press inevitably results in societal and communal benefits, facilitating the democratic decision-making process overall, creating a marketplace of ideas in which society as a whole can discover truth, and helping create a balance between change and stability. While these latter societal benefits are some of the same identified with the audience-based, communitarian model discussed below, the crucial difference is that the liberty model grounds freedom of expression in the value of autonomy, emphasizing the rights of individuals under the social contract. That theoretical framework limits governments' abilities to impose sanctions that would interfere with individuals' self-determination absent direct harm to others. As Scanlon and Baker noted, under a liberty model, even expression that results in others acquiring "false beliefs"[43] or acting on those beliefs cannot be sanctioned.[44] The general autonomy-based principles of this model can also apply to the institutional press, protecting the press against government censorship, licensing, or other actions that interfere with the press's autonomy or control over the content it publishes.[45]

Free Press Values: The Audience Model

While the liberty model recognizes both individual and societal interests served by each communicator's freedom of expression, the "audience model" focuses solely on the societal interests, the values expression serves for its audience. The audience-based values most often discussed in relevant literature are enabling effective self-governance, providing a check on government, creating a marketplace of ideas, facilitating a balance between societal stability and change, and fostering toleration. Some of those values overlap with values associated with the liberty model. However, where the liberty model associates those values with the right to communicate and disseminate information, the audience model connects those values to individuals' and society's rights to receive information or right to know.[46] The audience model grounds freedom of expression in audience members' rights to receive information.[47]

Audiences and self-governance

In 1948, Alexander Meiklejohn, a prominent philosopher who advocated for First Amendment freedoms, provided the foundation for theories that associate the scope of First Amendment coverage with the rights of message recipients.[48] Meiklejohn's seminal treatise, *Free Speech and Its Relation to Self-Government*, connected freedom for citizens to discuss government actions to American citizens' moral obligation to participate in self-governance and in public life.[49] He posited that the founding fathers protected freedom of speech and press to ensure that American citizens received the information necessary to cast informed votes.[50] Meiklejohn's self-governance rationale, while similar to Emerson's participation in decision-making value, provides narrower protection for free expression.[51] Meiklejohn proposed the First Amendment was intended to provide absolute protection for speech on matters of governing importance, matters that contribute to citizens' understanding of matters they need to know to remain sovereign over their governors.[52] He called that type of speech public speech and argued that all other types of speech, which he called private speech, fell under the protection of the Fifth Amendment's due process clause.[53] Under that rationale, the First Amendment right to publish would cover only the publication of information that promoted self-government.

Audiences and democracy

Another prominent First Amendment theorist, Harry Kalven, Jr., also connected freedom of speech to the necessity for individuals to receive information in a democratic society. [54] In 1964, Kalven contended that the Warren Court's unanimous ruling in *New York Times v. Sullivan* established a "central meaning" for the First Amendment: "a core of protection of speech without which democracy cannot function, without which, in [James] Madison's phrase, 'the censorial power,' would be in the Government over the people and not 'in the people over the Government.'"[55] Kalven explained that allowing speech to be sanctioned for government criticism would dissuade some speakers from making true, critical statements about the government.[56] That, in turn, would extinguish the political freedom that defines a democratic society.[57]

In 1971, Judge Robert H. Bork agreed that the First Amendment is central to "democratic organization" but proposed a much more restricted arena of protected speech, "expressly political" speech.[58] Bork said the First Amendment protects "speech about how we are governed, and the category therefore includes a wide range of evaluation, criticism, electioneering, and propaganda."[59] But, among other things, it would exclude speech "advocating forcible overthrow of the government or violation of law"[60] because such speech would not lead to the discovery and spread of political truth.[61]

<u>The press and self-governance</u>

Closely related to the self-government value is what commentators have referred to as the "checking value" or "watchdog function" of the press. This theory began to gain prominence after the Vietnam War and Watergate, when pessimism and distrust of "public power" underscored the necessity for an independent press to serve as a check on misconduct by powerful institutions.[62] Unlike the other values, which can be applied to both individual speech and the press, this value focuses directly on the Press Clause of the First Amendment. In a key 1974 law review article, Supreme Court Justice Potter Stewart acknowledged the social need for an autonomous press free to criticize and question government.[63] He said, "[T]he primary purpose of the constitutional guarantee of a free press was . . . to create a fourth institution outside the Government as an additional check on the three official branches."[64] That conception of press freedom acknowledges that the press protects the public's interest in learning about matters of public concern, which is essential for the participation in political decision-making value.[65] In an influential law review article published in 1977, "The Checking Value in First Amendment Theory," Professor Vincent Blasi described that value of freedom of the press as "the checking value," the value of the press serving as a check on the government and other powerful institutions.[66] The press was provided with freedom to serve as a watchdog that would warn citizens about threats to the balance of powers essential in a democracy. Like the self-government value, thBe checking value focuses on the audience's need to receive information.

The press and democracy

The audience model of freedom of expression has led several scholars to assert that the First Amendment protects a "right to know," a concept that emphasizes a right for citizens to receive information that promotes government accountability.[67] In 1976, Professor Emerson proposed that concept is an "integral part" of a well-functioning system of freedom of expression:

> Reduced to its simplest terms the concept includes two closely related features. First, the right to read, to listen, to see, and to otherwise receive communications; and second, the right to obtain information as a basis for transmitting ideas or facts to others. Together these constitute the reverse side of the coin from the right to communicate.[68]

Emerson suggested the concept could make the greatest contribution to society when asserted as a right of the public to obtain information stored, collected, or created by government actors, especially to obtain information "necessary or proper for the citizen to perform his function as ultimate sovereign."[69] That concept ultimately serves as a composite of rights associated with the self-governance and checking values of freedom of expression.

Audiences and the marketplace of ideas

As mentioned in the discussion of the liberty value above, the discovery of truth value has both an individual and societal dimension. The audience-based variation is often referred to as the marketplace of ideas value. Many twentieth-century theorists, [70] as well as the Supreme Court, have claimed that freedom of expression leads to a marketplace in which the audience benefits by having access to all manners of information and ideas.[71] Justice Oliver Wendell Holmes, Jr., first applied this concept to the First Amendment in his 1919 dissenting opinion objecting to the conviction of self-proclaimed "revolutionists" charged with espionage for printing leaflets encouraging resistance to the United States' war efforts.[72] Holmes wrote:

> [W]hen men have realized that time has upset many fighting faiths, they may come to believe even more than they believe the very foundations of their own conduct that the ultimate good desired is better reached by free trade in ideas – that the best test of truth is the power of the thought to get itself accepted in the competition of the market, and that truth is the only ground upon which their wishes safely can be carried out. That, at any rate, is the theory of our Constitution.[73]

Rodney Smolla, a major First Amendment scholar, suggested the ultimate benefit of the marketplace metaphor is its emphasis on the ongoing process of searching for and testing truth. The theory assumes that society benefits from a free flow of information that fosters public debate and allows speech to remedy harms caused by other speech.[74]

Some scholars have debated whether the marketplace theory is fundamentally flawed.[75] Proposing that the ultimate value served by the First Amendment is individual autonomy, Baker criticized key assumptions underlying the marketplace theory. He argued that the theory, based on laissez-faire economics fails in a society where individuals lack equal access to media channels.[76] He suggested that media monopolies, the wealthy, and powerful control access to national media, which could limit the range of viewpoints available from other sources. Baker criticized the market metaphor's assumptions about the quality of information provided and received, as well as the assumptions about the breadth of information available for public debate. He claimed that the theory erroneously assumed that the people providing and receiving information are capable of rational and rich debate.[77] Martin Redish, another theorist, acknowledged that Baker's criticism would be valid if the ultimate goal for freedom of speech is to discover truth.[78] Yet, Redish claimed that Baker's criticism "becomes irrelevant" when the marketplace theory is considered a means of facilitating another value, such as "self-realization."[79]

Audiences and balancing societal stability and change

Professor Emerson argued that freedom of expression also benefits audiences by facilitating a balance between societal stability and change.[80] That value overlaps with the marketplace and participation in public decision-making values. All three suppose that a free flow of information benefits society by ensuring that audiences receive information that enriches discussion and debate. Unlike the other values, however, the stability and change value could be compared to a safety valve. The theory assumes that suppression of discussion could lead to violence and weaken the social foundation essential for community building. Emerson described the value as "a method of achieving a more adaptable and hence a more stable community, of maintaining the precarious balance between healthy cleavage and necessary consensus."[81] In other words, freedom of expression encourages individuals to discuss and adapt to change rather than to resort to secrecy and violence. Emerson proposed that "suppression of discussion makes a rational judgment impossible, substituting force for reason." He continued, "[S]uppression promotes inflexibility and stultification."[82] Under the safety-valve value, freedom of expression benefits society, allowing individuals to resolve conflicts, promote progress, and strengthen community.[83]

Audiences and toleration

The final societal value, toleration, was articulated by Professor Lee C. Bollinger, who criticized mechanistic theorists for defining the scope of free speech in terms of political functions.[84] Bollinger suggested that a system of free speech should serve broad intellectual values by encouraging individuals to share and receive diverse opinions. He claimed that toleration is the key value for free speech: "Through toleration . . . we create the community, define the values of that community and affirm a commitment to and confidence in those values."[85] Toleration, which encourages individuals to listen to unpopular, as well as favored, messages, helps prepare individuals to participate in social and political decision-making. Listening to extreme viewpoints that may contradict their own beliefs may even help individuals to evaluate the truth of minority and majority views and promote stable change.[86] While individuals clearly can benefit from the toleration value of freedom of expression, Bollinger asserted, "[T]he ultimate aim of the First Amendment is the advancement of the public or collective good and not that of any single individual."[87] Thus, the toleration value, like the other values associated with the right to receive information, primarily benefits society as a whole.

Summary

Leading legal theorists have suggested that a right to receive and a right to know information are important parts of a well-functioning system of free expression. Under an audience model, the broad right to receive information serves five primary communal values: effective self-governance, the checking value, creation of a marketplace of ideas, societal stability and change, and toleration. The right to know primarily serves the societal values of effective self-governance and the checking value. All five values associated with an audience model benefit society as a whole because free speech fosters community building and democratic governance as members of society remedy harms through discussion and debate, rather than violence.

Free Expression Values Serving Individuals and Audiences

The audience model and the liberty model noticeably serve some of the same values considered essential to a well-functioning democratic society. The aforementioned scholarship has provided a foundation for those values to be assigned to an audience model when the underlying values are described as societal benefits associated with the receipt of information, or to the liberty model when the underlying values are described primarily as benefits resulting from an individual's communication. Of course, Professor Emerson clarified that those models and their underlying values are part of the larger system of freedom of expression protected by the First Amendment.[88]

Distinctions among those values and models, however, are essential to considering how much weight to assign to expression-based rights that conflict with privacy rights. For instance, Professor Meiklejohn assigned absolute protection to speech that effectuates self-governance that falls under the audience-based model, which would allow free speech to trump privacy.[89] On the other hand, Professor Scanlon's "Millian principle," which falls under the liberty-model, limits protection for expression to the expression that does not harm another individual.[90] In parallel, Professor Emerson suggested the societal right to receive information should yield to individual privacy interests that protect the autonomy of the individual.[91] The following section explores how scholarship has defined autonomy and other key values for privacy.

Defining Individual Values of Privacy

As is the case with freedom of expression, there is no single theory for privacy.[92] Nor is there a bright line distinction between the individual and societal values underlying privacy. By its very nature, privacy is more clearly an individual rather than a societal value; still some values serve society as well as individuals. Some literature, thus, has presented privacy values as primarily individual or, primarily societal, and both individual and societal.

Scholarship from law, philosophy, sociology, and psychology has addressed privacy as a condition,[93] space,[94] or claim[95] for individuals to enjoy a physical and emotional realm where they can flourish as autonomous individuals, a realm where they may be free from social or political pressure.[96] Fred C. Cate, a communication law expert, has claimed that it is important to explicate privacy values because "privacy is not an end in itself but rather an instrument for achieving other goals."[97] In a case book published in 2007, privacy law expert Anita Allen suggested that one meaningful way for theorists to advance privacy scholarship is to "clearly explicate the costs, benefits, and values associated with whatever 'privacy' is intended to denote."[98] Several important scholarly explications of privacy values are grounded in sociologist Erving Goffman's theory on the presentation of self,[99] psychoanalyst Sidney M. Jourard's theory on privacy,[100] and sociologist Alan F. Westin's theory on privacy in modern democratic societies.[101] While theorists have explored connections between some types of privacy and key individual and societal values, this section demonstrates that scholarship has suggested relationships exist between all of the key privacy values and at least one of the publication-based privacy torts.

One's core identity, or core self, is the fundamental individual privacy value, and that value is integrally related to other key individual privacy values: autonomy,[102] liberty,[103] emotional release,[104] personal growth and self-evaluation,[105] and psychic self-preservation.[106] Of course, several of those values also are related to the key societal privacy values of promoting civility and community,[107] fostering human relationships,[108] and encouraging participation in a democratic society.[109]

Individual Privacy Values

Scholarship from sociology, philosophy, and law has described an essential individual value for privacy as personhood or selfhood, or, alternately, the integrated values of personality, dignity, independence, individuality, and identity.[110] As noted in the introductory chapter, the Warren and Brandeis article, considered the metaphorical seedling for privacy law, blasted newspaper journalists and photographers for intruding in individuals' personal affairs and harming individuals' "inviolate personality."[111] That article called for the law to protect the right of individuals to be let alone, suggesting that privacy would protect individuals against intrusions by society and the demands of collective life.[112]

Personhood

In an article published in the New York University Law Review in 1964, Edward J. Bloustein, a legal authority on privacy, described Warren and Brandeis' vision for privacy law as a mechanism for protecting an "individual's independence, dignity and integrity."[113] Suggesting that privacy was a shield for individuals' interest in human dignity, Bloustein proposed that the key privacy value of personhood "defines man's essence as a unique and self-determining being."[114] In 2003, Jonathan Kahn, a legal and historical scholar of identity, suggested that maintaining and developing one's sense of dignity and integrity are key aspects of identity, a key underlying principle for privacy.[115] As such, the personhood value protects each individual's ability to define her own identity, or self, as she perceives herself as being distinct from other members of society.[116]

Autonomy

The core self or personhood value and the autonomy value are both grounded in sociologist Erving Goffman's suggestions that an individual desires to control others' perceptions of himself. [117] He claimed that each individual attempts to influence social conceptions of his identity by concealing personal attributes that would contradict social expectations for context-specific conduct or otherwise taint others' perceptions of his social identity. Political scientist Alan Westin observed, "Each person is aware of the gap between what he wants to be and what he actually is, between what the world sees of him and what he knows to be his much more complex reality."[118] Moreover, Sidney Jourard, a psychoanalyst, explained that adults are expected to perform certain social roles. When an adult's behavior noticeably deviates from the pattern of socially expected conduct, the nonconforming adult may be socially sanctioned.[119] Yet, an adult who strives to constantly conform to social expectations, suppressing contradictory desires, risks "self-alienation," which undermines one's physical and mental health.[120] Privacy, thus, protects each individual by providing opportunities for each to experience and to reflect on her uniqueness as a human being without exposing her core self to society.

The desire to protect one's individuality is integrally related to the value of autonomy.[121] Whereas the personhood value of privacy emphasizes one's essence as a unique person, the autonomy value stresses one's independence of judgment and one's ability to choose whether to resist pressures to conform to social norms.[122] Westin described autonomy as "the desire to avoid being manipulated or dominated wholly by others."[123] In an article published in 1979, legal expert Ruth Gavison asserted, "Autonomy requires the capacity to make an independent moral judgment, the willingness to exercise it, and the courage to act on the results of this exercise even when the judgment is not a popular one."[124] More than twenty years later, Jeffrey Rosen, a privacy scholar, suggested that the autonomy value of privacy presumes that each individual is capable of realizing "a self-actualized individual self," a self who chooses to assert her uniqueness as an individual and a member of her community.[125] According to those conceptions, privacy helps individuals exercise self-determination and make independent judgments.[126]

Liberty

The value of autonomy also is related to the third individual value of privacy—liberty.[127] While conceptions of privacy as control over information about oneself or access to oneself may relate to autonomy or personhood, some scholars have claimed that those conceptions relate more precisely to a liberty value of privacy.[128] In 1968, Charles Fried, a legal scholar, suggested that privacy allows individuals to do or say things that would be scorned or scrutinized by members of the general public without "fear of disapproval or more tangible retaliation."[129] Fifteen years later, W.A. Parent, a legal philosopher, argued that such conceptions of privacy as control over information about oneself ultimately relate to personal freedom, or liberty.[130] He asserted, "Whenever one person or group of persons tries to deprive another of control over some aspect of his life, we should recognize this as attempted coercion and should evaluate it as such, under the general concept of freedom-limiting action."[131] Gavison labeled that value "liberty of action," which incorporates the individual values of freedom from censure or ridicule, promotion of autonomy, and promotion of mental health.[132] The key underlying principle of the liberty value is that liberty insulates individuals from authoritarian interferences, such as government restraints or societal pressures, and allows individuals to challenge social norms in private, free from the pressures to conform in public.[133]

Emotional release

The fourth individual value of privacy, emotional release, has two key functions for individuals.[134] The first function allows an individual to escape the stress and tensions that result from one's performance of various social roles "depending on his audience and behavioral situation."[135] That function enables individuals to relax and drop their social personas, which is essential for physical and emotional health.[136] Westin compared the second function of the emotional release value to a safety valve that primarily benefits individuals, whereas the safety valve function of freedom of speech primarily benefits society. He suggested that privacy allows individuals to voice anger and frustration at authority figures to friends or family "without fear of being held responsible for such comments."[137] Such venting helps individuals to process emotions in a safe context, reducing the risk that individuals will spout off harmful statements in a context likely to violate their professional or broad social roles.[138] Both functions of the emotional release value ultimately benefit individuals' mental and physical health.[139]

Freedom to process one's thoughts and to reflect on one's emotions is also essential for the personal growth and self-evaluation value of privacy.[140] Westin claimed that privacy helps each individual find opportunities to process the deluge of information encountered during daily life and "to integrate his experiences into a meaningful pattern."[141] Reflecting on one's experiences is necessary for individuals to grow through self-discovery and self-criticism.[142] Evaluating one's thoughts, attitudes, and beliefs is also essential for individuals to practice and prepare how and when to present themselves to the general public.[143] The process of self-evaluation, then, ultimately helps each person feel confident in herself as an autonomous being.[144]

Self-preservation and emotional health

The final individual value for privacy, self-preservation and emotional health, is closely related to the individual values of personal autonomy, self-evaluation, and emotional release. For example, Westin described a function of limited and protected communication as "the means of psychic self-preservation for men in the metropolis."[145] In other words, individuals use reserve and discretion to decide which conduct and communications to share only within the parameters of trusted relationships because exposure to the general public would cause psychological pain. The value of psychic-self preservation has been associated with privacy for more than a century. When Warren and Brandeis called for a legal right of privacy, they asserted, "[M]odern enterprise and invention have, through invasions upon his privacy, subjected him to mental pain and distress, far greater than could be inflicted by mere bodily injury."[146] They argued that the underlying value for individual privacy, which allowed individuals to prevent the press from disclosing their information, is "peace of mind."[147]

Summary

Privacy is instrumental for individuals to achieve numerous personal goals.[148] The primary individual values of privacy are personhood, autonomy, liberty, emotional release, self-evaluation, and psychic self-preservation. Several of those values are synergistically related, and, at times, may even overlap. Nonetheless, each value has at least one unique primary attribute. For example, one's conception of oneself as a unique human being defines one's core identity or personhood.[149] Self-determination is a critical element for autonomy.[150] Freedom to act without interference by authorities is a key attribute of liberty.[151] The emotional release value serves two key functions: enabling individuals to express strong emotions without repercussions and allowing individuals to release the tensions experienced when donning their social personas.[152] Self-reflection and self-criticism are essential for the self-evaluation value.[153] The final value of psychic self-preservation promotes one's psychological well- being.[154] As mentioned previously, no bright lines separate those individual values.

Societal Privacy Values

While the privacy values of personhood, autonomy, liberty, and psychic self-preservation primarily benefit individuals, at times those values also have secondary benefits for society.[155] Likewise, the privacy torts may serve communitarian values that contribute to the wellbeing of modern democratic society as well as to the individual privacy values. Scholars primarily have identified those societal privacy values as maintaining civility and community in society,[156] fostering human relationships,[157] and encouraging evaluative decision-making and participation in a democratic society.[158]

<u>Maintaining civility and community</u>

In *The Limits of Privacy*, published in 1999, philosopher Amitai Etzioni claimed that no society could remain free for long without privacy.[159] Although Etzioni's book primarily focused on the constitutional right to privacy, the underlying philosophy for his work also is applicable to privacy recognized by the common law and statutory torts. Etzioni grounded his arguments in communitarian social philosophy, which presumes that "a good society crafts a careful balance between individual rights and the common good."[160] Under some circumstances, Etzioni suggested privacy can help individuals follow social norms, making sure their conduct is consistent with social virtues that promote the good of society.[161] Similarly, Professor Allen noted that scholarship has argued that "privacy makes us more fit for our social responsibilities and participation in group life."[162] And Daniel Solove argued in a book published in 2011 that privacy "is itself a form of social control that emerges from society's social norms."[163] He added, "Privacy thus shouldn't be weighed as an individual right against the greater social good. Privacy issues involve balancing societal interests on both sides of the scale."

Several legal scholars have connected privacy to the societal goals of promoting civilized communities.[164] In an article examining the significance of the Warren and Brandeis article between 1890 and 1990, Professor Bezanson said that the nineteenth-century conception of privacy "protected the individual's right to enjoy an identity forged by the existing social institutions of family and community, which embodied chosen social standards and morality."[165] Bezanson suggested that the nineteenth-century conception of privacy was based on communitarian values, and the right was asserted to protect the social institutions of family and community from pressures imposed by the culture of nineteenth-century mass media and society.[166] In *The Social Foundations of Privacy: Community and Self in the Common Law Tort*, published in 1989, Robert Post proposed that modern privacy law "safeguards the rules of civility" that define the social norms, or standards of propriety, each community member is expected to follow.[167] Post claimed that privacy law generally addresses violations of social rules that cause psychological injuries, including mental anguish or dignitary harms. He described the latter type of harms, dignitary injuries, as degradations of individuals and society that arise when one community member fails to extend to another a basic form of respect that standards of decency, which are social standards that may vary from community to community, suggest any member of a community deserves.[168] Such displays of disrespect demean the individuals involved and society by defying the fundamental level of moral treatment essential for individuals to coexist in a community that values personal growth, autonomy, and meaningful human relationships.[169]

Fostering human relationships

Several scholars also have connected the value of promoting and maintaining human relationships to a well functioning civil society, as well as to the mental health and personal growth of individuals.[170]

Westin claimed, "The greatest threat to civilized social life would be a situation in which each individual was utterly candid in his communications with others, saying exactly what he knew or felt at all times. The havoc done to interpersonal relations by children, saints, mental patients, and adult 'innocents' is legendary."[171] Fried has argued that privacy is a means of promoting fundamental human relations of respect, love, friendship, and trust. He wrote, "[W]ithout privacy they are simply inconceivable."[172] He suggested that privacy is a condition necessary for individuals to create and maintain levels of intimacy—sharing information about one's conduct, beliefs, thoughts, or feelings—that facilitates trust, respect, and the relations essential for civil interactions and, in turn, promotes the individual values of personhood, psychic self-preservation, and personal development.[173]

Encouraging evaluative decision-making and participation in American democratic society

The final societal privacy value is encouraging participation in the democratic process, which includes discussion of political issues and voting.[174] Professor Emerson argued:

> In its social impact a system of privacy is vital to the working of the democratic process. Democracy assumes that the individual citizen will actively and independently participate in making decisions and in operating the institutions of the society. An individual is capable of such a role only if he can at some points separate himself from the pressures and conformities of collective life.[175]

Ken Gormley said that the first vision of privacy law in America, which related privacy to maintaining control over information about oneself, was essential for democratic society.[176] Gormley explained, "[C]ontrol of information about oneself is critical in determining how and when (if ever) others will perceive us, which is in turn essential to maintaining our individual personalities."[177] That is essential to American democratic society's emphasis on individuality, autonomy, and liberty.[178]

In a law review article published in 2004, Solove wrote that much important discussion of political matters occurs within the bonds of trusted relationships, which allow individuals to frankly state and evaluate their opinions without fear of reprisal from the general public.[179] In an article published in 2006, Solove argued that privacy, which enables individuals to act anonymously, enables individuals to vote according to their consciences without fearing retaliation from individuals with other political biases.[180] Such arguments recognize that privacy enables individuals to act autonomously, allowing each person to reflect on the democratic process, evaluate conflicting opinions, and vote on political matters.[181] Thus, when privacy serves the societal privacy value of participation in self-government, privacy also facilitates the individual privacy values of autonomy and liberty.

Summary

Privacy serves the key societal goals of maintaining civility and community in society, fostering human relationships, and encouraging evaluative decision-making and participation in a democratic society. Applying Etzioni's communitarian philosophy, privacy primarily serves those values by stressing the common good of society. In a democratic society that emphasizes the importance of individual autonomy and liberty, some of the societal values of privacy inherently overlap with individual privacy values. For example, the societal goal of maintaining civility and community also promotes the individual value of mental health; promoting relationships also enhances the individual values of mental health and personal growth; and encouraging evaluative decision-making and participation in a democratic society also advances the individual values of personal autonomy and liberty. Although individual and societal values may intertwine at times, privacy theorists have recognized each as a distinct value worthy of legal protection through the tort of disclosure of private facts or appropriation.

Publication-Based Privacy Torts and Values They Protect

Scholars have indicated the publication-based privacy torts protect the individual privacy values — autonomy, liberty, emotional release, personal growth and self-evaluation, and psychic self-preservation — and the societal privacy values — promoting civility and community, fostering human relationships, and encouraging participation in a democratic society. Because the disclosure of private facts and appropriation are unique torts, this section examines each tort.

Disclosure of private facts and individual values

The disclosure of private facts tort protects the individual values of personality, autonomy, liberty, emotional release, mental health, self-evaluation, and reflection. Dean Prosser initially proposed that the disclosure tort protected one's interest in reputation, but Professor Bloustein argued, "The gravamen in the public disclosure cases is degrading a person by laying his life open to public view," which injures a person's individuality and personal dignity.[182] Professor Gerety claimed that Warren and Brandeis intended for privacy law to protect individual autonomy, which would be violated by disclosures of private, true facts “that embarrass or humiliate us.”[183] And Professor Post suggested that courts have treated the disclosure tort as a means of redress for "indecent and vulgar" communications that cause a reasonable person to feel emotional distress.[184] When mass media reports disclose private facts, Professor Gerety claimed the resulting harm makes autonomy and intimacy impossible.[185]

The disclosure tort also enables individuals to relax and to exercise what Westin called the “safety-valve” function of privacy by venting to friends or family members without judgment or retaliation.[186] Westin claimed, “Without the aid of such release in accommodating the daily abrasions with authorities, most people would experience serious emotional pressure.”[187] Losing control over the revelation of such information would sear through one’s liberty by searing through the insulation that is also necessary for one to experiment, reflect, and develop one’s personality without fear of censure.[188]

Disclosure of private facts and societal values

The disclosure tort also protects each of the societal privacy values. For instance, Professor Post suggested that the disclosure tort fosters rules of civility that “delineate information preserves” essential for members of a community to convey forms of respect that represent the basic moral obligations shared by each member of a community.[189] He argued that respecting those social norms, which define contexts in which disclosing private information to a third party would harm the subject of the disclosure, also safeguards “the ‘ritual idiom’ through which such respect finds social expression.”[190] Conveying respect for each person is essential for individuals to form meaningful relationships and to willingly participate in society.[191]

The disclosure tort encourages participation in a democratic society that emphasizes independence, plurality, tolerance, and self-governance.[192] Professor Westin asserted, “Such independence requires time for sheltered experimentation and testing of ideas, for preparation and practice in thought and conduct, without fear of ridicule or penalty, and for the opportunity to alter opinions before making them public.”[193] Recognizing social expectations that enable individuals and even groups to shield sensitive information from public disclosure, the tort ultimately helps individuals prepare to participate in public life by participating in political discussions,[194] enables individuals to associate with other persons or groups that share their political ideologies,[195] and increases one's willingness to run for public office.[196]

Appropriation of name or likeness and individual values

The *Restatement* describes an invasion of privacy under the appropriation theory as using "the name or likeness of another" for one's own benefit, either commercial or non-pecuniary.[197] The tort relates to the values of personhood, autonomy, liberty, and emotional health.

A comment on the *Restatement* section on appropriation suggests that the interest protected by appropriation is a person's "exclusive use of his own identity" and that protecting a person "against mental distress is an important factor leading to recognition of the rule."[198] Those interests clearly are related to the individual values of personality or identity, autonomy, and psychic self-preservation or mental health.[199] Bloustein claimed that every person has a right to control whether his name or likeness is used for the commercial benefit of another because "it would be demeaning to human dignity to fail to enforce such a right."[200] Bloustein argued that human dignity, a value that overlaps with autonomy, identity, and individuality, is the key value protected by privacy.[201]

The appropriation tort also protects the individual values of mental health and liberty.[202] Bloustein wrote, "The use of a personal photograph or a name for advertising purposes has the same tendency to degrade or humiliate as has publishing details of personal life."[203] Bloustein connected the emotional harms to a loss of liberty as the use of one's identity without one's consent diminishes "personal freedom."[204] In fact, the first state high court ruling to recognize invasion of privacy by appropriation described the harm from misappropriation as a "loss of liberty."[205] Losing control over the social presentation of one's personality, then, may diminish the individual's sense of individuality, identity, autonomy, and liberty.[206]

Appropriation of name or likeness and societal values

Moreover, the appropriation tort protects forms of respect that are essential for the key societal value of maintaining civility and community.[207] In an article published in 1991, Post suggested that emotional or dignitary harms resulted from misappropriation because the use of another's identity undermined "socialized expectations of respect."[208] As mentioned previously, expectations of respect are grounded in norms of propriety determined by members of a common community.[209] Post claimed, "Personality is violated when these forms of respect are transgressed."[210] Thus, the appropriation tort helps maintain community "by enforcing norms of propriety," which preserve "the community instantiated by those norms."[211] In 2001, Post clarified that such conceptions of privacy assume that social norms "constitute the decencies of civilization" and "govern" social interactions.[212]

Summary

Scholars have argued that the widely accepted mass publication-based privacy torts protect all of the individual and societal values of privacy. Scholarship from law, philosophy, psychology, and sociology suggests the appropriation tort protects most of the individual privacy values—personality, identity, autonomy, mental health, and liberty[213] —as well as one societal value—maintaining civility and community. [214] The literature associates each of the individual privacy values—personality, [215] which overlaps with autonomy [216] and liberty, [217] mental health, [218] and emotional release, [219] which can promote self-evaluation and reflection[220]—with the disclosure of private facts tort. The disclosure tort also protects each of the societal privacy valuesfostering civility and community,[221] enabling individuals to maintain the mental distance necessary to display the forms of respect essential to form and maintain relationships,[222] and providing individuals with the reserve necessary to participate in public life.[223]

Reconciling Clashes between Free Expression and Privacy Values

In addition to identifying and explicating the values served by freedom of expression and privacy, scholars have explored clashes between certain First Amendment values and several of the privacy values protected by the appropriation and disclosure torts, suggesting how such conflicts should be resolved. Literature also has examined how courts, especially the U.S. Supreme Court, have reconciled conflicts between press freedom and privacy values. Some of that scholarship suggests court rulings have favored freedom of expression.[224] Yet, as mentioned in the introduction, Jane Kirtley has claimed courts have favored privacy.[225]

Weighing select free expression and privacy values

Some scholarship suggests courts should weigh or balance free expression and privacy values when those come into conflict. Those efforts primarily suggest free expression values ought to outweigh privacy values, except in extremely rare circumstances. For instance, Thomas Emerson proposed that conflicts between freedom of expression and privacy should be resolved by examining the values of freedom of expression and privacy in a well-functioning system of freedom of expression.[226] He claimed the system would allow only "a very narrow" exception to the general rule of protection of speech.[227] Emerson said speech that is proscribed by the privacy torts, and thus is outside First Amendment protection, must harm the individual privacy value of "inner personality"[228] by "assaulting the dignity of the individual by depicting matters of a wholly personal and intimate nature."[229] That type of speech would harm personal autonomy, which the system presumes is essential for the development and maintenance of democratic society. Emerson proposed that in clashes among the societal freedom of expression values—discovery of truth, participation in decision making, and social change—and the individual privacy value of autonomy, the individual privacy value would prevail over the societal free expression values.[230] When the individual expression values of self-fulfillment or discovery of truth conflict with the autonomy value of privacy, Emerson claimed "privacy would prevail over freedom of expression."[231] He proposed the "guiding principle would be that the exercise of an individual right which injures another person would not be favored."[232] Still, Emerson said that invasions of privacy that caused only emotional injuries generally would not outweigh First Amendment protection for the expression.[233] Under Emerson's system, privacy would only trump freedom of expression values that clashed with the autonomy value of privacy.[234] In all other instances, free expression values would prevail.

C. Edwin Baker proposed a method for reconciling conflicts between the autonomy value of freedom of expression and privacy. That method is grounded in the presumption that freedom of expression and privacy serve two distinct types of autonomy: meaningful autonomy and formal autonomy.[235] The central premise of meaningful autonomy is that each person should be free to make the choices she desires.[236] That means each individual ought to have opportunities to make choices about her own life without unnecessary interference by others.[237] While meaningful autonomy suggests that each person should have the moral right to control whether her personal information is disclosed, formal autonomy assigns each person the agency to control whether such information is disclosed. Baker said formal autonomy "centers on the agent being the final authority over decisions about herself or, in the case of speech, about her speech."[238] He described formal autonomy as the "liberty of choice" that shields each individual from regulations that would prevent an individual from having the ultimate ability to determine what to disclose about herself.[239] While one individual's exercise of meaningful autonomy value may inhibit another person's meaningful autonomy, Baker claimed that one individual's exercise of the formal autonomy value would not inhibit another person's meaningful or formal autonomy. He declared that privacy serves meaningful autonomy and freedom of expression serves formal autonomy. Thus, Baker proposed freedom of expression should prevail over privacy when the autonomy value underlying freedom of speech or press collides with the autonomy value underlying privacy.[240]

Other scholarship has focused on reconciling conflicts between privacy values and the individual freedom of expression value of discovering truth or the societal freedom of expression value of the marketplace of ideas.[241] For instance, legal expert Frederick Schauer has claimed the very development of defamation and privacy torts implies that some individual or social interests might outweigh the value of acquiring knowledge, which underlies the freedom of expression values of discovery of truth and the marketplace of ideas.[242] Schauer compared the privacy interest likely to be harmed by a disclosure to the public interest likely to be served when audiences receive the information.[243] He noted that disclosures of information about a person's private life likely would harm more than the emotional health of the subject. Such disclosures, he wrote, would infringe on a private person's "interest in controlling certain aspects of his life" and, in turn, would undermine the individual privacy values of autonomy and liberty.[244] The public interest defense, however, recognizes the public benefit from receiving such information about a public figure, such as a celebrity, or a public official, a person elected to public office might override the individual's privacy interests. Schauer suggested that a public official or figure may relinquish some control over his social personality, decreasing his reasonable expectation of privacy "by placing his personality before the electorate for scrutiny" or by otherwise seeking to "benefit from publicity about [his] life."[245] That approach seeks to reconcile the individual privacy values of autonomy and liberty with the societal free expression values of self-governance and the marketplace-of-ideas.

Favoring free speech for matters of governing or public importance

Edward Bloustein published a pragmatic approach for reconciling speech-privacy conflicts. Bloustein asserted that Meiklejohn's audience-based free expression theory would provide a practical framework for reconciling collisions between tort-based privacy claims and the constitutional right of the public to receive information.[246] Bloustein relied on Meiklejohn's premise that the First Amendment protects the right of the public to hear information relevant to self-governance. Bloustein wrote, "[T]he weight to be given 'the public interest in obtaining information' should depend on whether or not the information is relevant to the public's governing purposes."[247] That would assign strong First Amendment protection to the disclosure of information about government officials, public issues, or other matters of governing importance.[248] The free expression value associated with society's right to learn information that enhances self-governance then would prevail over individual privacy interests, but the individual privacy value of dignity could trump a speaker's expression of information lacking governing importance.[249]

Another legal commentator, Eric B. Easton, wrote that the Supreme Court has reconciled clashes between freedom of press and privacy by creating tests that suggest audience members' rights to receive matters of "public importance" should trump individual privacy interests.[250] He suggested the Court's rulings in *Cox Broadcasting v. Cohn* and subsequent cases expanded First Amendment protection for the media to cover the publication of truthful information about matters of public significance, which includes matters of public importance,[251] "public interest," "legitimate public concern," and "newsworthiness."[252] Easton reasoned, "The public must know what is happening within official quarters, not only to maintain the ability to participate effectively but also for the purifying effect public scrutiny has on the decision-making process . . . ."[253] That public importance standard includes the self-governance, participation in decision-making, and watchdog values of freedom of expression. Easton's proposal suggests those audience-based freedom of expression values could prevail over individual privacy values as long as privacy is not considered essential to preserve freedom of speech and press.[254]

Summary

Relevant scholarship has reached some conflicting conclusions as to whether certain free expression values should trump certain privacy values. Baker proposed the freedom of expression values of autonomy, which he associated with liberty and self-fulfillment, should prevail over the privacy value of autonomy.[255] On the other hand, Emerson argued the individual privacy value of personhood or autonomy should prevail over the free expression values of self-fulfillment and discovery of truth.[256] Emerson would allow individual privacy values to outweigh the societal free expression values of participation in decision-making and stability and change, but Bloustein and Easton claimed that freedom to express matters related to self-governance, or of public importance, should prevail over privacy.[257]

Applying Newsworthiness or Public Significance Exceptions

Commentators also have assessed courts' applications of the newsworthiness or public interest defense to privacy invasion claims as a means of resolving conflicts between privacy and freedom of expression. Indeed, much of the literature on privacy and freedom of expression focuses on the constitutional defenses developed by U.S. Supreme Court rulings as a means of balancing the individual and societal values at stake. That scholarship generally suggests the newsworthiness or public interest defense might resolve conflicts between the values served by free expression and the appropriation or disclosure tort.

The newsworthiness defense

In their groundbreaking 1890 law review article, Warren and Brandeis suggested that disclosures of newsworthy information could not be considered actionable invasions of privacy: "The right to privacy does not prohibit any publication of matter which is of public or general interest."[258] Samuel Warren and Louis Brandeis grounded that exemption in the premise that privacy laws should protect individuals in "whose affairs the community has no legitimate concern from being dragged into an undesirable and undesired publicity."[259] They claimed that privacy laws would not apply equally to those individuals and to "others who, in varying degrees, have renounced the right to live their lives screened from public observation."[260] For example, they suggested that an ordinary individual's "peculiarities of manner and person" would be matters inappropriate to discuss publicly, but those same peculiarities could become "matters of public importance" if that person were seeking a political office or other public position.[261] They also suggested that publishing matters related to the proceedings of courts, government bodies, or other organizations formed to serve the general interest of society would be exempted from liability.[262] Those suggestions provided a basis for courts and commentators to recognize a public interest, or newsworthiness, exemption from liability for the appropriation and disclosure torts.

Rodney Smolla contended the First Amendment provides a direct and a derivative right for news organizations to use a person's name or likeness in connection with a newsworthy event. Freedom of speech or press, he said, "overrides the law of torts" that would otherwise make the unauthorized use of one's name or likeness for another person's commercial benefit a tortious invasion of privacy by appropriation.[263] The direct First Amendment newsworthiness exception protects the use of one's identity in connection with a report on a newsworthy event in which members of society are likely to express interest. The derivative First Amendment right extends to a secondary use of that report to advertise the news item or entity. In both instances, the newsworthiness exception would prevent the publisher from being held liable for appropriation and would promote the free flow of information.[264] The free expression value of the marketplace of ideas, then, would prevail over the individual privacy values of autonomy and liberty.

The newsworthiness exception, however, would not exempt a publisher from liability for an exploitative use of one's name or likeness for commercial purposes. For example, Smolla proposed the actual malice standard of liability would be applied when a magazine printed a celebrity's picture on its cover in connection with a false news story. If the magazine published the celebrity's image and the associated news report with knowledge or reckless disregard of falsity, the publisher would be liable for invasion of privacy by appropriation. Under those circumstances, the individual privacy values of autonomy and liberty would prevail over the freedom of expression value of the marketplace of ideas.

The public significance privilege

Several commentators have claimed the U.S. Supreme Court's development of a public significance defense for disclosure of private facts cases has allowed courts to favor press freedom over privacy.[265] They suggested the Court's ruling in *Florida Star v. B.J.F.* in 1989 signaled the inevitable demise of the disclosure tort.[266] The Court held: "[W]here a newspaper publishes truthful information which it has lawfully obtained, punishment may lawfully be imposed, if at all, only when narrowly tailored to a state interest of the highest order . . . ."[267] For example, Peter Edelman claimed that ruling continued the Court's tendency to avoid the collision between press and privacy rights "by finding that the disclosed information was lawfully obtained."[268] He suggested the Court favored a free expression value of liberty in the *Florida Star* ruling and failed to acknowledge the privacy values protected by the disclosure tort.[269] Edelman proposed the Court should have weighed the public's interest in learning about information held in government records against the privacy values of autonomy, emotional health, and forming meaningful relationships.[270]

Edelman and other commentators have even argued that courts' reliance on defenses that favor freedom of expression threatens the viability of the disclosure tort.[271] Communications law scholar Deckle McLean wrote in 2000 that the *Florida Star* ruling "makes success in a public disclosure suit even more unlikely than it was prior to the ruling."[272] McLean concluded that a subsequent Michigan appeals court ruling, which "frankly admitted the importance of balancing privacy interests against First Amendment interests," provided a more effective approach for considering privacy interests than was provided by the *Florida Star* ruling.[273] Such an approach would encourage courts to give greater consideration to privacy and free expression values.

Summary

Scholarship focusing on the newsworthiness, public interest, or matter of public significance exceptions primarily encourages courts to focus on the degree to which information benefits audiences and the character of the use of identifying information. Such approaches could allow courts to favor the audience-based free expression values of the marketplace of ideas, self-governance, and checking values over individual privacy values.

Seeking Alternative Approaches to Reconcile Clashes

As indicated by the literature reviewed in this chapter, many scholars have identified and described individual and societal values served by both freedom of expression and privacy. How to reconcile the two sets of values when they come into conflict has drawn some, but considerably less, scholarly attention, with a couple authors looking at small samples of cases to describe how courts undertake this difficult task.[274]

While scholarship has focused primarily on U.S. Supreme Court rulings, defenses, or legal theory, two articles provided especially valuable analysis of how select lower court rulings have weighed privacy and free expression values. Those articles, published by Professor McLean and by Professor Diane Zimmerman, suggest that systematic analysis of lower court rulings may illustrate alternative approaches to reconciling privacy and free speech values.[275]

Examining state and federal appellate courts' approaches

This study attempts to provide a systematic review of post-*Florida Star* state high court and federal appellate court rulings to determine if and how courts address free expression and privacy values when deciding cases involving the disclosure of private facts and appropriation torts. The analysis includes disclosure of private facts and appropriation cases decided by U.S. Courts of Appeals and state high courts between June 1989 and July 2011 to determine whether and, if so, how courts identify and attempt to reconcile individual free expression values — autonomy, self-fulfillment, self-realization, discovery of truth, and participation in the social and political decision-making process—societal free expression values—effective self-governance, check on government, marketplace of ideas, balance between societal stability and change, and toleration—and the individual and social privacy values associated with each tort.

Chapter three examines disclosure of private facts cases for discussion of freedom of expression values and the individual privacy values—autonomy, liberty, and emotional health—and social privacy values—fostering civility and community, helping individuals maintain relationships, and providing individuals with the reserve necessary to participate in public life—associated with disclosure. [276] Chapter four examines appropriation cases for discussion of the individual and social freedom of expression values and the individual privacy values—personality, autonomy, liberty, and emotional health—and the social privacy value—maintaining civility and community—underlying the appropriation tort.[277] Chapter five analyzes trends found in courts' discussion of free expression and privacy values in disclosure of private facts or appropriation rulings.

Identifying relevant rulings

The case analysis focused on state high courts' rulings and U.S. Courts of Appeals' rulings because state high courts have binding authority over all lower state courts within their respective states and federal circuit courts of appeals have binding authority over all federal district courts within their respective circuits. State courts have subject-matter jurisdiction on state law claims such as disclosure of private facts under state common law or appropriation under state statutory law.[278] But federal courts have subject-matter jurisdiction to hear federal issues, including conflicts between the First Amendment and privacy law. Federal courts also have diversity jurisdiction to hear cases involving disputes between residents from different states when the claimed damages exceed $75,000.[279] In any cases that do not involve federal issues, federal courts are constitutionally required to apply and to interpret state law.[280]

Cases for analysis were identified by searching the online versions of three reporting services: Westlaw, LexisNexis Academic, and *Media Law Reporter*.[281] All three databases were used to minimize the likelihood of missing relevant cases. Searches were limited to disclosure of private facts cases and appropriation cases reported between June 21, 1989, when the U.S. Supreme Court ruled in *Florida Star v. B.J.F.*, and July 31, 2011.[282] After *Florida Star*, some scholars criticized the Court's method of analysis for focusing on speech interests without adequately considering countervailing privacy interests.[283] For example, Paul Gewirtz wrote: "The Court gives only token recognition to the value of implementing legal protections of privacy. This extreme solicitude for the one and sharply limited solicitude for the other is what should be reversed."[284]

Analyzing disclosure of private facts and appropriation rulings

Traditional textual analysis was used to assess if and how courts discussed free expression values and/or privacy values when explaining the rationales for their holdings, concurrences, or dissents. Opinions were categorized as 1) discussing free expression values and privacy values; 2) discussing free expression values but not privacy values; 3) not discussing free expression values but discussing privacy values; 4) discussing neither free expression values nor privacy values. When values were discussed in the opinions, those values were categorized as individual or social free expression values or individual or social privacy values found in the literature on free expression and privacy theory.

Identifying discussions of individual freedom of expression values

The individual freedom of expression values are autonomy, self-realization or self-fulfillment, attainment of truth, and participation in social and political decision-making. The following explications of those values guided the analysis:

The autonomy value is assigned to discussion of an individual's or autonomous press's personal agency or self-determination, individuality, ability to choose what to communicate or publish, or liberty from authoritarian pressure to publish particular information.[285] The self-realization or self-fulfillment value also overlaps with autonomy. Thus, the value of autonomy includes discussion of the individual sphere of life Mill described as 1) "the inward domain of consciousness," 2) "liberty of conscience, in the most comprehensive sense," 3) "liberty of thought and feeling," and 4) "absolute freedom of opinion and sentiment on all subjects."[286] That value also includes writings that tie freedom of speech to personal growth, personal salvation, personal dignity, and the equal worth of individuals.[287]

The attainment of truth value includes discussions tying freedom to communicate to liberty to express opinions, to seek true information, to test one's opinions, or to engage in discussions to seek greater personal understanding.[288] Descriptions that grounded freedom of expression with freedom to discuss or debate information or to seek greater truth or personal understanding are categorized under the individual value of attainment of truth when rulings emphasized the personal benefit to individual communicators.

The participation in decision-making value includes discussions connecting freedom to communicate to one's ability to form judgments about government and society, to evaluate political decisions, and to contribute to culture. As Thomas Emerson explained, the principle also "includes freedom of expression in religion, literature, art, science, and all areas of human learning and knowledge."[289]

<u>Identifying discussions of societal freedom of expression values</u>

The societal values for free expression are self-governance, check on government, marketplace of ideas, stability and change, and toleration. The following explications of those values guided the analysis:

The marketplace of ideas value includes discussions connecting audiences' freedom to receive information, to listen to discussions, or even to take part in debate that allows individuals to receive multiple points of view. The value also includes writings that declare a free flow of information is essential for audiences to receive the information needed for speech to remedy other harmful speech.

The balance between change and stability value includes discussion indicating freedom of expression serves as a safety valve, facilitating stable political or social change, or serves as a general mechanism for society to address matters likely to cause violence or social unrest if not debated or discussed.[290]

The self-governance value is assigned to discussions that connect freedom of expression to the benefits to democracy that result from audiences receiving information necessary to cast informed votes, to evaluate information and opinions about political or public life, or to debate political issues. In other words, this value is assigned to rationales that recognize Alexander Meiklejohn's argument tying freedom of expression to audiences' need to receive speech on matters of governing importance that advance society's sovereignty over its governors.[291]

The checking value, or watchdog value, is applied to references to the role that freedom of speech or press plays in alerting the public to corruption, incompetence, malfeasance or other abuses of power by government or other powerful entities in society.[292]

The final free expression value, toleration, includes discussions tying freedom of expression to message recipients' abilities to respect the equal worth of all individuals, to receive information relevant to a broad range of intellectual values, to encourage societies to allow extreme views to challenge social norms, and to consider messages that challenge common fears, biases, beliefs, and assumptions. [293] In other words the toleration value considers freedom of expression, as Lee C. Bollinger explained, as "a social context in which basic intellectual values are developed and articulated, where assumptions about undesirable intellectual traits are offered and remedies proffered."[294]

Identifying discussions of individual privacy values

The individual privacy values are autonomy, emotional release or emotional health, and liberty. Following are explications of each of those values that guided the analysis:

References to protection of a person's inner personality, personal identity, individuality, dignity, or integrity are categorized as discussion of the autonomy value of privacy.[295] The privacy value of autonomy also includes references to self-determination, personal agency, individuality, or the ability to avoid being controlled by others.[296]

The emotional health value includes references to an individual's emotional well-being, emotional release, and peace of mind. The emotional health value is assigned to descriptions of privacy as a means of facilitating emotional self-preservation, providing opportunities to reflect on emotions, overcoming psychic harms, and growing as an emotionally mature individual.[297] Emotional release benefits individuals by encouraging relaxation, which includes releasing stress and escaping from social pressures to conform one's conduct or persona to others' expectations. Emotional release also serves a safety valve function that allows individuals to vent strong opinions or emotions in an environment he controls.[298]

The liberty value includes mentions of control over information about one's self and freedom to choose if and how sensitive information is disclosed without undue pressure from government or social interference. Liberty promotes autonomy and mental health, but it is unique because it focuses on the individual's ability to make decisions without fear of censorship or even social pressures intended to coerce individuals to conform to social expectations. That individual value stresses personal freedom.

Identifying discussions of societal privacy values

The societal privacy values are civility and community, forming relationships, and promoting democratic processes. Following are explications of each of those values that guided the analysis:

The civility and community value include discussion of social norms or standards of decency intended to promote harmony and participation in collective life. That value includes discussions of social virtues, such as respect for others as members of a community of individuals, considered essential for individuals to engage in collective life.[299]

A closely related value, forming and maintaining relationships, includes mentions of friendship, intimacy, trust, and respect for individual persons. Whereas the civility and community value emphasizes collective life, the latter value focuses on forming individual relationships with friends, co-workers, or family. The value of forming and maintaining relationships includes references to personal actions or attributes that promote one person's ability to connect with at least one other person in a meaningful, perhaps even intimate, manner.[300]

The final privacy value, promoting democratic processes, includes discussions that tie privacy to individuals' willingness to vote, engage in debates on public issues, discuss political issues, evaluate information relevant to self-governance and public life, or to run for public office.[301]

Of course, the analysis of case law reveals language that at times simultaneously relates to more than one of the aforementioned values. When that occurred in a case, each of the appropriate values was assigned to that case.

Limitations

This study has several limitations. First, the purpose of the study is to examine how courts with binding authority over lower state courts or federal district courts in their circuits have identified free expression and/or privacy values when attempting to reconcile clashes between freedom of speech or press and privacy. Thus, the case analysis excluded cases that involved solely the right of publicity, as opposed to the right of privacy. Publicity is viewed as a property right, the right to profit or not from commercial uses of one's identity and, thus, involves significantly different values than the personal right of privacy.

Second, this study was restricted to cases reported by Westlaw, LexisNexis Academic, or *Media Law Reporter* using the search tools. It is possible that some relevant cases were not included in one of those databases or were not associated with the search, case categorization, or indexing mechanisms or used by the editors for those case services. Also, limiting state cases to those decided by state high courts and federal cases to those decided by the circuit courts of appeals may have resulted in the study missing some significant discussions of how to reconcile competing values by lower courts. The sheer volume of cases, however, precluded including trial courts and state intermediate appellate courts in the analysis. Trial court rulings only were included for cases that a state high court or federal circuit court of appeals remanded for trial.

Third, textual analysis inherently introduced subjectivity into this study. Even though individual and societal values were explicated on preceding pages, deciding which language fits in which category requires interpretation and judgment. It is possible that another person who reads the cases analyzed for this study would place language from the cases in different categories. Recognizing those limitations, the author and trained coders carefully read a sample of disclosure of private facts and appropriation cases and applied the value explications to each one in an attempt to recognize and minimize challenges to consistent applications of the coding scheme.

Chapter 2 Notes

---

1 GEORGE KATEB, THE INNER OCEAN: INDIVIDUALISM AND DEMOCRATIC CULTURE 3-4 (1992). *See also* RODNEY A. SMOLLA, FREE SPEECH IN AN OPEN SOCIETY 119 (1992). Smolla wrote:

> Privacy, like freedom of expression, has both an individual and a collective dimension. Laws protecting privacy are the means through which the collective acknowledges rules of civility that are designed to affirm human autonomy and dignity. If conscience and consciousness are the roots of free expression, they are also the roots of privacy.

2 C. Edwin Baker, *Autonomy and Informational Privacy, or Gossip: The Central Meaning of The First Amendment*, 21 SOC. PHIL. & POL'Y 215, 220-21 (2004). The U.S. Supreme Court first recognized an autonomy-based constitutional right to privacy in *Griswold v. Connecticut* in 1965. Thomas I. Emerson, *The Right of Privacy and Freedom of The Press,* 14 HARV. C.R.-C.L. L. REV. 328, 328 (1979) (citing Griswold v. Connecticut, 381 U.S. 479 (1965)).

3 For the sake of clarity, the term common law torts will be used to refer to privacy torts recognized under state common law and statutory laws throughout this study.

4 Emerson, *supra* note 2, at 330-31.

5 C. Edwin Baker, *Scope of the First Amendment Freedom of Speech*, 25 UCLA L. REV. 964, 964 (1977).

6 *Id.* at 964, 990-92. *See also* FREDERICK SCHAUER, FREE SPEECH PRINCIPLE 71 (1982) ("In order for the argument from autonomy to hold up, it must be rooted in social contract theory").

7 Baker, *supra* note 5, at 991.

8 *Id.*

9 *Id.*

10 Baker explained, "The emphasis on 'self' in self-fulfillment requires the theory to delineate a realm of liberty for self-determined processes of self-realization. The participation in change value requires the theory to specify and protect activities essential to a democratic, participatory process of change." *Id.*

11 *Id.* at 966.

12 *Id.* at 1013 (quoting JOHN STUART MILL, ON LIBERTY 13 (1956)).

13 Thomas Scanlon, *A Theory of Freedom of Expression*, 1 PHIL. & PUB. AFF. 204, 214 (1972).

14 *Id.* at 213.

15 *Id.* at 214-15.

16 THOMAS I. EMERSON, SYSTEMS OF FREEDOM OF EXPRESSION 6-9 (1969).

[17] *Id.* It is important to note that Baker referred to Emerson's functions as values because he defined values as purposes. Baker, *supra* note 5, at 990-91.

[18] EMERSON, *supra* note 16, at 6. It is also important to note that Professor Martin H. Redish later argued that "the constitutional guarantee of free speech ultimately serves only one true value," which Redish called "individual self-realization." That value encompasses "development of the individual's powers and abilities" and "the individual's control of his or her own destiny through making life-affecting decisions." Redish, *The Value of Free Speech*, 130 U. PA. L. REV. 592, 604 (1981). *Cf.* Eric B. Easton, *Public Importance: Balancing Proprietary Interests and the Right to Know*, 21 CARDOZO ARTS & ENT. 139, 159 (2003) (arguing that the value of self-fulfillment underlying the right to speak "is utterly hollow if there is no audience.").

[19] EMERSON, *supra* note 16, at 6.

[20] *Id.* at 6-7.

[21] *Id.* at 7.

[22] Baker, *supra* note 5, at 992.

[23] EMERSON, *supra* note 16, at 7.

[24] *Id.*

[25] Randall P. Bezanson, *Means and Ends and Food Lion: The Tension between Exemption and Independence in Newsgathering by the Press*, 47 EMORY L.J. 895 (1998); Randall P. Bezanson, *The Right to Privacy Revisited: Privacy, News, and Social Change*,1890-1990 , 80 CALIF . L. REV. 1133, 1153 (1992); Randall P. Bezanson, *Political Agnosticism, Editorial Freedom, and Government Neutrality Toward the Press*, 72 IOWA L. REV. 1359 (1987); Randall P. Bezanson, *The New Free Press Guarantee*, 63 VA. L. REV. 731 (1977).

[26] JOHN MILTON, AREOPAGATICA: A SPEECH TO THE PARLIAMENT OF ENGLAND, FOR THE LIBERTY OF UNLICENSED PRINTING 3 (Cambridge" Chadwyck-Healey, 1999) (1644). He wrote:

> If ye be thus resolv'd, as it were injury to thinke ye were not, I know not what should withhold me from presenting ye with fit instance wherein to shew both that love of truth which ye eminently prosesse, and that uprightnesse of your judgement which is not wont to be partial to your selves; by judging over again that Order which ye have ordain'd to *regulate Printing. That no* Book *pamphlet, or* [*p*]*aper shall be henceforth Printed, unlesse the same be first approv'd and licenc't by such*, or at least one of such, as shall be thereto appointed.

[27] *Id.*

---

[28] JOHN STUART MILL, ON LIBERTY 28 (David Bromwich & George Kateb, eds., Yale Univ. Press 2003) (1859). Mill offered the utilitarian rationale that individuals would need to pit truth against falsehoods if they wished to find "the clearer and livelier perception of truth." He wrote:

> [T]he peculiar evil of silencing the expression of an opinion is that it is robbing the human race: posterity as well as the existing generation; those who dissent from the opinion, still more than those who hold it. If the opinion is right, they are deprived of the opportunity of exchanging error for truth; if wrong, they lose what is almost as great a benefit, the clearer perception and livelier impression of truth, produced by its collision with error.

[29] *Id.* at 26.
[30] *Id.*
[31] *Id.* at 82-83.
[32] *Id.* at 83.
[33] *Id.* at 73-74.
[34] Bezanson, *New Free Press Guarantee*, *supra* note 25, at 732, 761; Bezanson, *Means and Ends*, *supra* note 25, at 897-899, 927 n.22.
[35] Bezanson, *New Free Press Guarantee*, *supra* note 25, at 734.
[36] *Id.* at 762 (1977) (citing 420 U.S. 469, 495-96 (1975).
[37] *Id.*
[38] *Id.* at 763 (citing Pell v. Procunier, 417 U.S. 817 (1974); Saxbe v. Washington Post Co., 417 U.S. 843 (1974); noting that the U.S. Supreme Court's rulings on access to prisons "support the propriety of such a neutral ban on access to sources of information under governmental control").
[39] *Id.*
[40] Bezanson, *New Free Press Guarantee*, *supra* note 25,at 757 (citing Miami Herald v. Tornillo, 418 U.S. 241, 257-58 (1974)).
[41] 418 U.S. at 257-58.
[42] Bezanson, *New Free Press Guarantee*, *supra* note 25, at 757 (citing 418 U.S. at 257-58).
[43] Scanlon, *supra* note 13, at 217.
[44] *Id. See also* Baker, *supra* note 5, at 1028-29. Baker wrote:

> By protecting substantively valued conduct from abridgement by general prohibitions, the liberty model provides for a process of public decision making and a search for, or creation of, truth that avoids the problems and improper assumptions of both the market models. Thus, the liberty model better promotes the key value that justified the classic marketplace of ideas theory of freedom of speech: the value of furthering the search for truth or best premises, a value

that, due to a failure of assumptions, the classic theory could not adequately serve.

[45] Potter Stewart, *Or of the Press*, 26 HASTINGS L.J. 631, 632 (1975); Bezanson, *New Free Press Guarantee*, *supra* note 25, at 762.

[46] Gerald J. Baldasty & Roger A. Simpson, *The Deceptive 'Right to Know': How Pessimism Rewrote the First Amendment*, 56 WASH. L. REV. 365 (1981); Thomas I. Emerson, *The First Amendment and the Right to Know*, 1976 WASH. U. L.Q. 1; James C. Goodale, *Legal Pitfalls in the Right to Know*, 1976 WASH. U. L.Q. 29; Michael J. Hayes, *What Ever Happened to 'the Right to Know'?: Access to Government-Controlled Information Since* Richmond Newspapers, 73 VA. L. REV. 1111 (2007); William E. Lee, *The Supreme Court and the Right to Receive Expression*, 1987 SUP. CT. REV. 303; David M. Obrien, *The First Amendment and the Public's 'Right to Know,'* 7 HASTINGS CONST. L.Q. 579 (1979).

[47] *Id.*

[48] ALEXANDER MEIKLEJOHN, FREE SPEECH AND ITS RELATION TO SELF-GOVERNMENT (1948).

[49] *Id.*at 33.

[50] *Id.*

[51] Thomas I. Emerson, *Toward a General Theory of the First Amendment*, 72 YALE L.J. 877, 878 (1963) (describing freedom of expression as a "method of securing participation by the members of society in social, including political, decision-making").

[52] MEIKLEJOHN, *supra* note 48, at 25-26. Responding to criticism that his original view was too narrow, Professor Meiklejohn later expanded his definition of political speech to include many forms of communication "from which the voter derives the knowledge, intelligence, sensitivity to human values," that inform voting. He said education, "achievements of philosophy and the sciences," "literature and the arts," and "the spreading of information and opinions" related to public issues. Alexander Meiklejohn, *The First Amendment Is an Absolute*, 1961 SUP. CT. REV. 245, 257.

[53] MEIKLEJOHN, *supra* note 48, at 36-40.

[54] Harry Kalven, *The New York Times Case: A Note on "The Central Meaning of The First Amendment,"* 1964 SUP. CT. REV. 191, 208 (citing 376 U.S. 254, 273-276 (1964)).

[55] *Id.*

[56] *Id.* at 212-13.

[57] *Id.* at 205.

[58] Robert H. Bork, *Neutral Principles and Some First Amendment Problems*, 47 IND. L.J. 1, 28 (1971).

[59] *Id.*

[60] *Id.* at 29-30.

[61] *Id.* at 28-31.

[62] Vincent Blasi, *The Checking Value in First Amendment Theory*, 1977 AM. B. FOUND. RES. J. 522, 541-42 (warning "if modern government were ever to gain complete control of the channels of mass communication or to incapacitate its professional critics in some other way, there would be no effective check on official misconduct").

[63] Stewart, *supra* note 45, at 632.

[64] *Id.* at 634.

[65] *Id.* at 636.

[66] Blasi, *supra* note 62, at 541-42.

[67] Thomas I. Emerson, *Colonial Intentions and the Current Realities of the First Amendment*, 125 U. Pa. L. Rev. 737, 754-56 (1977); Emerson, *supra* note 47, at 2; O'Brien, *supra* note 46, at 590; Wallace Parks, *The Open Government Principle: Applying the Right to Know Under the Constitution*, 26 GEORGE WASH. L. REV. 1 (1957). *But see* David M. O'Brien, *Reassessing the First Amendment and the Public's Right to Know in Constitutional Adjudication*, 26 VILL. L. REV. 8 (1980) (claiming proponents of a constitutional right to know "confuse the political ideal of freedom of information and an informed public with a directly enforceable right to know under the first amendment.")

[68] Emerson, *supra* note 46, at 2.

[69] *Id.* 17.

[70] *See, e.g.*, Redish, *supra*, note 18, at 617-19 (1981) ("[I]f viewed as merely a means by which the ultimate value of self-realization is facilitated, the concept may prove quite valuable in determining what speech is deserving of constitutional protection."); Neil M. Richards, *Intellectual Privacy*, 87 TEX. L. REV. 387, 394-96 (2008) (explaining that the theory "has been enormously influential in both free speech theory and jurisprudence."); SCHAUER, *supra* note 6, at 19-20 (explaining the marketplace concept as a "process of discussion" through which truth emerges); SMOLLA, *supra* note 1, at 8 ("While the marketplace of ideas is far from perfect, in the long run it is overwhelmingly superior to a system of regulated expression, and is by itself enough to make the case for a preferred position in an open culture."). *But see* Baker, *Scope*, *supra* note 5, at 974-81 (asserting that the marketplace model relies on faulty assumptions); Stanley Ingber, *The Marketplace of Ideas: A Legitimizing Myth*, 1984 DUKE L.J. 1, 7-8 ("On the whole, current and historical trends have not vindicated the market model's faith in the rationality of the human mind, yet this faith stands as a foundation block for most recent free speech theory.").

[71] *See, e.g.*, Shapero v. Ky. Bar Ass'n, 486 U.S. 466, 483 (1987) (O'Connor, J., dissenting) (asserting that the marketplace metaphor "has become almost as familiar as the principle that it sought to justify."); Wolston v. Reader's

Digest Assn., Inc., 443 U.S. 157, 171 (1978) (Blackmun, J., concurring); Pac. Gas & Elec. Co. v. Pub. Utils. Comm'n of Cal., 475 U.S. 1, 8 (1985) ("By protecting those who wish to enter the marketplace of ideas from government attack, the First Amendment protects the public's interest in receiving information."); Lamont v. Postmaster Gen., 381 U.S. 301, 308 (1964) (Brennan, J., concurring) ("The dissemination of ideas can accomplish nothing if otherwise willing addresses are not free to receive and consider them. It would be a barren marketplace of ideas that had only sellers and no buyers.").

[72] Abrams v. United States, 250 U.S. 616, 630 (1919) (Holmes, J., dissenting).

[73] *Id.* at 630.

[74] Baker, *supra* note 5, at 965-66; Melville B. Nimmer, *The Right to Speak from Times to Time: First Amendment Theory Applied to Libel and Misapplied to Privacy*, 56 CAL. L. REV. 935, 955-7 (1968).

[75] *See, e.g.*, Baker, *supra* note 5, at 965-66; Jerome A. Barron, *Access to the Press—A New First Amendment Right*, 80 HARV. L. REV. 1641 (1966).

[76] Baker, *supra* note 5, at 965-66.

[77] *Id.* at 966.

[78] Redish, *supra* note 18, at 619.

[79] *Id.*

[80] EMERSON, *supra* note 16 at 7.

[81] *Id.*

[82] *Id.*

[83] *Id.*

[84] Lee C. Bollinger, *Free Speech and Intellectual Values*, 92 YALE L.J. 438, 438 (1983).

[85] *Id.* at 460.

[86] *Id.*

[87] *Id.* at 439.

[88] Emerson, *supra* note 46, at 2-3.

[89] MEIKLEJOHN, *supra* note 48, at 25-26.

[90] Scanlon, *supra* note 13, at 214.

[91] Emerson, *supra* note 46, at 22.

[92] *See, e.g.*, Edward J. Bloustein, *Privacy as an Aspect of Human Dignity: An Answer to Dean Prosser*, 39 N.Y.U.L. REV. 962, 966 (1964); ("[I]f [Dean Prosser] is right, the social value or interest we call privacy is not an independent one, but is only a composite of the value our society places on protecting mental tranquility, reputation, and intangible forms of property."); Charles Fried, *Privacy [A Moral Analysis]*, *in* PHILOSOPHICAL DIMENSIONS OF PRIVACY 205 (Ferdinand David Schoeman ed., 1984) ("It is my thesis that privacy is not just one possible means among others to insure some other value, but that it is necessarily related to ends and relations of the most

fundamental sort: respect, love, friendship, and trust."); Ken Gormley, *One Hundred Years of Privacy*, 1992 WIS. L. REV. 1335, 1339 ("[L]egal privacy consists of four or five different species of legal rights which are quite distinct from each other and thus incapable of a single definition, yet heavily interrelated as a matter of history, such that efforts to completely sever one from another are (and have been) disastrous."); Judith Jarvis Thomson, *The Right to Privacy*, *in* PHILOSOPHICAL DIMENSIONS OF PRIVACY 272 (Ferdinand David Schoeman ed., 1984) ("Perhaps the most striking thing about the right to privacy is that nobody seems to have any very clear idea what it is.").

[93] *See, e.g.*, Hyman Gross, *The Concept of Privacy*, 42 N.Y.U.L. REV. 33, 36 (1967) (describing privacy as "the condition of human life" in which a person limits her acquaintance with another person and limits the other person's knowledge of her personal affairs.); W.A. Parent, *A New Definition of Privacy for the Law*, 2 LAW & PHIL. 305, 306 (1983) (defining privacy as "the condition of not having undocumented personal information about oneself known by others.").

[94] Bezanson, *The Right to Privacy*, *supra* note 25. Bezanson argued that the legal right to privacy rested, "at its core, on the need of the individual for a space free from the demands of the larger social order in which to develop beliefs, attitudes, and behavioral norms."

[95] ALAN WESTIN, PRIVACY AND FREEDOM 7 (1967) ("Privacy is the claim of individuals, groups, or institutions to determine for themselves when, how, and to what extent information about them is communicated to others.").

[96] *Id.*at 32-33; Jonathan Kahn, *Privacy as a Legal Principle of Identity Maintenance*, 33 SETON HALL L. REV. 371, 372 (2003).

[97] FRED CATE, PRIVACY IN THE INFORMATION AGE 23 (1997).

[98] ANITA ALLEN, PRIVACY LAW & SOCIETY 3 (2007).

[99] ERVING GOFFMAN, THE PRESENTATION OF SELF IN EVERYDAY LIFE 4 (1959) ("[W]hen an individual appears in the presence of others, there will usually be some reason for him to mobilize his activity so that it will convey an impression to others which it is in his interests to convey."). *See* Robert C. Post, *The Social Foundations of Privacy: Community and Self in the Common Law Tort*, 77 CALIF. L. REV. 957, 962-64 (1989) (quoting Erving Goffman, *The Nature of Deference and Demeanor*, *in* INTERACTION RITUAL: ESSAYS ON FACE-TO-FACE BEHAVIOR 47, 47, 56, 77, 84-85, 90-91 (1967)); Daniel Solove, *The Virtues of Knowing Less: Justifying Privacy Protections Against Disclosure*, 53 DUKE L.J. 966, 1037 (2003) (citing GOFFMAN, THE PRESENTATION OF SELF IN EVERYDAY LIFE (1959)); WESTIN, *supra* note 95, at 33, 35.

[100] Sidney M. Jourard, *Some Psychological Aspects of Privacy*, 31 LAW & CONTEMP. PROBS. 307, 307 (1966).

> Privacy is an outcome of a person's wish to withhold from others certain knowledge as to his past and present experience and action and his intentions for the future. The wish for privacy expresses a desire to be an enigma to others or, more generally, a desire to control others' perceptions and beliefs vis-à-vis the self-concealing person.

See Ruth Gavison, *Privacy and the Limits of Law*, 89 YALE L.J. 421, 448-49 (1979); Daniel J. Solove, *Conceptualizing Privacy*, 90 CAL. L. REV. 1087, 1106 (2002).

[101] WESTIN, *supra* note 95, at 7. *See* CATE, *supra* note 97, at 22-28; Gavison, *supra* note 100, at 412 n.1 ("The best general treatment of privacy is still [Westin's] PRIVACY AND FREEDOM."); Tom Gerety, *Redefining Privacy*, 12 HARV. C.R.-C.L. L. REV. 233, 261-63 (1977).

[102] WESTIN, *supra* note 95, at 33-34. *But see* C. Keith Boone, *Privacy and Community*, 9 SOC. THEORY & PRAC. 1, 4 (1983). Boone contended viewing privacy as protecting autonomy is "commonplace" and "plausible" but not always applicable: "[S]ocial norms as well as legal statutes require that some 'private' acts not be performed in public," and "[T]he implementation of some 'private rights' are, by collective fiat, restricted to specified contexts, and thus are forms of social control over behavior." Boone defined privacy as "the state of limited access by others—most of the time voluntary, but sometimes imposed—to certain modes of being in a person's life." *Id.* at 6.

[103] Gavison, *supra* note 100, at 438-39; Jourard, *supra* note 100, at 308.

[104] WESTIN, *supra* note 95, at 34-35.

[105] Gavison, *supra* note 100, at 445; WESTIN, *supra* note 95, at 36-37.

[106] Gavison, *supra* note100, at 442; WESTIN, *supra* note 95, at 37-38.

[107] Gavison, *supra* note 100, at 442.

[108] *Id.* at 442; Fried, *supra* note 92, at 205-207; James Rachels, *Why Privacy Is Important*, 4 PHIL. & PUB. AFF. 323, 326-29 (1975).

[109] Gavison, *supra* note 100, at 421.

[110] *See, e.g.*, Bloustein, *supra* note 92, at 971; Kahn, *supra* note 96, at 377; Jeffrey H. Reiman, *Privacy, Intimacy, and Personhood*, *in* PHILOSOPHICAL DIMENSIONS OF PRIVACY 272 (Ferdinand David Schoeman ed., 1984); WESTIN, *supra* note 95, at 34-38.

---

[111] Samuel D. Warren and Louis D. Brandeis, *The Right to Privacy*, 4 HARV . L. REV . 193, 205 (1890).

[112] *Id.* at 195-96.

[113] Bloustein, *supra* note 92, at 971.

[114] *Id.*

[115] Kahn, *supra* note 96, at 377 ("The harm to dignity caused by invasions of privacy ultimately implicates the integrity of individual identity.").

[116] *See* Jed Rubenfeld, *The Right of Privacy*, 102 HARV. L. REV. 737, 761 (1989). Criticizing the vagueness of the personhood value for constitutional privacy, Rubenfeld proposed that an individual could consider any act to be self-defining. He claimed, "The premise of such freedom is an individualist understanding of human self-definition: a conception of self-definition as something that persons are, and should be, able to do apart from society."

[117] GOFFMAN, PRESENTATION OF SELF, *supra* note 99, at 4 ("[W]hen an individual appears in the presence of others, there will usually be some reason for him to mobilize his activity so that it will convey an impression to others which it is in his interests to convey."); WESTIN, *supra* note 95, at 33.

[118] WESTIN, *supra* note 95, at 33.

[119] *Id.*

[120] Jourard, *supra* note 100, at 309.

[121] Professor Gerety defined privacy as "autonomy or control over the intimacies of personal identity." Gerety, *supra* note 101, at 236.

[122] Gavison, *supra* note 100, at 449-50; WESTIN, *supra* note 95, at 34.

[123] WESTIN, *supra* note 95, at 33.

[124] Gavison, *supra* note 100, at 449.

[125] Jeffrey Rosen, *The Purposes of Privacy: A Response*, 89 GEO. L.J. 2117, 2124 (2001).

[126] Gerety, *supra* note 101, at 266.

[127] Gavison, *supra* note 100, at 448-49.

[128] Fried, *supra* note 92, at 202; Parent, *supra* note 93, at 316.

[129] Fried, *supra* note 92, at 202-03.

[130] Parent, *supra* note 93, 328.

[131] *Id.*

[132] Gavison, *supra* note 100, at 448-49.

[133] *Id.* at 448.

[134] WESTIN, *supra* note 95, at 34-35.

[135] *Id.* at 34.

[136] Gavison, *supra* note 100, at 448-49; Jourard, *supra* note 100, at 309-310; WESTIN, *supra* note 95, at 34-35.

[137] WESTIN, *supra* note 95, at 35.

[138] *Id.*

[139] *Id.* at 36. *See also* Jourard, *supra* note 100, at 309 ("Enactment of any social role appropriate to one's sex, age, or occupation calls upon one to suppress inappropriate action and to repress inappropriate experience. These praxes culminate in physical sickness or 'role-check-outs' (mental illness).").

[140] CATE, *supra* note 97, at 25; WESTIN, *supra* note 95, at 36.

[141] WESTIN, *supra* note 95, at 36.

[142] JOSEPH H. KUPFER, AUTONOMY AND SOCIAL INTERACTION 135 (1990).

[143] CATE, *supra* note 97, at 26; KUPFER, *supra* note 142, at 135; WESTIN, *supra* note 95, at 34.

[144] KUPFER, *supra* note 142, at 135; WESTIN, *supra* note 95, at 34.

[145] WESTIN, *supra* note 95, at 38.

[146] Warren and Brandeis, *supra* note 111, at 196.

[147] *Id.* at 200.

[148] Gavison, *supra* note 100, at 441 ("The best way in which to understand the value of privacy is to examine its functions. This approach is fraught with difficulties, however. These justifications are instrumental, in the sense that they point out how privacy relates to other goals."); Solove, *supra* note 100, at 1145 ("[A]long with other scholars, I contend that privacy has an instrumental value—namely, that it is valued as a means for achieving certain other ends that are valuable.").

[149] Reiman, *supra* note 110, at 272; Bloustein, *supra* note 92, at 971.

[150] Gavison, *supra* note 100, at 449-50; WESTIN, *supra* note 95, at 34.

[151] Parent, *supra* note 93, 328.

[152] WESTIN, *supra* note 95, at 34-35.

[153] CATE, *supra* note 97, at 25; WESTIN, *supra* note 95, at 36.

[154] WESTIN, *supra* note 95, at 38.

[155] *See, e.g.*, DANIEL J. SOLOVE, NOTHING TO HIDE: THE FALSE TRADEOFF BETWEEN PRIVACY AND SECURITY 50 (2011) (stating "Privacy isn't the trumpeting of the individual against the society's interests but the protection of the individual based on society's own norms and values.").

[156] Gavison, *supra* note 100, at 442.

[157] *Id.*, at 442; Fried, *supra* note 92, at 205-07; James Rachels, *supra* note 108, at 326-29.

[158] Gavison, *supra* note 100, at 421; Paul M. Schwartz, *Privacy and Democracy in Cyberspace*, 52 VAND. L. REV. 1609, 1664-70 (1999).

[159] AMITAI ETZIONI, THE LIMITS OF PRIVACY 1 (1999).

[160] *Id.* at 5.

[161] *Id.* at 196.

[162] ALLEN, *supra* note 98, at 7-8.

[163] DANIEL J. SOLOVE, NOTHING TO HIDE, *supra* note 155, at 50 (2011).

[164] *See, e.g.*, Julie Cohen, *Examined Lives: Informational Privacy and the Subject as Object*, 52 STAN. L. REV. 1373, 1427-28 (2000) ("Informational privacy, in short, is a constitutive element of a civil society in the broadest sense of the term."); Gavison, *supra* note 100, at 455; Post, *supra* note 99, at 957.

[165] Randall P. Bezanson, *supra* note 25, at 1133.

[166] *Id. at* 1138-39 ("The concept of privacy represented an attempt to protect the functioning of those discrete social institutions from the monolithic, impersonal, and value-free forces of modern society by channeling that which is personal to these discrete institutions and foreclosing it to society at large.").

[167] Post, *supra* note 99, at 963.

[168] *Id.* at 967.

[169] Fried, *supra* note 92, at 475 ("It is my thesis that an essential part of the morality which underlies these realizations is the constraint of respect for the privacy of all, by the state and citizen alike."); Gavison, *supra* note 100, at 445; Post, *supra* note 99, at 985 ("The civility rules which delineate information preserves must therefore be understood as forms of respect that are integral to both individual and social personality. They comprise an important part of the obligations that members of a community owe to each other.").

[170] Fried, *supra* note 92, at 475; Gerety, *supra* note 101, at 245; Rachels, *supra* note 108, at 326; WESTIN, *supra* note 144, at 37.

[171] WESTIN, *supra* note 95, at 37.

[172] Fried, *supra* note 92, at 477.

[173] *Id.* at 477-78. *See* Rachels, *supra* note 108, at 326 ("[P]rivacy is necessary if we are to maintain the variety of social relations with other people that we want to have."). *But see* Reiman, *Privacy, Intimacy, and Personhood*, 6 PHIL. & PUB. AFFAIRS 26, 34-35, 38-44 (1976). Reiman criticized Rachels' definition of intimacy. Reiman argued that one's willingness to share information is only one aspect of intimacy. Sharing information is dependent

on the condition of caring unique to each relationship. For Reiman, privacy is a social ritual that enables individuals to choose whether to share information with others. He proposed that privacy is a right "because it enables me to make the commitment that underlies caring as *my* commitment uniquely conveyed by *my* thoughts and witnessed by *my* actions." *Id.* at 44.

[174] EMERSON, *supra* note 16, at 546; Gavison, *supra* note 100, at 444; Daniel J. Solove, *Taxonomy of Privacy*, 154 U. PA. L. REV. 477, 514 (2006) ("Anonymity and pseudonymity protect people from bias based on their identities and enable people to vote, speak, and associate more freely by protecting them from danger of reprisal.").

[175] EMERSON, *supra* note 16, at 546.

[176] Gormley, *supra* note 92, at 1356-57.

[177] *Id.* at 1356.

[178] *Id.* at 1356-57.

[179] Solove, *supra* note 174, at 993-94.

[180] *Id.* at 514.

[181] Gavison, *supra* note 100, at 455. Gavison wrote:

> Privacy is also essential to democratic government because it fosters and encourages the moral autonomy of the citizen, a central requirement of a democracy. Part of the justification for majority rule and the right to vote is the assumption that individuals should participate in political decisions by forming judgments and expressing preferences. Thus, to the extent that privacy is important for autonomy, it is important for democracy as well.

[182] Robert C. Post, *Three Concepts of Privacy*, 89 GEO. L.J. 2087, 2093 (2001).

[183] Gerety, *supra* note 101, at 291.

[184] Post, *supra* note 99, at 985.

[185] Gerety, *supra* note 101, at 292.

[186] WESTIN, *supra* note 95, at 35-36 ("Most persons need to give vent to their anger at 'the system,' 'city hall,' 'the boss,' and various others who exercise authority over them, and to do this in the intimacy of family or friendship circles . . . without fear of being held responsible for such comments."). *See also* DANIEL J. SOLOVE, THE FUTURE OF REPUTATION 130 (2007) ("Privacy permits individuals to express unpopular ideas to people they trust without

having to worry how society will judge them or whether they will face retaliation.").

[187] WESTIN, *supra* note 95, at 35.

[188] *See* Gavison, *supra* note 100, at 364 ("In addition to providing freedom from distractions and opportunities to concentrate, privacy also contributes to learning, creativity, and autonomy by insulating the individual against ridicule and censure at early stages of groping and experimentation.").

[189] Post, *supra* note 99, at 984.

[190] *Id.*

[191] Gerety, *supra* note 101, at 266 (stating that individuals need control over their identities and the availability of information about themselves. "Without such control, much that we take as distinctively human – love, reflection, choice—cannot flourish or perhaps even survive in our society.").

[192] WESTIN, supra note 95, at 34 ("This development of individuality is particularly important in democratic societies, since qualities of independent thought, diversity of views, and non-conformity are considered desirable traits for individuals.")

[193] *Id.*

[194] SOLOVE, *supra* note 186, at 131 ("Political discussions often take place between two people or in small groups rather than at public rallies or nationwide television broadcasts. . . . Without privacy, many people might not feel comfortable having these candid conversations.").

[195] Although this study will not address constitutional privacy, it is important to recognize that First Amendment jurisprudence acknowledges a constitutional right of associational privacy. Professor Solove explained:

> The First Amendment protects freedom of association, which is integral to the formation of political views and the execution of political action. Protection against disclosure protects freedom of association, for it enables people to join together and exchange information without having to fear loss of employment, community shunning, and other social reprisals.

Solove, *Virtues*, *supra* note 99 at 994.

[196] *See, e.g.*, Gavison, *supra* note 100, at 421 ("[I]t can be argued that respect for privacy will help a society attract talented individuals to public life."); Solove, *Virtues*, *supra* note 99, at 992 ("In fact, privacy protections against

disclosure strongly promote democratic self-governance," and "[t]hus, privacy can contribute to a robust public life rather than detracting from it.").

[197] RESTATEMENT (SECOND) TORTS § 652C (1977).

[198] RESTATEMENT (SECOND) TORTS § 652C cmt a (1977).

[199] During the past six decades many appropriation suits have been based on the right of publicity rather than right of privacy. Right of publicity-based appropriation suits conceptualize identity as a property right rather than personal right. The harm claimed by the plaintiff is pecuniary rather than emotional or psychological. *See, e.g.*, Richard S. Murphy, *Property Rights in Personal Information: An Economic Defense of Privacy*, 84 GEO . L.J. 2381, 2390 (1995) (explaining that the use of another's identity for one's own benefit typically is done for commercial gain); Nimmer, *supra* note 74, at 957-58 ("This right, sometimes called the right of publicity, involves the commercial appropriation of values which, whether or not labeled as 'property,' may not be freely plundered under the banner of the first amendment."); Parent, *supra* note 93, at 324 ("It is a mistake to conceptualize these kinds of cases in terms of privacy for they don't involve the finding out of personal facts about anyone. Most of them have essentially to do with the issue of financial remuneration and consequently should be handled as property cases."). This study is concerned with the ways in which courts balance free expression and privacy values and, thus, does not focus on right of publicity-based cases except to the extent courts address privacy values.

[200] Bloustein, *supra* note 92, at 989.

[201] *Id.*

[202] *Id.* at 986; Parent, *supra* note 93, at 324 ("If the gravamen of petitioner's complaint is not financial but concerns the preemption of choice—she wasn't asked whether her name or likeness could be used –the right to liberty becomes the focus of attention.").

[203] Bloustein, *supra* note 92, at 986.

[204] *Id.*at 990.

[205] Pavesich v. New England Life Ins. Co., 122 Ga. 190, 220 (1905).

[206] Solove, *Taxonomy*, *supra* note 174, at 549.

[207] Post, Robert C. Post, *Rereading Warren and Brandeis*, 41 CASE W. RES . L. REV . 647, 652 (1990).

[208] *Id.*

[209] *Id.*

[210] *Id.*

[211] *Id.*

[212] Robert C. Post, *supra* note 182, at 2093.

[213] Bloustein, *supra* note 92, at 986; Parent, *supra* note 93, at 324; Solove, *Taxonomy*, *supra* note 174, at 549.

[214] Post, *supra* note 207, at 652.

[215] Bloustein, *supra* note 92, at 981.

[216] Gerety, *supra* note 101, at 292.

[217] Gavison, *supra* note 100, at 364

[218] Post, *supra* note 99, at 985.

[219] SOLOVE, *FUTURE*, *supra* note 186, at 130; WESTIN, *supra* note 95, at 35-36.

[220] Gavison, *supra* note 100, at 364.

[221] Post, *supra* note 99, at 984.

[222] *See* Gerety, *supra* note 101, at 292 (stating that after the mass disclosure of private information "neither privacy, nor autonomy, nor intimacy is any longer possible).

[223] Gavison, *supra* note 100, at 421; Solove, *Virtues*, *supra* note 99, at 994; WESTIN, *supra* note 95, at 34.

[224] *See, e.g.*, Paul Gewirtz, *Privacy and Speech*, 2001 SUP. CT. REV. 139, 140; Nadine Strossen, *Protecting Privacy and Free Speech in Cyberspace*, 89 GEO. L. J. 2103, 2104 (2000) at 2104.

[225] Jane Kirtley, *Freedom of the Press: The Most Serious Threat Is ... The Cloak of Privacy*, 30 COLUM. JOURNALISM REV. 46 (1991).

[226] EMERSON, *supra* note 16, at 550.

[227] *Id.* at 556.

[228] *Id.*

[229] *Id.* at 562.

[230] Emerson, *supra* note 2, at 341.

[231] *Id.*

[232] *Id.*

[233] EMERSON, *supra* note 16, at 556.

[234] Emerson, *supra* note 2, at 341.

[235] Baker, *supra* note 2, at 220-225.

[236] *Id.* at 220-23.

[237] *Id.* at 220.

[238] Baker, *supra* note 2, at 232

[239] *Id.* at 262.

[240] *Id.* at 215-16, 253-54.

[241] *See,e.g.*, EMERSON, *supra* note 16, at 556; Emerson, *supra* note 2, at 341.

[242] SCHAUER, *supra* note 6, at 175-76.

[243] *Id.*

[244] *Id.*

[245] *Id.* at 177.

[246] Edward J. Bloustein, *The First Amendment and Privacy: The Supreme Court Justice and the Philosopher*, 28 RUTGERS L. REV. 41, 42 (1974). *See* Lillian BeVier, *An Informed Public, an Informing Press: The Search for a Constitutional Principle*, 68 CAL .L. REV. 482, 503 (1980) (stating that the principle of representative self-government "does not support the conclusion that the Court's rhetorical affirmations of the values of the public being informed about government and the press's role in bringing such information to the public *ought* to be conceived of as acceptable elaborations of constitutional principle.").

[247] *Id.* at 56.

[248] *Id.* at 46 (quoting ALEXANDER MEIKLEJOHN, POLITICAL FREEDOM 37-38 (1969).

[249] *Id.* at 46. Bloustein explained that under Meiklejohn's theory, the Fifth Amendment protected private speech.

[250] Easton, *supra* note, 18, at 167-68.

[251] *Id.* (citing 420 U.S. 469 (1975).

[252] *Id.* at 143.

[253] *Id.* at 168.

[254] *Id.* at 174, 196 (explaining a "privacy interest will never prevail when the information is a matter of public importance.").

[255] Baker, *supra* note 2, at 220.

[256] Emerson, *supra* note 2, at 341; Emerson, *supra* note 46, at 22.

[257] Bloustein, *supra* note 246, at 56; Emerson, *supra* note 2 at 341; Emerson, *supra* note 46, at 22, Easton, *supra* note 18, at 174.

[258] Warren and Brandeis, *supra* note 111, at 214.

[259] *Id.*

[260] *Id.* at 215.

[261] *Id.*

[262] *Id.* at 217.

[263] SMOLLA, *supra* note 1, at 141.

[264] *Id.* at 141-44.

[265] *See, e.g.*, Peter B. Edelman, *Free Press v. Privacy: Haunted by the Ghost of Justice Black*, 68 TEX . L. REV . 1195, 1207 (1989), at 1207-08; Strossen, *supra* note 224, at 2104.

[266] Florida Star v. B.J.F., 491 U.S. 524 (1989); Edelman, *supra* note 265, at 1199 (condemning the Court for "its gradual erosion of the right to privacy in this area."); Gormley, *supra* note 92, at 1389 (arguing the Court's *Florida Star* ruling "once again flattened the privacy interest under a rubble of First Amendment language."); Diane L. Zimmerman, *Requiem For a Heavyweight: Farewell to Warren and Brandeis's Privacy Tort*, 68 CORNEL L. REV. 292, 29 303-04.

[267] 491 U.S. 524, 541.

[268] Edelman, *supra* note 265, at 1201.

[269] *Id.* at 1198-1204.

[270] *Id.* at 1208.

[271] Geof Dendy, Note, *The Newsworthiness Defense to the Public Disclosure Tort*, 85 KY. L.J. 147, 148 (1997); Edelman, *supra* note 265, at 1208; Jacquelin Rolfs, Note, Florida Star v. B.J.F.*: The Beginning of the End for the Tort of Public Disclosure*, 1990 WIS. L. REV. 1107. *See also* Kalven, *supra* note 54, at 336 (stating the newsworthiness defense had become "so overpowering" as to virtually "swallow the tort.").

[272] Deckle Mclean, *Lower Courts Point the Way on Press and Privacy Rights*, 22 COMM. & L. 41, 45 (2000).

[273] *Id.* at 54 (citing Winstead v. Sweeney, 517 N.W.2d 874 (Mich. Ct. App. 1994)).

[274] *See, e.g.*, Gerald G. Ashdown, *Media Reporting and Privacy Claims—Decline in Constitutional Protection for the Press*, 66 KY. L.J. 759, 778-81 (1978); Solove, *Virtues*, *supra* note 99, at 970.

[275] Mclean, *supra* note 272, at 45; Zimmerman, *supra* note 266.

[276] Gavison, *supra* note 100, at 364; Gerety, *supra* note 101, at 266, 292; Post, *supra* note 99, at 984; WESTIN, supra note 95, at 34-35.

[277] Post, *supra* note 207, at 652; Solove, *Taxonomy*, *supra* note 174, at 549.

[278] Benjamin C. Glassman, *Making State Law in Federal Court*, 41 GONZ. L. REV. 237, 241 (2006).

[279] *Id.*

[280] *Id.* at 242 (citing Erie R.R. Co. v. Tompkins, 304 U.S. 64, 78 (1938)).

[281] Westlaw is a collection of databases in which editors at West Publishing Company organize legal documents for storage and searching by topic. The LexisNexis Academic legal database is organized and maintained by editors at LexisNexis. *Media Law Reporter* publishes and indexes case law and legal news that editors at the Bureau of National Affairs (BNA) consider relevant to mass communication law.

[282] 491 U.S. 524 (1989).

Cases were identified by using the Westlaw Key Number system and Key Cite function. Westlaw editors assign "key numbers" to legal terms or phrases commonly mentioned in the headnote summaries that Westlaw editors add to each case. Appropriation cases were identified by searching the Key Number 379IV(C), "Use of Name, Voice or Likeness; Right to Publicity."[282] Disclosure cases were identified by searching Key Number 379IV, "Privacy," and Key Number 379IV(B), "Privacy and Publicity." Relevant cases also were identified by performing a Key Cite search, which identified all cases that have cited the *Restatement (Second) Sections* 652C "Appropriation of Name or Likeness" or 652D "Publicity Given to Private Life" Appropriation cases also were identified by performing a Key Cite search for all rulings that cited state appropriation statutes.

Relevant case law was found by using the topic search function in the LexisNexis Academic databases of U.S. Courts of Appeals' rulings and rulings by the highest courts in all states. Appropriation cases were identified by using two search strings. The first is "privacy AND appropriation." The second search string is "(privacy AND ("use of name" OR "use of likeness" OR "use of image"))." Disclosure cases were found by searching for "privacy AND ("public disclosure" OR "public disclosure of private facts")." The index term of privacy was used to limit the search in *Media Law Reporter*'s indexed weekly case digests online. *Media Law Reporter*'s case annotations were used to identify relevant rulings by U.S. circuit courts of appeals and state high courts.

283 Edelman, *supra* note,265, at 1204; Gewirtz, *supra* note 224, at 180; Strossen, *supra* note 8, at 2104.

284 Gewirtz, *supra* note 224, at 180.

285 Baker, *supra* note 5 at 990-92; Scanlon, *supra* note 13, at 214; SCHAUER, *supra* note 6, at 71.

286 MILL, *supra* note 28, at 82-83.

287 Baker, *supra* note 5, at 991.

288 *Id.* at 965-66; EMERSON, *supra* note 16, at 6-7; Nimmer, *supra* note 74, at 955.

289 EMERSON, *supra* note 16, at 7.

290 *Id.*

291 MEIKLEJOHN, *supra* note 48, at 25-26; Meiklejohn, *supra* note 52, at 257.

292 Blasi, *supra* note 62, at 541-42

293 Bollinger, *supra* note 84, at 458-60.

294 *Id.* at 473.

[295] *See, e.g.*, Bloustein, *supra* note 92, at 971; Jonathan Kahn, *supra* note 96, at 377; Reiman, *supra* note 110, at 272; WESTIN, *supra* note 95, at 34-38.
[296] Bloustein, *supra* note 92, at 971.
[297] CATE, *supra* note 97, at 25; Gavison, *supra* note 100 at 448-49; Jourard, *supra* note 100, at 309-310; WESTIN, *supra* note 95, at 34-35.
[298] WESTIN, *supra* note 95, at 34-35.
[299] Bezanson, *Privacy Revisited, supra* note 25, at 1138-39; Post, *supra* note 148, at 963; WESTIN, *supra* note 95, at 37.
[300] Gavison, *supra* note 100, at 45; Rachels, *supra* note 108, at 326.
[301] EMERSON, *supra* note 16, at 546; Gormley, *supra* note 92, at 1356-57.

CHAPTER 3

Favoring Free Expression: Disclosure of Private Facts

Most states and the District of Columbia have recognized the disclosure of private facts tort either under common law or statutory law.[1] Since the U.S. Supreme Court's *Florida Star v. B.J.F.* ruling in 1989, appellate courts in New Hampshire, Minnesota, and Colorado have indicated for the first time that their respective states recognize the disclosure of private facts tort.[2] To prevent confusion about the status of the disclosure tort in Washington, that state's supreme court declared, "[W]e explicitly hold the common law right of privacy exists in this state and that individuals may bring a cause of action for invasion of that right."[3]

On the other hand, the highest courts in three states have either questioned or rejected outright the disclosure of private facts branch of privacy law.[4] Almost a year before the U.S. Supreme Court ruling in *Florida Star*, the North Carolina Supreme Court declined to recognize the tort under state common law. Calling the tort "constitutionally suspect,"[5] the court reasoned that adopting the disclosure branch of privacy law "would add to the existing tensions between the First Amendment and the law of torts and would be of little practical value to anyone."[6] In 1993, the New York Court of Appeals affirmed that its state common law did not recognize a right to privacy and that the state legislature had only recognized misappropriation under the state's statutory law.[7] Four years later, a Supreme Court of Indiana plurality opinion cast considerable doubt on whether Indiana ever has or will recognize the disclosure tort.[8] A plurality of the court reasoned that punishing the disclosure of true information could conflict with a provision in the Indiana Bill of Rights recognizing truth as a defense to libel. This provision, Chief Justice Randall Shepard wrote, "commands real caution about proposals to recognize a civil cause of action for libel that impose liability for truthful statements."[9]

Looking to Lower Courts

This chapter examines if and how state high court and federal appellate court decisions filed after the U.S. Supreme Court's *Florida Star* ruling have analyzed clashes between free expression and privacy values in disclosure of private facts cases. Eighty-two state high court and federal appellate court rulings issued after June 1989, when the Supreme Court decided *Florida Star*, involving claims of invasion of privacy by disclosure of private facts were identified by this study.[10]

Appellate courts have taken a number of approaches when considering disclosure of private facts cases. Only one of the rulings included in this study upheld an award of damages for a plaintiff.[11] A few courts reversed trial courts' summary judgment motions for defendants,[12] and some decided cases on procedural grounds.[13] Other appellate courts that addressed the substantive issues crafted narrow rulings, following the U.S. Supreme Court's example of how to handle clashes between privacy and freedom of expression.[14] Not surprisingly, more than half of the rulings examined lower courts' summary judgment awards by focusing on the elements of the tort or the newsworthiness defense.[15]

Similar to U.S. Supreme Court rulings, lower courts' rulings suggest that important interests exist on the free expression as well as the privacy side of the balance in disclosure of private facts cases. Several circuit courts of appeals and state high court rulings referred to either individual-based values—autonomy, self-realization or self-fulfillment, attainment of truth, and participation in decision-making—or society-based free expression values—marketplace of ideas, balance between stability and change, self-governance, the checking value, and toleration—when considering the applicability of First Amendment or common law privileges.[16] Some opinions also made reference to individual-based privacy values—autonomy, emotional health, and liberty—or society-based privacy values—civility and community, forming and maintaining relationships, and promoting democratic processes—when discussing the elements of the tort or its viability.[17] Few rulings, however, truly attempted to reconcile clashes between the two sets of values. Indeed, most rulings suggested that the elements of the tort, newsworthiness defense, and public importance privileges struck the proper balance between freedom of expression and privacy.

Elements of the Disclosure of Private Facts[18]

During the past twenty years, most state high court and federal circuit courts of appeal rulings on disclosure of private facts cases focused primarily on whether the facts at hand satisfied at least one of four common elements of the tort as a matter of law. Analysis of each element usually was guided by the *Restatement (Second) of Torts* § 652D. The *Restatement* says that a disclosure may be an actionable invasion of privacy when 1) widespread publicity is given to 2) a true, private fact 3) the disclosure of which would be highly offensive to a reasonable person 4) and that is not a matter of legitimate public concern.[19] Most of the rulings turned on the courts' interpretation of one or two elements from the *Restatement*, implicating privacy values in relation to the publicity and private facts elements and free expression values in relation to the matter of legitimate public interest element.[20] Of the rulings focused on the elements, few were found to include questions of fact suitable to remand for a new trial.[21]

Widespread publicity

More than one-fourth of the rulings turned on whether the plaintiff satisfied the requisite level of publicity.[22] The *Restatement (Second) of Torts* states publicity "means that the matter is made public, by communicating it to the public at large, or to so many persons that the matter must be regarded as substantially certain to become one of public knowledge."[23]

In 2000, for example, the Supreme Court of Alabama in *Ex parte The Birmingham News, Inc.* called publicity the threshold element for a disclosure of private facts claim.[24] That case arose after a male employee of the newspaper made a comment to the plaintiff about a sexual harassment complaint she had filed that involved another employee. She claimed he also made a similar comment to one other employee. The court reasoned, "To comment to the plaintiff about the plaintiff's private life is not to give publicity to her private life; to give publicity to one's private life, a person has to make a communication to third persons."[25] Because the information was not conveyed to numerous individuals in addition to the plaintiff, the court determined, "[w]e need not address the other elements of the tort of invasion of privacy by 'giving publicity to private information' because the absence of the publicity element is dispositive."[26]

Three state high courts considered the vitality of a broader interpretation of the publicity element, which would be met by disclosing a matter to a small number of people who have a special relationship with the plaintiff.[27] The Supreme Court of Minnesota and the Supreme Court of South Carolina rejected that special relationship rationale.[28] Those courts applied the more stringent standard from the *Restatement*, which requires a matter be disclosed to the public at large.[29] On the other hand, a 1997 plurality opinion by the Supreme Court of Indiana applied a "particular relationship" rationale in its evaluation of whether one postal worker's communication of a colleague's HIV status to two people could be an actionable invasion of privacy.[30] The plurality indicated that none of the facts conveyed indicated that the plaintiff and a second letter carrier, who was previously unaware of the plaintiff's health condition, "have a special relationship with the plaintiff such that the disclosure would be particularly damaging."[31] That suggests recognition of the particular relationship rationale hinges on the likelihood that the plaintiff would endure the severe type of emotional harm that typically results from disclosing information to the general public, a more extreme level than the plaintiffs could demonstrate in the aforementioned cases.

Private facts

A few of the relevant post-*Florida Star* rulings turned on whether the disclosed information was factual.[32] Courts have found that rhetorical hyperbole and falsehoods cannot be considered actionable private facts.[33] For example, in a 1992 ruling the Supreme Court of Delaware treated the true private facts element as dispositive.[34] That case, *Barker v. Huang*, resulted from a newspaper's publication of false statements originally made during a deposition. The court explained that the appellant's "pleadings complain only of *false* accusations by Huang and therefore fail to state a cognizable claim under the 'unwanted publicity' variety of the tort of invasion of privacy."[35] That ruling affirmed the superior court's award of summary judgment to the defendant.[36]

More rulings discussed whether the disclosure at issue actually revealed private information that included intimate, intensely personal, or embarrassing details of an individual's private life.[37] Two considered whether the disclosed information was so "intimate" that its disclosure would cause embarrassment, shame, or humiliation.[38] For example, in 1995, the Fifth Circuit Court of Appeals sitting en banc and applying Texas law found that a press release Internal Revenue Service agents sent to newspapers did not include private facts about a man who pled guilty to tax evasion. The release included the man's middle name and home address—information often available from public records—that the court did not consider "highly intimate or embarrassing material."[39] In a 2007 ruling, the Supreme Court of California found that information disclosed at an academic conference during discussion of an article on repressed memories of childhood abuse was not private information.[40] That discussion revealed that a woman, who was the unnamed subject in several studies, engaged in destructive behavior and later worked for the U.S. Navy. The court held those facts "were not of an '[i]ntensely personal or intimate' nature."[41] Four years later, a panel of three Eleventh Circuit Court of Appeals judges applying Florida common law focused on an appellant's failure to allege "intimate details of the family unit" or "information regarding her health or well-being" were disclosed in a television program that portrays law enforcement officers activities while on patrol.[42] That unpublished per curiam ruling in *Spilfogel v. Fox Broadcasting Co.* found that Fox publicized neither private nor intimate information when broadcasting film of a woman discussing her alleged traffic violations while she was on a public street.[43] Thus, courts have suggested that private information comprises very personal, sensitive, or intimate details of a person's individual or family life.[44]

Other rulings determined whether information was private by focusing on whether the information was available to the public through widespread knowledge or public sources prior to the disclosure at issue.[45] In 2006, the Alabama Supreme Court found discussions of sexually explicit photographs of female high school students were not private facts.[46] The court reasoned that "knowledge of the photographs was pervasive" among the students and faculty prior to the faculty members' disclosures to students, faculty, and parents, thus "the matter was no longer private."[47] Likewise, the Supreme Court of Idaho held in

Steele v. Spokesman Review that facts readily observable or "readily available from public sources," such as that Edgar J. Steele was a licensed attorney who used a post office box for his representation of the Aryan Nations, were too easily accessible to be considered private information.[48] The court concluded that Steele failed to satisfy the elements of a prima facie disclosure case against the newspaper because the information at issue was not private.[49] In other words, private information pertains to secrets or sensitive details one strives to prevent other individuals from knowing.

Reasonable expectation of privacy

In 1999, the Supreme Court of Idaho assessed whether plaintiffs had a reasonable expectation of privacy pertinent to facts disclosed by Robert Howard, a deputy sheriff, and his wife, Linda, who monitored and recorded telephone conversations between their neighbor, Sandy Hoskins, and her friend.[50] Alleging that Hoskins threatened to kill his wife in a recorded phone call, the deputy took a copy of the recording to work and placed it in an investigation file. The Howards contended that the conversation was not private, in part, because the alleged "murder-plot" was a "matter of public concern."[51] Idaho's high court said plaintiffs' disclosure of private facts claim, as well as their intrusion upon seclusion claim, would turn on whether a reasonable person would find a privacy interest in the conversation. The court said this required a two-step analysis: 1) whether the speaker engaged in the conversation had an expectation that the information would remain private and 2) whether society would consider that expectation reasonable.[52] In other words, the court held that a trial court must determine whether a subjective and an objective expectation of privacy existed.[53]

More than a decade later, the Supreme Court of New Jersey's 2011 ruling in *G.D. v. Kenny* focused on objective societal expectations for privacy. The court indicated that an expungement order for G.D.'s conviction record could not recreate a reasonable expectation of privacy for information that was once publicly available. The issue arose after G.D. claimed that a political campaign flyer posted during a New Jersey State Senate primary contest violated G.D.'s privacy by disclosing G.D. was ""a DRUG DEALER who went to JAIL for FIVE YEARS for selling coke near a public school"" prior to G.D.'s employment by Brian Stack, a candidate for the Democratic nomination. The court reasoned that G.D. had plead guilty to second-degree possession with intent to distribute cocaine and the conviction information was posted on the Department of Corrections' website. It wrote:

> This is not a case in which a defendant peered through closed curtains into a bedroom or wrongly acquired a personal diary and made highly private information available to the public. A person has a reasonable expectation of privacy in the sanctity of his or her bedroom and personal diary from peeping toms intent on making private facts titillating fodder for the public. This case, however, deals with public facts, a guilty plea and sentence in a public courtroom, and public facts, courts records available to the public over many years."

Thus, information once made available to the public could not be converted into the type of "hidden secret" for which society would recognize a reasonable expectation of privacy.

Unreasonable and highly offensive disclosures

Few rulings focused on whether the disclosure at issue would be highly offensive to a person of ordinary sensibilities.[54] In 2010 in *Boring v. Google Inc.*, the Third Circuit Court of Appeals held that no publicity that "would be highly offensive to a reasonable person" was given to private life when the Google Street View function of Google Maps allowed Internet users to view images of the Boring home, which is located on a private road in Pittsburgh.[55] The Court reasoned, "No person of ordinary sensibilities would be shamed, humiliated, or have suffered mentally as a result of a vehicle entering into his or her ungated driveway and photographing the view from there." That discussion clearly relates to the emotional harm value underlying privacy.

Two appellate court rulings included in this study suggested tests of reasonableness ought to be used to determine whether a matter disclosed by a government employee would be highly offensive to a reasonable person.[56] A 1997 Supreme Court of Rhode Island ruling in *Pontbriand v. Sundlun* treated the unreasonableness of the disclosure at issue as "the gravamen of the tort."[57] The court described the applicable standard as a requirement of plaintiffs to demonstrate that they expected the disclosed information would remain private and that individuals from the community would consider that expectation "reasonable" as well as "be willing to respect it."[58] The case arose after Bruce Sundlun, then-governor of Rhode Island, sent a newspaper a list including the account balances, Social Security Numbers, and names of people with more than $100,000 in financial institutions in 1991. At that time, he declared a banking emergency that closed "all state-chartered banks and credit unions" without Federal Deposit Insurance and sought passage of a bill that would allow the state to use public money to reimburse account holders' losses that exceeded the federal coverage of $100,000 for individuals' deposits in closed financial institutions. Newspapers subsequently published the names of two of those people and their account balances, which the individuals claim gave unreasonable publicity to private matters. Reasoning that application of the two-part test of reasonableness combined questions of fact and law, the Rhode Island Supreme Court remanded the case for trial. That case, however, was settled out of court.

Applying Louisiana law in *Zaffuto v. City of Hammond*, a 2002 ruling in a disclosure of private facts case, the Fifth Circuit Court of Appeals used a reasonableness test that balances a plaintiff's privacy interest "with the defendant's interest" in disclosing the information at issue.[59] The court affirmed a trial court's award of $2 in damages for an unreasonable disclosure of private facts involving the disclosure of a secretly recorded personal phone call from a police officer to his wife. At trial, two police officers testified that the assistant police chief played the recording for them. That disclosure was considered an unreasonable disclosure because the defendant's "only interest was apparently to embarrass" the plaintiff and to "curry favor" with his peers.[60] Thus, disclosing the information in a manner that might benefit the defendant but did not benefit the public or the plaintiff could be found unreasonable and objectionable.

Reasonableness is at the heart of a special element that the Supreme Court of Colorado added to the traditional disclosure of private facts tort when Colorado adopted the tort in 1997. In *Ozer v. Borquez*, which involved invasion of privacy and wrongful discharge claims, the court defined a reckless disregard requirement for a common law tort claim of unreasonable publicity given to private life claim in Colorado. That element requires a plaintiff to demonstrate a "defendant acted with reckless disregard of the private nature of the fact or facts disclosed." The ruling clarified, "A person acts with reckless disregard if, at the time of the publicity, the person knew or should have known that the fact or facts disclosed were private in nature."[61] The court carefully explained that element because it was the first time the state supreme court had recognized the common law disclosure of private facts tort. That case involved unquestionably sensitive facts. Robert Borquez sued his former employer, the Ozer law firm, for disclosure of private facts after Robert Ozer, the president and shareholder in the firm, told a couple of firm employees that Borquez was a homosexual who needed to be tested for HIV after Borquez's partner had been diagnosed as HIV positive. But the court did not discuss whether Ozer recklessly disregarded the private nature of those facts prior to disclosing them to a few employees at the law firm. The court held the trial court had misinterpreted the first element of the tort—widespread publicity—as being synonymous with publication. That error would have allowed the jury could to interpret the disclosure as unreasonable if "Ozer disclosed to any single individual the fact of Borquez'[s] homosexuality and exposure to [HIV]."[62] The court indicated that factual questions remained about whether the information was disclosed to such a large number of people that it could be considered public knowledge. The parties reached a settlement out of court before a second trial commenced to consider the reasonableness or recklessness of that disclosure of private facts.[63]

<u>Legitimate matters of public interest</u>

About one-third of the state high court and federal circuit court of appeals rulings in the disclosure of private facts cases focused on whether the information disclosed was a legitimate matter of public interest.[64]

Some courts have found that matters of importance to the public include the use of taxpayers' dollars,[65] acts of law enforcement officers,[66] activities of courts or public officials,[67] reports of crime,[68] reports of public records,[69] reports of public controversies,[70] or "matters called to public attention."[71] For instance, in 1998, the Supreme Court of South Carolina held that "the commission of a violent crime between inmates of a county jail is a matter of public significance," even when that crime is a sexual assault.[72] Seven years later in *Ayash v. Dana-*

Farber Cancer Institute, the Supreme Judicial Court of Massachusetts determined that disclosure of information about the professional performance of a doctor responsible for an experimental chemotherapy protocol under which two patients received chemotherapy overdoses, one of which was fatal, was a matter of "public scrutiny and interest."[73] More recently, in 2011 in *Smith v. Borough of Dunmore*, the Third Circuit Court of Appeals held that a firefighter's alleged failure to complete mandatory training is not a confidential personnel matter because that information "involves public safety and, therefore, is a matter of public concern."[74] Thus, sensitive information that may be considered private under different circumstances may be a matter of public importance when the information sheds light on public safety or health.

Notably, some courts that found disclosed information pertained to public concerns specifically stated that the courts did not need to consider constitutional questions about the disclosure tort because plaintiffs failed to demonstrate the disclosures were not of legitimate public concern.[75] For instance, in *Veilleux v. National Broadcasting Co.*, the First Circuit Court of Appeals wrote:

> The constitutional validity of the unreasonable publication tort is unclear. To date, the Supreme Court has declined to decide "whether truthful publications may ever be subjected to civil or criminal liability consistently with the First and Fourteenth Amendments, or to put it another way, whether the State may ever define and protect an area of privacy free from unwanted publicity in the press." We need not consider whether this tort is constitutionally viable, because we conclude that plaintiffs did not establish its state law elements.[76]

Applying Maine common law, that court assessed whether NBC invaded the privacy of a professional truck driver by broadcasting that one of his drug tests was positive for amphetamine and marijuana. The court found that the general subject matter of the report, highway safety and regulations pertinent to truck drivers, was of public interest. The court, accordingly, concluded that the identity of the driver was newsworthy because discussing his professional experience and test results illustrated the subject of the broadcast.[77]

In 1993 in *Haynes v. Alfred A. Knopf*, the Seventh Circuit Court of Appeals suggested the matter of public interest element is related to the offensiveness element under Illinois common law. Writing for the majority, Judge Posner stated, "An individual, and more pertinently perhaps the community, is most offended by the publication of intimate personal facts when the community has no interest in them beyond the voyeuristic thrill of penetrating the wall of privacy that surrounds a stranger."[78] The court defined the line between a newsworthy and an offensive disclosure by clarifying the link between the disclosed information and the author's purpose for a book about black migration to the North. Luther Haynes claimed that excerpts of that book that disclosed information about the dissolution of his marriage to one woman and later marriage to another woman at issue was an offensive invasion of his privacy. The majority ruling, however, found the information was a matter of public interest because it clearly related to at least one of the major themes of the book, "the transposition" of sharecropper morality to a "matriarchal and elastic" family structure.[79] The details about Haynes' relationships were relevant to the sociological transformation explored in the book, thus Judge Posner wrote the details disclosed were "not only of legitimate but of transcendent public interest."[80]

<u>Summary</u>

Most rulings examined whether summary judgment was properly granted on the grounds that the plaintiff could not prove that widespread publicity was given to information that was not a legitimate matter of public interest.[81] Fewer cases turned on whether the information disclosed was truly private or whether the disclosure would be highly offensive to a reasonable person.[82] When reviewing the publicity, private facts and offensiveness elements, some courts' discussions implicated privacy values, which will be discussed later in this chapter. When reviewing the matter of public concern element, some courts' rationales mentioned free expression values, which also will be discussed later in this chapter.[83]

Free Expression Values

Since June 1989, state high court and federal circuit courts of appeals primarily have discussed audience-based free expression values and rarely have discussed liberty-based free expression values.[84] One unpublished ruling implicated the liberty-based value of autonomy for individual speakers.[85] Most cases, however, focused more specifically on audience-based values for freedom of expression, namely the marketplace of ideas, self-governance, and check on government values, or some combination of those values.[86] Regardless of which values were mentioned in courts' rationales, most of the decisions followed the U.S. Supreme Court's tendency to issue narrow holdings rather than categorical rules of law.

Liberty and autonomy values

In a 2003 unpublished opinion, the Supreme Court of Idaho discussed the importance of individuals having the freedom to express themselves to the public without censorship.[87] Jane Doe and her husband claimed that Tarek Haw and *The Idaho Statesman* invaded their privacy by printing a letter that Doe wrote to the executive director of the Board of Medicine at the request of her psychiatrist, Dr. Haw. Her doctor included the letter in advertisements he placed in the newspaper to express grievances against the Board of Medicine.[88] Idaho's high court affirmed a trial court's summary judgment finding for Dr. Haw and the newspaper because a different conclusion could deter newspapers from publishing issue or editorial advertisements relevant to newsworthy matters.[89] The court wrote:

> Issue or editorial advertisements are commonly used by members of the public to give direct voice to their views on issues of public concern and are a long recognized tool for the expression of free speech. The issue or editorial advertisement gives its maker the opportunity to speak directly to the general public, not filtered through a particular reporter or lost in a broader story in which other views are expressed. The choice of words, the form of the advertisement belongs to its maker.[90]

Thus, the court emphasized the liberty-based value of autonomy for individuals addressing matters of legitimate public interest.[91]

A 1997 ruling by the Eight Circuit Court of Appeals incorporates elements from the liberty-based model and audience-based model.[92] In that ruling, *Coplin v. Fairfield Public Access Television Committee*, the court applied an autonomy-based rationale that incorporated the Millian principle associated with liberty model.[93] Applying Iowa law, the court held that "speech that reveals truthful and accurate facts about a private individual can, consistently [sic] with the First Amendment, be regulated because of its constitutionally proscribable content," but only "in the 'extreme case.'"[94] That case arose from Randy Coplin's claim that the committee violated his First Amendment rights by sanctioning him for broadcasting sensitive information during a "Sex Survey" call-in show.[95] The court explained that exposing the sexual habits of a private person to "public ridicule" typically would be highly offensive and not a matter of legitimate public interest.[96] The court implicated the audience-based self-governance value by stating a different conclusion could be reached if the individuals discussed were public officials.[97] That tied the press's editorial freedom to its ability to inform audiences about public officials.

<u>Autonomy value and a right to know</u>

Another group of rulings linked press freedom to a form of liberty-based editorial autonomy and either a general audience-based right to know or a specific audience-based checking value.[98] For instance, the Fifth Circuit Court of Appeals' ruling in *Lowe v. Hearst* noted that court had declined to evaluate "the newsworthiness of specific details in a newsworthy story," preserving the editorial control of the press.[99] Applying Texas law, the court refused "to circumscribe the paper's coverage in this case by imposing judicial rules on what is relevant and appropriate in a story that is based on very personal" details that "became newsworthy by their connection to the alleged crimes."[100]

A few rulings have tied a general right to know or to receive information to the audience-based marketplace of ideas value.[101] For instance, in *Young v. Jackson*, the Supreme Court of Mississippi ruled that Jackson did not invade the privacy of Young by revealing to Young's colleagues that she collapsed and was hospitalized because of complications from a hysterectomy—not from radiation poisoning, which her colleagues feared also could affect them.[102] The majority reasoned that under those circumstances, it is "'more important that information should be given freely than that a man should be protected from what under other circumstances would be an actionable wrong.'"[103] In other words, that ruling indicated that Young's co-workers' interest in learning about their potential health risks outweighed Young's privacy interest, even when the matter disclosed involved intimate details about Young's reproductive health. That ruling favored the free flow of information to individuals, but the limited holding ultimately provides little guidance on how much gravity that court would assign to the marketplace of ideas value for freedom of expression under different circumstances.

Marketplace of ideas and checking values

Another ruling provides a more classic conception of the marketplace of ideas value by discussing the importance of allowing an audience to receive more than one side of a debate.[104] In *Howell v. Tribune Entertainment Co.*, Tammy Howell claimed that the Tribune Company invaded her privacy by broadcasting her stepmother reading from a police report during a television talk show on how stepparents and their stepchildren "have had trouble getting along."[105] Howell, who was 16 at that time, countered her stepmother had engaged in adultery.[106] Applying Wisconsin law, the Seventh Circuit Court of Appeals reasoned, "Tammy may not hide behind Wisconsin's privacy law and from that shelter pelt her stepmother with defamatory accusations with impunity. Such a privilege would distort the terms of public debate by giving an unjustified advantage to the juvenile contestant."[107] Adding that Howell waived her right to privacy by volunteering to appear on the talk show, the court found that the show's producer broadcast that material "to prevent the audience from obtaining a one-sided view of the quarrel."[108] Writing for the majority, Judge Posner suggested that finding the company liable for broadcasting the stepmother's rebuttal "would place quite a damper on the media's taste for public controversy, in rather clear violation of the free speech clause of the First Amendment."[109]

The U.S. Court of Appeals for the Fourth Circuit's rationale in *Reuber v. Food Chemical News*, which it decided in 1991, involved both the marketplace of ideas and checking values for freedom of expression.[110] Melvin Reuber claimed that the publication invaded his privacy by publishing a letter of reprimand his supervisor at the National Cancer Institute wrote criticizing Reuber for publishing his own research on whether the Institute had changed its position on the carcinogenic nature of a pesticide.[111] Applying Maryland law, the court reversed the district court award of damages to Reuber. The court alluded to the marketplace value when it stated that the First

Amendment "protects the public's right to learn about both sides of the controversy through the press,"[112] and to the checking-value for the First Amendment when it declared, "To uphold Reuber's manifold claims would be to disable the government from rebutting charges by employees that the positions taken by government agencies were ill-founded, ill-motivated, or even corrupt." The court added, "We think the First Amendment protects the right of persons both within and without government to challenge vigorously the conclusions of public agencies."[113] Connecting free expression to the ability of individuals and the press to challenge potential government ineptitude or malfeasance implicates the need to keep the power assigned to government agencies in check through the potential for public exposure and debate.[114]

Self-governance and checking values

A few rulings, which examined whether the disclosure of information relevant to criminal justice proceedings was privileged from liability for invasion of privacy, implicated the audience-based self-governance and checking values for free expression.[115] When discussing the public's right to know about judicial proceedings, those opinions primarily referred to the U.S. Supreme Court's rationale in its 1975 ruling in *Cox Broadcasting Corp. v. Cohn.*[116] In that case, the Court held that a television station could not be held liable for invasion of privacy resulting from the broadcast of a rape victim's name obtained from open judicial records of a public prosecution. The interest in privacy fades for information that is available to the public, the Court said.[117] Writing for the majority, Justice White asserted:

> Without the information provided by the press most of us and many of our representatives would be unable to vote intelligently or to register opinions on the administration of government generally. With respect to judicial proceedings in particular, the function []the press serves to guarantee the fairness of trials and to bring to bear the beneficial effects of public scrutiny upon the administration of justice.[118]

State high court and federal circuit courts of appeals rulings have tied similar reasoning to brief discussions of the importance of exposing government agents and agencies to public scrutiny.[119]

In one of the earliest relevant rulings, decided in October 1989, the Florida Supreme Court recognized the self-governance and government watchdog values of the First Amendment.[120] The court, however, discussed a more general right to know when discussing precedent under state common law. In that case, *Cape Publications v. Hitchner*, the court found that a newspaper could not be held liable for invasion of privacy "for publishing lawfully obtained and confidential child abuse information in a story on a related child abuse trial."[121] The court suggested that *Cox Broadcasting* indicated that the public's right to receive information "assumes special importance where judicial proceedings are concerned,"[122] and reasoned that Cape Publications was serving the checking function by publishing an article the purpose of which was "to scrutinize the judicial function."[123]

The U.S. Court of Appeals for the Tenth Circuit's ruling in *Avalardo v. KOB-TV* primarily relates to the self-governance and checking values.[124] Applying New Mexico law in 2007, that court found the First Amendment protected a New Mexico news station from liability for publishing the identities of two undercover police officers allegedly involved in sexual assault when they were off duty.[125] Refusing to provide an exception for undercover police officers, the court reasoned that such action would "run afoul of the First Amendment" because allegations of "police misconduct" and commentary on the qualifications of police officers are matters of public interest protected by the First Amendment.[126] The court stated, "To be sure, any rule of law adopted in this area would implicate core and vital First Amendment values, and it is far from clear whether and how such a law might coexist with the freedom of the press."[127] The court's discussion relates to the self-governance and checking values, although the opinion does not explicitly mention those values.

Summary

Since 1989, state high court and federal appellate court rulings on disclosure of private facts claims primarily involve the audience-based marketplace of ideas, self-governance and checking values.[128] A couple of rulings also implicate the liberty-based autonomy value for free expression,[129] which include brief discussion of the free expression values with little or no discussion of privacy values.

Privacy Values

Privacy literature indicates that individual-based privacy values—liberty, autonomy, and emotional health—and society-based privacy values—civility and community, fostering relationships, and promoting democratic processes—underlie privacy torts. Since June 1989, most relevant appellate court opinions in disclosure cases did not include specific discussion of privacy values. A few rulings on disclosure of private facts appeals have recognized the right to privacy as the "right to be let alone,"[130] sometimes linking that phrase to the famous Warren and Brandeis article.[131] Such statements could be interpreted as linking privacy to most of the individual or societal values of privacy, especially the liberty and autonomy values. More obvious connections to privacy values primarily arose when courts discussed key elements of the plaintiff's case, mentioned the type of harm addressed by the tort, or compared the disclosure tort to intentional infliction of emotional distress, breach of confidentiality, or defamation. Those rulings primarily implicated the individual values of liberty, autonomy, or emotional health and mental well-being with little or no discussion of the societal values of promoting civility and community or fostering relationships.

<u>Liberty and autonomy values</u>

Rulings that connected the general right to be let alone to a right to be free from undue pressure or "unwarranted publicity" typically suggested that a liberty value underlies privacy.[132] For instance, the Supreme Judicial Court of Massachusetts' 2005 ruling in *Ayash v. Dana-Farber Cancer Institute*[133] quoted the *Restatement (Second) of Torts*, "'every individual has some phases of his life and his activities and some facts about himself that he does not expose to the public eye, but keeps entirely to himself or at most reveals only to his family or to close personal friends.'"[134] Using that comment in its interpretation of the state's privacy statute, the court said the statute protected the plaintiff against interference with her right to control the disclosure of sensitive, highly personal, or intimate information, such as "matters concerning her health or her lifestyle."[135] Connecting privacy to control over the publicity given to one's personal information and freedom from interference with that control implicates the liberty value for privacy.

Because the autonomy and liberty values may overlap, it is not surprising to find some descriptions of privacy relate to both individual values.[136] The Supreme Court of Minnesota's commentary on the disclosure of private facts tort suggested an autonomy and a liberty value for privacy.[137] When the court first recognized the disclosure tort in *Lake v. Wal-Mart Stores, Inc.*, in 1998, it wrote: "[T]he right to privacy is an integral part of our humanity; one has a public persona, exposed and active, and a private persona, guarded and preserved. The heart of our liberty is choosing which parts of our lives shall become public and which parts we shall hold close."[138] The first part of that statement relates to personal agency and identity, which are part of the autonomy value.[139] The second part of that statement suggests individuals have freedom to choose if and how personal information is exposed to others.[140] That statement, however, clearly identifies the liberty value by name as well as description.

The individual autonomy and liberty values for privacy are only implicated when an individual loses control over the disclosure of truly sensitive or personal information not pertinent to matters of public importance. In 2011 in *Lovejoy v. Linehan*, the Supreme Court of New Hampshire explained that the public disclosure tort """involves the invasion of something secret, secluded or private pertaining to the plaintiff.""""[141] Although David Lovejoy claimed that the publication of his annulled assault charges was a tortious disclosure of private information, the court disagreed. The court reasoned that Lovejoy, by choosing to run for county sheriff, """rendered his annulled assault conviction a matter of legitimate public concern.""""[142] Willingly exposing himself to scrutiny as a candidate for public office, accordingly, prevented the disclosure of that information from undermining his personal autonomy or liberty values for privacy.

Emotional health and mental well-being values

In 2009, the federal D.C. Circuit Court of Appeals indicated that the individual liberty, autonomy, and emotional health values underlie privacy.[143] In *Randolph v. ING Life Insurance and Annuity Co.*, the court held that plaintiffs failed to demonstrate that widespread publicity was given to private facts.[144] Quoting prior cases, the court said, "[A] cause of action for the invasion of privacy 'represents a vindication of the right of private personality and emotional security.'"[145] The disclosure branch protects individuals "'from undue and unreasonable publicity.'"[146] The court mentioned emotional security when responding to the defendant's assertion that the District of Columbia "Consumer Personal Information Security Breach Notification Act of 2006," which excluded pain and suffering from the actual damages plaintiffs could recover for a violation of that Act, "creat[ed] 'incongruity'" with the common law invasion of privacy tort.[147]

Some discussions of the elements of the disclosure tort clearly have connected privacy to the emotional health of individuals. In fact, the common law in a few states requires that a plaintiff must demonstrate likelihood for a disclosure to cause emotional harm.[148] For example, in 1999, the South Carolina Supreme Court wrote that the elements of the tort require the disclosure be of such a kind that would "bring shame or humiliation to a person of ordinary sensibilities."[149] Nine years earlier, the Supreme Court of Mississippi reasoned that a defendant cannot be held liable for disclosure of private facts "unless he should reasonably have foreseen that the person would be likely offended."[150] Of course, some states incorporate that more general description of emotional harm by requiring the disclosure be highly offensive or objectionable to a reasonable person, a requirement that relates to emotional harm.[151]

A couple of rulings have discussed the mental well-being value for privacy when attempting to distinguish the harm redressed by the disclosure of private facts tort from the harm redressed by the tort of defamation.[152] In 2009, the Supreme Court of Pennsylvania found that a medical clinic's release of confidential medical information to the plaintiff's employer did not constitute the level of widespread publicity necessary for the disclosure to be actionable.[153] As the level of publicity required for the tort of defamation is distinct from the level of publicity required for the tort of disclosure, the court indicated that the primary harm addressed by each of those torts is distinct. The court wrote, "[A] libel claim primarily involves damage to reputation, while in an action for invasion of privacy, the central harm to be redressed is mental suffering due to public exposure."[154] The court acknowledged that damages for invasion of privacy torts could include harm to personal reputation. Nonetheless, that ruling emphasized emotional harm, suggesting emotional health is the primary value underlying the disclosure tort.

In an aforementioned plurality opinion suggesting that Indiana does not recognize the disclosure of private facts tort, the state supreme court's comparison of the disclosure and emotional distress torts emphasized the emotional health value for privacy.[155] Chief Justice Randall Shepard wrote that the tort protects an individual's "interest in mental well-being, in avoiding the emotional distress that could result from disclosures."[156] But the plurality was not convinced that a disclosure tort was necessary to protect individuals' emotional health in the 1990s as it had been in the 1890s.[157] The plurality reasoned that that American society had grown "more open and tolerant," leaving individuals with modern sensibilities less susceptible to devastation than were individuals with Victorian sensibilities.[158] Even if modern individuals were likely to become devastated by disclosures, Shepard suggested the tort of outrage provided remedies for severe emotional distress. Because the tort of outrage includes more stringent requirements for the plaintiff than disclosure, the plurality rejected the need to accept the disclosure of private facts tort, which it called "outrage 'lite.'"[159]

Another state high court's comparison of the disclosure tort and the breach of confidentiality tort implies the individual emotional health value relates to disclosure of private facts and the societal value of maintaining relationships relates to breach of confidentiality.[160] In *Swinton Creek Nursery v. Edisto*, the Supreme Court of South Carolina affirmed an intermediate court of appeals' conclusion that invasion of privacy and breach of confidentiality address distinct harms. The court reasoned: "Warren and Brandeis envisaged a privacy right that would occupy ground not already covered by contract and confidentiality theories. In this sense, if a plaintiff has a claim for breach of contract or confidentiality, there is no justification for reviving an otherwise invalid invasion of privacy claim."[161] In the explanatory footnote following that statement, the court suggested that breach of confidentiality focuses on the harm resulting from betrayal by the source of the disclosure rather than the emotional harm resulting from the disclosure of the information itself. That note concluded, "[I]t is irrelevant in a breach of confidentiality claim whether the disclosure of the information would bring shame to a person of ordinary sensibilities."[162] Thus, whereas the breach of confidentiality tort relates to one's connections to the person who disclosed information, the disclosure tort primarily focuses on the emotional damages suffered by the subject of the disclosure.

Promoting civility and fostering relationships

Comparing the disclosure and defamation torts, however, the Indiana Supreme Court plurality opinion discussed above suggests the disclosure tort may relate to the societal values of promoting civility and community or forming and maintaining relationships.[163] Discussing a reputational interest for the disclosure tort, the plurality claimed: "Truthful disclosures can be socially disruptive and personally dangerous. In many real-life situations, the maintenance of a social organization—such as a workplace—sometimes depends upon the ability of individuals to censor themselves and minimize internecine strife."[164] Concerns about personal danger can encompass desires to promote an individual's physical and mental well-being as well as emotional health. But the overall focus on the potential for discordant relations to disrupt organizations, or micro-communities, implicates the societal value of promoting civility and community.[165] The interest in reputation also inherently connects the discussion to relationships, as persons may choose not to associate with an individual based on her tarnished public image. Recognizing defamation torts traditionally have addressed such harms, Chief Justice Shepard suggested the disclosure tort acted as a libel law for truthful information. He reasoned that recognizing disclosure, therefore, would contradict the Indiana Constitution.[166]

The Washington Supreme Court focused primarily on individual privacy values although it also implicated relational privacy values when it reaffirmed the state's recognition of the disclosure tort under common law.[167] The court's quotation of a 1988 decision implicates the individual values of liberty and emotional health by mentioning control over the dissemination of information when the disclosure would cause offense: "Every individual has some phases of his life and his activities and some facts about himself that he does not expose to the public eye, but keeps entirely to himself or at most reveals to his family or to close friends." It added, "When these intimate details of his life are spread before the public gaze in a manner highly offensive to a reasonable man, there is an actionable invasion of privacy."[168]

That case focused on dignitary harm endured by individuals whose loved-ones' autopsy photographs were casually displayed by county employees. The ruling implied that releasing intimate details about each decedent harmed survivors precisely because decedents and their surviving relatives had formed special relationships, making intimate details about decedents' intimate details for the survivors.[169] The court held "the immediate relatives of a decedent have a protectable privacy interest in the autopsy records of the decedent. That protectable privacy interest is grounded in maintaining the dignity of the deceased."[170] The court's finding suggests that survivors have an interest in protecting the integrity of individuals for whom they care, an interest clearly connected to the societal values of forming relationships and maintaining civility as well as individual liberty and emotional health.

<u>Summary</u>

Disclosure rulings primarily have discussed individual values rather than societal values for privacy. Most rulings have indicated that a liberty, autonomy, or emotional health value underlies privacy.[171] In fact, those values at times overlap in courts' discussion of emotional distress resulting from a loss of control over the disclosure of sensitive information. Each of those values was implicated in the U.S. Fifth Circuit Court of Appeals' rationale for upholding a $2 damage award in the only binding post-*Florida Star* disclosure of private facts ruling found in which a circuit court upheld a damage award. The individual values of liberty and emotional health also were implicated in both rulings related to the societal privacy values of promoting civility and community and fostering relationships. Other societal values for privacy were not explicitly discussed in the disclosure of private facts rulings included in this study.

Reconciling Clashes among Free Expression and Privacy Values

Although both freedom of expression and privacy are highly valued in a democratic society, appellate court rulings suggest that disclosure of private facts plaintiffs should expect to prevail only in "extreme cases."[172] Rulings that attempt to reconcile potential conflicts between freedom of expression and privacy primarily have implicated select societal free expression values—marketplace of ideas, self-governance, and the checking function—and the individual privacy value of liberty. Most rulings that acknowledge a clash between freedom of speech or press and privacy have focused on the applicability of the common law newsworthiness defense or a similar First Amendment privilege. The balancing test applied to assess the newsworthiness of the facts at issue in each case generally has resulted in the public's interest in learning information outweighing the individual privacy interest.[173]

Individual privacy and audience-based free press values

The 1993 Georgia Supreme Court opinion in *Macon Telegraph v. Tatum* indicates that the clash between privacy and press freedom necessitates weighing "the individual's right to privacy against the public's right to know and the press's right to publish."[174] The opinion does not identify any specific privacy values, but it clearly implicates three freedom of expression values. Quoting its own 1905 ruling that first recognized a common law right to privacy, the Georgia Supreme Court wrote that privacy "'is limited by the right to speak and print.'"[175] That quotation and text included in a footnote implicate a liberty-based autonomy value for individuals and the institutional press.[176] The opinion also ties press freedom to the audience-based self-governance and checking values for free expression: "A free press is necessary to permit public scrutiny on the conduct of government and to ensure that government operates openly, fairly, and honestly."[177] Extending that rationale to the facts of the case, the court found that Tatum could not prevail in her disclosure of private facts claim against the newspaper that published articles identifying her as the sexual assault victim found to have acted in self-defense when she shot and killed a man who broke into her home and exposed himself to her.[178]

Two years later, the Supreme Court of Texas also found that a newspaper could not be held liable for invasion of privacy for disclosing information that would identify a rape victim.[179] That court's examination of the newsworthiness of the disclosed matter implicated individual privacy and audience-based free expression values. The majority opinion grounded the right to privacy in personal liberty pertaining to one's self and one's property,[180] and it assessed whether Doe's right to privacy was violated by asking if a "logical nexus" existed between the information disclosed about Doe and the subject of the news report—her rape.[181] The court explained that private details might not be newsworthy if they "are not uniquely crucial to the case" or are just related to "a general, sociological issue."[182] But Doe's identifying information, including the general area in which she lived and the fact that she had a security alarm, was sufficiently relevant to the reported crime, the subject of the news report, for the published information to be of public concern.[183]

Despite that conclusion, the court warned in dictum that it might find the publication of identifying information about a sexual assault victim to be an actionable invasion of privacy under other circumstances. The court wrote:

> Newspapers and other media should take precautions to avoid unwarranted public disclosure and embarrassment of innocent individuals who may be involved in otherwise newsworthy events of legitimate public interest. . . . Facts which do not directly identify an innocent individual but which make that person identifiable to persons already aware of uniquely identifying personal information, may or may not be of legitimate public interest.[184]

That court indicated that statement was a warning rather than a legal rule because requiring the media to assess the "individual and cumulative impact (of facts) under all circumstances" could have a "chilling effect" on press freedom.[185] The liberty-based value of autonomy for the institutional press clearly relates to that statement. Audience-based values also underlie the court's rationale that such a requirement "foreseeably could cause critical information of legitimate public interest to be withheld until it becomes untimely and worthless to an informed public."[186] That statement connects the disclosure of newsworthy information to a public right to receive information implicating the audience-based marketplace of ideas, self-governance, and checking values for freedom of expression.

In 1997, the Colorado Supreme Court wrote that balancing must be used when an individual's right to privacy clashes with the free expression rights guaranteed by the Constitutions of the United States and Colorado.[187] Guided by earlier rulings by the U.S. Ninth and Tenth Circuit Courts of Appeals, the state high court applied a newsworthiness test to balance press freedom and privacy.[188] The court described newsworthy information as information the public has a legitimate interest in learning. The court wrote, "In determining whether a subject is of legitimate public interest, '[t]he line is to be drawn when the publicity ceases to be the giving of information to which the public is entitled, and becomes a morbid and sensational prying into private lives for its own sake.'" [189] That rationale implicates the audience-based values for freedom of expression and the individual liberty value for privacy.

A 1998 plurality opinion by the Supreme Court of California focused on audience-based values for free expression by drawing the boundary between privacy and press freedom where Warren and Brandeis drew the line in 1890.[190] Warren and Brandeis indicated that disclosing matters of public and general interest would not constitute an invasion of privacy.[191] More than a century later, California's high court wrote in *Shulman v. Group W. Productions, Inc.*:

> The sense of an ever-increasing pressure on personal privacy notwithstanding, it has long been apparent that the desire for privacy must at many points give way before our right to know, and the news media's right to investigate and relate facts about the events and individuals of our time.[192]

The court asserted that courts historically determined whether an invasion of privacy was actionable by "balancing privacy interests against the press's right to report, and the community's interest in receiving, news and information."[193] It indicated that privacy interests could outweigh the public's right to know when disclosed details "bear only slight relevance to a topic of legitimate public concern."[194] Rather than discussing specific privacy values or free expression values, the opinion focuses on whether the disclosed information was newsworthy or "of legitimate public concern."[195] The court conceded that the analysis of newsworthiness requires courts to engage "to some degree in a normative assessment of the 'social value'" of a publication.[196] The analysis also requires courts to compare the extent to which the information revealed is private in nature and "the extent to which the plaintiff played an important role in public events."[197] That connects the editorial autonomy for the press to the general right for the public to receive information, which could incorporate any values from the audience-based model.[198]

One unpublished and later withdrawn and superseded opinion that applied a similar balancing method suggested that a plaintiff's individual liberty-based privacy interest in the context of the case was sufficient to merit a trial.[199] In 2001 in *Uranga v. Federated Publications, Inc.*, the Idaho Supreme Court ruled that a trial court erred in granting summary judgment for a newspaper corporation based on the newsworthiness of information contained in a photograph of a forty-year-old statement. The court found that the published information did not implicate the public's right to scrutinize judicial proceedings because the statement that Uranga had engaged in a sexual experience with his homosexual cousin, Fred, was not the subject of any judicial proceedings.[200] That sensitive information was only "tangentially" related to the subject of the newspaper's report.[201] Thus, the court concluded that a reasonable person might disagree with the trial court's assessment that Fred Uranga lacked a "legitimate expectation of privacy in a statement regarding his sexuality contained in a forty-year-old court file."[202] The court's rationale indicated the disclosure was not protected because the disclosed statement was not used in any judicial proceedings that would implicate the checking value for freedom of expression.[203]

In the published opinion that superseded the 2001 *Uranga* ruling, the Supreme Court of Idaho focused solely on the constitutional guarantee of freedom of expression without balancing free speech and privacy values.[204] In the 2003 *Uranga* ruling, Idaho's high court held that the First Amendment as applied to the states via the Fourteenth Amendment would not permit a court to hold the newspaper liable for "accurately publishing a document contained in a court record open to the public."[205] The court reasoned that the age of the documents and the lack of a significant public interest in Uranga's identity did not sufficiently distinguish the facts of Uranga's case from those in *Cox Broadcasting v. Cohn*[206] to merit finding the newspaper liable for invasion of privacy.[207] The court asserted that the U.S. Supreme Court "was concerned about the chilling effect upon the freedoms of speech and press if liability for invasion of privacy could be based upon the reporting of information contained in records open to the public."[208] It also applied the Supreme Court's recognition that reports on crime, prosecutions, and judicial proceeds are of "significant public interest."[209] The court indicated that the unique circumstances in the case "certainly evoke sympathy for Uranga," but it did not discuss the privacy interests at issue.[210] Rather, the ruling turned on the constitutional issues that implicate a liberty-based autonomy value and audience-based checking value for freedom of speech and of the press.

Individual privacy and editorial autonomy

In 2003, the U.S. Fourth Circuit Court of Appeals applied a broad definition of newsworthiness to determine whether disclosing a sexual abuse victim's name was an invasion of privacy or a matter of public concern under South Carolina law. In *Doe 2 v. Associated Press*, the court stated, "[T]here is some justification for the complaint" arising from a reporter's public identification of a sexual abuse victim, information the reporter learned during a sentencing hearing, but courts "do not sit as censors of the manners of the Press."[211] Although the ruling suggests that the AP might have exercised bad judgment,[212] the court found the news service did not invade Doe's liberty-based privacy, or "right to be let alone," by reporting a fact Doe voluntarily disclosed in an open court proceeding.[213] The court wrote:

> Without some indication from South Carolina courts to the contrary, we cannot understand how the voluntary disclosure of information in an unrestricted open court room setting could be anything but a matter of public interest. The nature of the information disclosed here does not change our legal analysis: "if a person, whether willingly or not, becomes an actor in an event of public or general interest, then the publication of his connection with such occurrence is not an invasion of his right to privacy."[214]

The court connected the reporter's presence in an open court proceeding to the public's interest in learning about the administration of justice.[215] Thus, identifying the victim of a crime in that case related to the checking value for freedom of expression, which outweighed the liberty value for privacy in this case.

Four years later, a California Supreme Court ruling relied on the *Shulman* newsworthiness test when weighing freedom of speech against an individual's privacy interests.[216] The majority opinion balanced the public's right to know information about "Jane Doe," the subject of a child maltreatment study, and the individual's privacy interest. As mentioned in section A, the court reasoned that the disclosed information was connected to a matter of public interest and was not of an "[i]ntensely personal or intimate" nature such that disclosing it "would be offensive and objectionable to the reasonable person."[217] Rather than discuss the potential for the disclosure to cause emotional harm that could be redressed by the disclosure tort, the court focused on the rights of academics to receive information on the subject matter. The court indicated that articles discussing the original study had shown "it would be important and of interest from an academic standpoint to learn the effects of the events described in the case study upon Jane's future development."[218] The majority decided that a researcher's subsequent statements that Jane Doe "'engaged in 'destructive behavior'" as a teenager and later joined the Navy were relevant to academic analysis of a prominent case study on memories of childhood sexual abuse.[219] Notably, that rationale implicates a marketplace of ideas value for freedom of expression and an emotional health value for privacy by recognizing a limited right for academics to learn information that is not sufficiently sensitive to cause extreme emotional harm.[220]

Summary

Most of the courts that mentioned a balancing of interests test or a clash between freedom of expression and privacy issued rulings suggesting audience-based free expression values outweighed the individual privacy values at issue.[221] If those rulings implicated privacy values, the discussion related primarily to the individual liberty or emotional health values for privacy.[222] Most relevant rulings focused on whether disclosed information was a matter of legitimate public concern with discussions of newsworthiness implicating audience-based free expression values.[223] The majority opinions from a few of those cases assessed whether the disclosed information related to the public's right to learn or scrutinize criminal justice proceedings, which relates to the self-governance and checking values for freedom of expression.[224] Only one ruling involving a balancing of interests test suggested that a reasonable person could find that a plaintiff's privacy was invaded by the disclosure of information.[225] That ruling, the Supreme Court of Idaho's unpublished opinion in *Uranga v. Federated Publications*, was superseded two years later by a published ruling that connected the autonomy-based value of editorial freedom with the press's ability to inform the public.[226] The court wrote:

> We are reluctant to embark on a course that would make public records generally available to the media but forbid their publication if offensive to the sensibilities of the supposed reasonable man. Such a rule would make it very difficult for the media to inform citizens about the public business and yet stay within the law. The rule would invite timidity and self-censorship and very likely lead to the suppression of many items that would otherwise be published and that should be made available to the public.[227]

In the aforementioned binding rulings, freedom of speech or press outweighed the privacy interests at issue in the cases.[228]

Neither Dead nor Obliterated

Although one prominent commentator has argued that "it is probably time to admit defeat, give up the efforts at resuscitation, and lay the noble experiment in the instant creation of common law to a well-deserved rest,"[229] some appellate court rulings published since 1989 suggest the disclosure tort is neither dead nor was it obliterated by *Florida Star*. During the 1990s, only two states' high courts suggested their states' common law did not recognize the disclosure branch of invasion of privacy.[230] The highest courts in four states have clarified that the common law of their respective states does recognize invasion of privacy by the disclosure of private facts in the past twenty-two years.[231] Most state court rulings included in this study did not involve a question that would require a court to address whether the disclosure tort unconstitutionally abridged freedom of expression. Two federal circuit courts of appeals rulings, however, imply that state courts and circuit courts of appeals question might not need to answer that question.[232] Quoting an earlier Seventh Circuit decision, the Eighth Circuit stated, "[T]he [U.S. Supreme] Court was not 'being coy in *Cox* or *Florida Star* in declining to declare the tort of publicizing intensely personal facts totally defunct.'"[233]

Yet, a media defendant was only involved in one of the five appellate court rulings that reversed lower courts' summary judgment orders for defendants.[234] That unpublished ruling in *Uranga v. Federated Publications* was superseded two years later by a second Supreme Court of Idaho ruling.[235] On the other hand, the Supreme Court of Texas ruling in *Star-Telegram, Inc. v. Doe* warns media defendants that protection for the press is not absolute, although the court stated reluctance to impose restrictions that would chill editorial autonomy. Despite those concerns about a liberty-based autonomy value for press freedom, that ruling suggests media could be vulnerable to liability for disclosures that do not serve audience-based free expression values associated with a public right to receive matters of public interest.

<u>Liberty-based free expression values</u>

Courts have discussed the liberty-based autonomy value for freedom of expression, [236] at least one audience-based value for freedom of expression,[237] or a combination of those values.[238] Discussion of the autonomy value arose in two cases involving freedom of speech.[239] Courts tied the marketplace of ideas, self-governance, and checking function values to freedom of speech and to freedom of the press.[240] When courts mentioned the autonomy value and at least one of the audience-based values, their rationales related to either freedom of speech or press.[241]

When courts discussed the autonomy value undergirding freedom of expression, their discussions of the liberty-based value primarily related to John Stuart Mill's connection of freedom of speech to freedom from censorship. The Supreme Court of Idaho emphasized the individual benefits associated with communicating "to the public without censorship," explaining issue advertisements as a "tool for the expression of free speech" by individuals, speech that is free from others' filtering.[242] The U.S. Eighth Circuit Court of Appeals' ruling in a case that involved another important venue for individuals' unfiltered speech, public television, also implied that freedom of speech for individuals is very important, and thus can only be proscribed in "the extreme case."[243]

<u>Audience-based free expression values</u>

Post-*Florida Star* state high court and federal circuit court rulings generally have recognized strong protection exists for the institutional press against disclosure of private facts claims involving accurate publicity given to matters of public interest or public significance, which inherently implicates audience-based free expression values. Some courts have indicated that the newsworthiness test separates disclosures that are actionable invasions of privacy from disclosures protected by the First Amendment.[244] One court has even quoted a Tenth Circuit Court of Appeals' decision issued almost eight years prior to the U.S. Supreme Court's *Florida Star* ruling to assert that adopting a common law newsworthiness privilege or legitimate public interest element "properly restricts liability for public disclosure of private facts to the extreme case, thereby providing the breathing space needed by the press."[245] That rationale echoes the reasoning from *New York Times v. Sullivan*, a landmark defamation case that limited tort liability imposed on the press when the press was information readers about matters of public concern involving a public official, connecting protection to audience-based self-governance and checking function values free expression values.[246]

A few rulings discussed a general audience-based right to know information, a concept that implicated the marketplace of ideas or checking function values. The Mississippi Supreme Court mentioned another aspect of the marketplace of ideas value for freedom of speech when it discussed the importance of allowing individuals to receive information "freely."[247] The U.S. Seventh Circuit Court of Appeals discussed another attribute of the classic marketplace of ideas value, allowing audiences to receive more than one side of a debate or argument.[248] The Fourth Circuit related press freedom to the marketplace of ideas value when it discussed "the public's right to learn about both sides of a controversy" involving a research institute's response to a researcher's claims that the institute changed its position on a potential carcinogen.[249] That court also tied press freedom to the checking value when it identified a right to challenge public agencies.

Several other rulings implied the audience-based self-governance and checking values for freedom of expression when discussing the public's right to receive information about alleged crimes or judicial proceedings.[250] A few cited the U.S. Supreme Court's rationale from *Cox Broadcasting Corp. v. Cohn*, tying freedom of expression to "the beneficial effects of public scrutiny of the administration of justice."[251] The Florida Supreme Court mentioned the self-governance and check on government values when it discussed the First Amendment protection for a newspaper that published "lawfully obtained and confidential child abuse information" in an article related to a criminal trial on that topic.[252] The U.S. Tenth Circuit Court of Appeals discussion of a television station's broadcast of the identities of two undercover police officers accused of sexual assault also related to the self-governance and checking values for press freedom.[253] That ruling provided one of the most explicit discussions of First Amendment values and acknowledged the conflict between privacy law and press freedom and concluded that "police misconduct allegations" and "officer qualifications" are matters of public importance, thus the officers were unable to state a viable claim for invasion of privacy by the disclosure of sensitive sexual information.[254]

Individual privacy values

Courts primarily provided implicit discussion of privacy values, which might explain why more than one individual value for privacy often related to courts' mentions of the individual privacy values of liberty, autonomy, and emotional health.[255] Courts rarely discussed societal values for privacy, and if they did, their discussions implicated the values of promoting civility and community or forming and maintaining relationships.[256]

Courts mentioned the liberty and autonomy values for privacy when discussing the history of the disclosure tort or the publicity element.[257] When discussing the development of the legal right to privacy in America, one even quoted Warren and Brandeis' definition for privacy as "'the right to be let alone.'"[258] In some cases, courts' discussion of the plaintiff's loss of control over sensitive information implicated the liberty value and the autonomy value.[259] The Supreme Court of Minnesota wrote, "The heart of our liberty is choosing which parts of our lives shall become public and which parts we shall hold close."[260] The court connected that interest to one's control over her "private persona" and her "public persona," which also implicates the autonomy value for privacy. It is not surprising that a court's discussion of individuals' loss of control over the exposure of intimate aspects of their lives would implicate the liberty value and the autonomy value for privacy, considering that both values relate to personal agency, which understandably is prized where persons praise individualism.

Courts primarily discussed the emotional health value undergirding privacy when indicating disclosures of private information cause emotional harm.[261] The South Carolina Supreme Court indicated that the elements of the tort require that a disclosure of private facts would "bring shame or humiliation to a person of ordinary sensibilities."[262] The D.C. Circuit Court of Appeals quoted earlier case law when it described privacy as a right of "emotional security." [263] Although a broad conception of emotional security could relate to the emotional release and emotional injury aspects of the emotional health value, the court's mention of emotional security responded to the defendant's assertion that a D.C. statute that excluded pain and suffering from the actual damages plaintiffs could recover for breaches of electronic security contraindicated the ability for a plaintiff to collect damages for emotional harm resulting from a disclosure of private facts.[264]

Societal privacy values

If courts implied a societal significance for privacy, their discussions of privacy also involved at least one individual privacy value.[265] The South Carolina Supreme Court's comparison of the disclosure of private facts and breach of confidentiality torts related to the forming and maintaining relationships value.[266] But that ruling indicated that an emotional health value undergirded privacy and the value of forming and maintaining relationships undergirded breach of confidentiality.[267] The Supreme Court of Washington's conclusion that individuals have a privacy interest that may be invaded by the disclosure of autopsy records of their immediate relatives implicated the societal values of forming and maintaining relationships and promoting civility as well as the individual values of liberty and emotional health.[268] No discussion of the other societal privacy values was found in the cases included in this study.

Reconciling conflicts between free expression and privacy

Few courts suggested that they attempted to reconcile conflicts between freedom of expression and privacy, or even acknowledged the tension between First Amendment interests and privacy interests that Justice Marshall mentioned in *Florida Star*.[269] In one sense, courts followed the U.S. Supreme Court's practice of relying on principles "that sweep no more broadly than the appropriate context of the case."[270] But most state high courts and federal courts of appeals did not balance free expression and privacy interests or apply the limited First Amendment privilege from *Florida Star* that protects the truthful reporting of lawfully obtained information on matters of public significance. Nor did many quote the limited First Amendment principle from *Bartnicki v. Vopper* that stated, "privacy concerns give way when balanced against the interest in publishing matters of public importance."[271] A few courts applied the First Amendment privilege from *Cox Broadcasting*, which prevents states from sanctioning the press for truthfully reporting matters of public interest that are available from publicly available judicial records.[272] The latter standard, in addition to the common law privilege for matters of public interest or general interest, provided much broader protection for free expression than the aforementioned limited First Amendment privileges.

Several rulings referred to at least one individual value undergirding privacy law—most commonly the liberty value— and the marketplace of ideas, self-governance, and checking values for freedom of expression.[273] Some suggested the free expression interests outweighed the privacy interests at issue, but only gave lip-service to the traditional concept of balancing competing interests. Most of those rulings engaged in definitional balancing, suggesting that publishing information on a matter of public interest automatically outweighed any privacy interests at stake. Those rulings practically provided absolute protection for the free expression interests associated with the broad common law privilege that exempts matters of public or general interest from liability for disclosure of private facts.

In a few cases, the courts' reasoning implicated key free expression values and privacy values.[274] Those opinions identified either the liberty-based autonomy value or audience-based marketplace of ideas, self-governance, and checking values for free expression.[275] After mentioning at least one of those values undergirding freedom of expression, most courts did not discuss any of the values scholars tie to privacy. Some cases related to at least one free expression value and the individual liberty, autonomy, or emotional health values for privacy.[276] Nonetheless, courts did not truly balance the competing free expression and privacy interests.[277] Their discussions focused on freedom of expression without actually weighing free expression values against privacy values when members of the public had a right to receive information at issue in that case.[278]

Privacy interests only trumped free expression interests when no audience-based free expression values were served by disclosure at issue in the post-*Florida Star* rulings included in this study. In three cases remanded for trial, the disclosure of private information also did not serve any public interests, but the disclosures harmed individual privacy interests associated with the liberty, autonomy, and emotional health values.[279] Even those cases rarely resulted in awards of damages for plaintiffs.[280] For instance, in *Lake v. Wal-Mart*, the Clay County Superior Court stated that a Wal-Mart employee, who was not listed as a party in the case, did invade the plaintiff's privacy by distributing photographs of two nude young women showering together. The court reasoned, however, that employee was not acting in his capacity as a Wal-Mart employee when distributing the images, thus the corporation was not liable for damages.[281] The only appellate court ruling that upheld a jury's finding for a plaintiff after June 1989 involved a public entity and its employees—not a media defendant. In that case, the U.S. Fifth Circuit Court of Appeals applied Louisiana law, which allowed a plaintiff's privacy interests to prevail when no public interests were served by the disclosed "embarrassing" private information.[282] Thus, this study suggests that post-*Florida Star* state high court and federal circuit court rulings have limited the disclosure of private facts tort to providing redress for exploitative disclosures that harm individual liberty, autonomy, and emotional health without serving any public interests. In that respect, courts provided some consistent charting in this area of law, charting that appropriately allows constitutional free expression rights to limit the successful disclosure of fact claims to "extreme cases."[283]

Chapter 3 Notes

---

[1] Ozer v. Borquez, 940 P.2d 371, 377 (Colo. 1997) (en banc) ("It is generally recognized by a majority of jurisdictions that the right of privacy may be invaded . . . by unreasonable publicity given to another's private life . . . .").

[2] *Ozer*, 940 P.2d at 379; Lake v. Wal-Mart Stores, Inc., 582 N.W.2d 231, 235 (Minn. 1998) (en banc); Karch v. Baybank, 794 A.2d 763, 774 (N.H. 2002).

[3] Reid v. Pierce County, 961 P.2d 333, 339 (Wash. 1998). The First Circuit Court of Appeals also indicated that the state of New Hampshire likely would recognize the tort. Riley v. Harr, 292 F.3d 282, 298 (1st Cir. 2002).

[4] Doe v. Methodist Hosp., 690 N.E.2d 681, 691 (Ind. 1997) (plurality); Howell v. New York Post Co., Inc., 612 N.E.2d 699, 703 (N.Y. 1993); Hall v. Post, 372 S.E.2d 711, 716 (N.C. 1988).

[5] *Hall*, 372 S.E. 2d at 716.

[6] *Id.* at 715.

[7] *Howell*, 612 N.E.2d at 703 ("[W]e have no common law of privacy. Balancing the competing policy concerns underlying tort recovery for invasion of privacy is best left to the Legislature, which in fact has rejected proposed bills to expand New York law . . . .").

[8] *Methodist Hosp.*, 690 N.E.2d at 691.

[9] *Id.* at 691. Reasoning that reputation is one of the interests protected by the disclosure theory of invasion of privacy, the plurality suggested that the disclosure tort could clash with the state Constitution. *Id.*

[10] Searches for the key words of "privacy" and "disclosure of private facts" in LexisNexis, Westlaw and the Media Law Reporter found 740 court rulings from June 1989 through July 31, 2011. Most of those rulings are not considered relevant to this study because they were handed down by state courts at the intermediate appellate level, involved other invasion of privacy torts, or involved statutory claims unrelated to the disclosure of private facts tort. Circuit Court of Appeals rulings for the District of Columbia are equated to state high court rulings in this study as those rulings are in the LexisNexis and Westlaw state case law databases.

The relevant rulings are: Spilfogel v. Cox Broad. Co., No. 10-12507, *4 (11th Cir. July 5, 2011); Equal Employment Opportunity Comm'n v. C.R. England, Inc., 2011 U.S. App. LEXIS 8971, No. 09-4207, at *72 (10th Cir. 2011); Boring v. Google Inc., 362 Fed. App'x. 273, 278-80 (3d Cir. 2010); Alvarado v. KOB-TV, 492 F.3d 1210, 1219-21 (10th Cir. 2007); Anderson v. Suiters, 499 F.3d 1228, 1235-37 (10th Cir. 2007); Baldwin v. Blue Cross/Blue Shield of Alabama, 480 F.3d 1287, 1308-09 (11th. Cir. 2007); Lowe v. Hearst Newspapers P'ship L.P., 497 F.3d 246, 251-52 (5th Cir. 2007); Karraker v. Rent-A-Center, Inc., 411 F.3d 831, 838 (7th Cir. 2005); Doe 2 v. Associated Press, 331 F.3d 417, 421 (4th Cir. 2003); Dasey v. Anderson, 304 F.3d 148 (1st Cir. 2002) (citing Mass.Gen.Laws ch. 214 § 1B); Green v. CBS Inc., 286 F.3d 281, 283 (5th Cir. 2002); Willan v.

Columbia Cnty, 280 F.3d 1160, 1162 (7th Cir. 2002); Zaffuto v. City of Hammond, 308 F.3d 485, 491 (5th Cir. 2002); Phillips v. Grendahl, 312 F.3d 357, 371-72 (8th Cir. 2001); Campbell v. Lyon, 26 Fed. App'x 183, 186 (4th Cir. 2001)(unpublished per curiam); Parry v. Mohawk Motors of Mich., Inc., 236 F.3d 299, 313 (6th Cir. 2000); Veilleux v. Nat'l Broad. Co., 206 F.3d 92, 107 (1st Cir. 2000); Dickinson v. Chitwood, No. 98-1446, 1998 U.S. App'x LEXIS 32569, at *6-7 (1st Cir. 1998); Coplin v. Fairfield Pub. Access Television Comm., 111 F.3d 1395, 1405-06 (8th Cir. 1997); Roe v. Cheyenne Mountain Conference Resort, Inc., 124 F.3d 1221, 1236 (10th Cir. 1997), *appeal after remand,* 127 F.3d 879 (10th Cir. 1999); Howell v. Tribune Entm't Co., 106 F.3d 215, 220 (7th Cir. 1997); McNewmar v. Disney Store, Inc., 91 F.3d 610, 622 (3d Cir. 1996); Johnson v. Sawyer, 47 F.3d 716, 731-33 (5th Cir. 1995)(en banc); Cinel v. Connick, 15 F.3d 1338, 1346 (5th Cir. 1994); Merlo v. United Way of Am., 43 F.3d 96, 104 (4th Cir. 1994); Tichenor v. Roman Catholic Church, 32 F.3d 953, 963 (5th Cir. 1994); Haynes v. Alfred A. Knopf, Inc., 8 F.3d 1222, 1232-35 (7th Cir. 1993); Thomas v. Pearl, 998 F.2d 447, 452 (7th Cir. 1993); Lee v. Calhoun, 948 F.2d 1162, 1165 (10th Cir. 1991); S.B. v. St. James Sch., 959 So. 2d 72, 91-92 (Ala. 2006); Rosen v. Montgomery Surgical Ctr., 825 So.2d 735, 739 (Ala. 2001); *Ex parte* The Birmingham News, Inc., 778 So.2d 814, 818-19 (Ala. 2000); Finebaum v. Coulter, 854 So. 1120, 1129 (Ala. 2003); Johnston v. Fuller, 706 So.2d 700, 703 (Ala. 1997); Milam v. Bank of Cabot, 937 S.E.3d 653 (Ark. 1997); Taus v. Loftus, 151 P.3d 1185, 1208-09 (Cal. 2007); Gates v. Discovery Commc'ns, Inc., 101 P.3d 553, 562-63 (Cal. 2005); Barker v. Huang, 610 A.2d 1341, 1350 (Del. 1991); Ozer v. Borquez, 940 P.2d 371, 377 (Colo. 1997) (en banc); Elliott v. Healthcare Corp., 629 A.2d 6, 9 (D.C. 1993); Cape Publ'ns, Inc. v. Hitchner, 549 So. 2d 1374, 1378-79 (Fla. 1989); Macon Telegraph v. Tatum, 6 S.E.2d 655, 657 (Ga. 1993); Nation v. State of Idaho Dept. of Corrections, 158 P.3d 953, 967 (Idaho 2007); Doe v. Haw, 2003 WL 21015143, at *6 (Idaho Feb, 5 2003)(unpublished); Uranga v. Federated Publ'ns, No. 27118, at *26-27 (2001 LEXIS) (Idaho June 21, 2001) (unpublished), *superseded by* Uranga v. Federated Publ'ns, Inc. v. Idaho Statesman, 67 P.3d 29, 35 (Idaho 2003); Hoskins v. Howard, 971 P.2d 1135, 1142 (Idaho 1998); Doe v. Methodist Hosp., 690 N.E.2d 681, 691 (Ind. 1997) (plurality); Loe v. Town of Thomaston, 600 A.2d 1090, 1093 (Me. 1991); Ayash v. Dana-Farber Cancer Inst., 822 N.E.2d 667, 682-84 (Mass. 2005); Mulgrew v. City of Taunton, 574 N.E.2d 389, 393 (Mass. 1991); Warner-Lambert Co. v. Execuquest Corp., 691 N.E.2d 545, 548 (Mass. 1998) (stating that a corporation does not have a right to privacy); Gauthier v. Police Comm'r of Boston, 557 N.E.2d 1374, 1376 (Mass. 1990); Bodah v. Lakeville Motor Express, Inc., 663 N.W.2d 550, 551-58 (Minn. 2003); Lake v. Wal-Mart Stores, Inc., 582

N.W.2d 231, 235 (Minn. 1998) (en banc); Young v. Jackson, 572 So.2d 378, 384-85 (Miss. 1990); Nazeri v. Missouri Valley Coll., 860 S.W.2d 303, 303 (Mo. 1993); Svaldi v. Anaconda-Deer Lodge County, 106 P.3d 548, 553 (Mont. 2005); Lovejoy v. Linehan, 161 N.H. 483, 486, No. 2010-343 (N.H. 2011); Karch v. Baybank, 794 A.2d 763, 774 (N.H. 2002); G.D. v. Kenny, 15 A.3d 300, 309-10 (N.J. 2011); Howell v. New York Post Co., Inc., 612 N.E.2d 699, 703 (N.Y. 1993); Hadnot v. Shaw, 826 P.2d 978, 986 (Okla. 1992); Burger v. Blair, 964 A.2d 374, 380 (Pa. 2009); Lamarque v. Centreville Savings Bank, No. 2010-67, 2011 R.I. LEXIS 86, at *11(R.I. 2011); Swerdlick v. Koch, 721 A.2d 849, 859 (R.I. 1998); Pontbriand v. Sundlun, 699 A.2d 856, 864 (R.I. 1997); Swinton Creek Nursery v. Edisto Farm Credit, 514 S.E.2d 126, 131-32 (S.C. 1999); Doe v. Berkeley Publishers, 496 S.E.2d 636, 637 (S.C. 1998); Shattuck-Owen v. Snowbird Corp., 16 P.3d 555, 558 (Utah, 2000).

[11] *Zaffuto*, 308 F.3d at 491 (affirming the award of $2 in compensatory damages and remanding for a new trial on punitive damages.).

[12] *See,e.g.*, *Uranga*, No. 27118, at *26-27 (2001 LEXIS), *superseded by* Uranga v. Federated Publ'ns, Inc. v. Idaho Statesman, 67 P.3d 29, 35 (Idaho 2003); *Hoskins*, 971 P.2d at 1142; *Lake*, 582 N.W.2d at 232; *Karch*, 794 A.2d at 774; *Reid*, 961 P.2d at 342.

[13] *See, e.g.*, *Steinbuch*, 518 F.3d at 589-91 (asserting that Steinbuch had not established personal jurisdiction and Steinbuch failed to state a claim against Home Box Office and Time Warner Cable because no publicity had occurred); *Tichenor*, 32 F.3d at 963 (finding the disclosure of private facts claim was time-barred); *Milam*, 937 S.E.3d at 653 ("[T]he Milams do not state which theory of privacy invasion applies to their case. . . . [W]e will not develop this claim for the Milams. That was their responsibility."); *Foncello*, 931 A.2d at 928 (asserting that the plaintiff's claim on appeal for disclosure of private facts had little to do with the original claims for identity theft and intrusion upon seclusion).

[14] *See, e.g.*, *Alvarado*, 492 F.3d at 1219-21; *Doe 2*, 331 F.3d at 421; *Taus*, 151 P.3d at 1208-09; *Gates*, 101 P.3d at 562-63; *Shulman*, 955 P.2d at 486; *Ozer*, 940 P.2d at 378; *Cape Publ'ns, Inc.*, 549 So. 2d at 1378-79; *Macon Telegraph*, 6 S.E.2d at 657 (Ga. 1993); *Uranga*, 67 P.3d at 34-6.

[15] *See infra* note 82 and accompanying text.

[16] *See infra* notes 85-130 and accompanying text.

[17] *See infra* notes 131-171 and accompanying text.

[18] Most state high courts have recognized the disclosure of private facts under state common law, adopting the elements recorded in the RESTATEMENT (SECOND) TORTS § 652D (1977). Most states that have recognized the disclosure tort under statutory law have adopted at least the first three of the four elements described in Section 652D of the Restatement.

[19] A few rulings, however, discussed a fifth element: whether the disclosure was reckless. For example the Supreme Court of Colorado has indicated, "A person acts with reckless disregard if, at the time of the publicity, the person knew or should have known that the fact or facts disclosed were private in nature." *Ozer*, 940 P.2d at 379.

[20] *See infra* notes 23-49, 65-81, and accompanying text.

[21] *See, e.g., Ozer*, 940 P.2d at 380; *Hoskins*, 971 P.2d at 1142; *Lake*, 582 N.W.2d at 236; *Pontbriand*, 699 A.2d at 864.

[22] *C.R. England, Inc.*, 2011 U.S. App. LEXIS 8971, No. 09-4207, at *72; *Steinbuch*, 518 F.3d at 591 (stating that Steinbuch failed to state a claim against Home Box Office and Time Warner Cable because no publicity had occurred); *Karraker*, 411 F.3d at 838; *Willan*, 280 F.3d at 1162 (7th Cir. 2002); *Parry*, 236 F.3d at 313; *Roe*, 124 F.3d at 1236, *appeal after remand*, 127 F.3d 879 (10th Cir. 1999); *McNewmar*, 91 F.3d at 622; *S.B.*, 959 So. 2d at 91-92; *Rosen*, 825 So.2d at 739; *The Birmingham News*, 778 So.2d at 818-19; *Johnston*, 706 So.2d at 703; *Ozer*, 940 P.2d at 377-79; *Elliott*, 629 A.2d at 9; *Nation*, 158 P.3d at 967; *Bodah*, 663 N.W.2d at 551-58; *Hadnot*, 826 P.2d at 986; *Burger*, 964 A.2d at 380; *Lamarque*, No. 2010-67, 2011 R.I. LEXIS 86, at *11; *Swinton*, 514 S.E.2d at 131-32; *Shattuck-Owen*, 16 P.3d at 558.

[23] RESTATEMENT (SECOND) TORTS §652D cmt. a. (1977). *But see Pontbriand*, 699 A.2d at 864 (explaining that Rhode Island has adopted the publication standard commonly applied in libel and slander claims).

[24] 778 So. 2d at 818-19.

[25] *Id.* at 818-19.

[26] *Id.* at 819.

[27] *Methodist Hosp.*, 690 N.E.2d at 693; *Bodah*, 663 N.W.2d at 553-54; *Swinton*, 514 S.E.2d at 131-32.

[28] *Bodah*, 663 N.W.2d at 553-54; *Swinton*, 514 S.E.2d at 131-32.

[29] Restatement (Second) of Torts ß 652D cmt. a.

[30] *Methodist Hosp.*, 690 N.E.2d at 693 (citing McSurely v. McClellan, 753 F.2d 88, 112-13 (D.C. Cir. 1985).

[31] *Id.* at 693.

[32] *Campbell,* 26 Fed. App'x at 186; *Barker*, 610 A.2d at 1350; *Nazeri*, 860 S.W.2d at 303 (stating that the plaintiff filed a disclosure of private facts claim, but the disclosed information was not true).

[33] *Finebaum*, 854 So. at 1129; *Nazeri*, 860 S.W.2d at 303.

[34] *Barker*, 610 A.2d at 1350.

[35] *Id.*

[36] *Id.*

[37] *See, e.g., Showler*, 222 Fed. App'x at 764; *Dasey*, 304 F.3d at 148 (citing MASS.GEN.LAWS ch. 214 § 1B); *Green*, 286 F.3d at 283; *Dickinson*, No. 98-

1446, 1998 U.S. App'x LEXIS 32569, at *6-7; *Johnson*, 47 F.3d at 731-33; *Merlo*, 43 F.3d at 104; *Haynes*, 8 F.3d at 1232-35; *Puckett*, 1990 U.S. App'x LEXIS 19761, at *5-6; *Reuber*, 925 F.2d at 719, *cert. denied*, 501 U.S. 1212 (1991); *S.B.*, 959 So. 2d at 92; *Taus*, 151 P.3d at 1208-09; *Steele*, 61 P. 3d at 607; *Warner-Lambert Co.*, 691 N.E.2d at 548 (stating that a corporation does not have a right to privacy); *Svaldi*, 106 P.3d at 553.

[38] *Johnson*, 47 F.3d at 732-33; *Haynes*, 8 F.3d at 1232-35.

[39] *Johnson*, 47 F.3d at 732-33. The court applied Texas common law, which requires "the plaintiff to prove (1) that the publicized information 'contains highly intimate or embarrassing facts about a person's private affairs, such that its publication would be highly objectionable to a person of ordinary sensibilities.'"

[40] *Taus*, 151 P.3d at 1208-09.

[41] *Id.* (quoting *Shulman*, 955 P.2d at 486.

[42] *Spilfogel*, No. 10-12507, *4.

[43] *Id.*

[44] *See, e.g.*, *Steele*, 61 P. 3d at 607; *Warner-Lambert Co.*, 691 N.E.2d at 548.

[45] *See, e.g.*, *Campbell*, 26 Fed. App'x. at 186; *Johnson*, 47 F.3d at 731-32; *Reuber*, 925 F.2d at 719; *Steele*, 61 P.3d at 610.

[46] *S.B.*, 959 So. 2d at 93.

[47] *Id.* at 93.

[48] *Steele*, 61 P.3d at 610.

[49] *Id.*

[50] *Hoskins*, 971 P.2d at 1136-41.

[51] *Id.* at 1140.

[52] *Id.* at 1141.

[53] *Id.*

[54] *Boring*, 362 Fed. App'x. at 278-80; *Zaffuto*, 308 F.3d at 486; *Pontbriand*, 699 A.2d at 866.

[55] *Boring*, 362 Fed. App'x. at 278-80.

[56] *Zaffuto*, 308 F.3d at 486; *Pontbriand*, 699 A.2d at 866.

[57] *Pontbriand*, 699 A.2d at 866. The court ruled the claim should go to trial to determine whether a disclosure "could be expected to inflict harm on the person whose private affairs are made points of public discussion. This issue, of course, involves a factual determination of what would be offensive or objectionable in the context of this case."

[58] *Id.* at 864.

[59] *Zaffuto*, 308 F.3d at 486.

[60] *Id.* at 491.

[61] 940 P.2d 371, 377 (Colo. 1997).

[62] *Id.*

[63] Peggy Lowe, *Lawyer wins discrimination suit*, DENVER POST B-08 Jan. 7, 1999.

[64] *See, e.g.*, *Anderson*, 499 F.3d at 1235-37; *Doe 2*, 331 F.3d at 417; *Veilleux*, 206 F.3d at 132-33; *Cinel*, 15 F.3d at 1346; *Thomas*, 998 F.2d at 452; *Haynes*, 8 F.3d at 1232-35; *Purnell*, 1992 U.S. App. LEXIS 24313, at *4; *Reuber*, 925 F.2d at 703; *Lee*, 948 F.2d at 1165; *Taus*, 151 P.3d at 1207-08; *Cape Publ'ns, Inc.*, 549 So. 2d at 1379; *Macon Telegraph*, 436 S.E.2d at 679; *Ayash*, 822 N.E.2d at 682-84; *Mulgrew*, 574 N.E.2d at 393; *Gauthier*, 557 N.E.2d at 1376; *Loe*, 600 A.2d at 1093; *Swerdlick*, 721 A.2d at 859; *Berkeley Publishers*, 496 S.E.2d at 637; *Star-Telegram, Inc.*, 915 S.W.2d at 473-74.

[65] *Loe*, 600 A.2d at 1093.

[66] *Gauthier*, 557 N.E.2d at 1376.

[67] *Doe 2*, 331 F.3d at 421; *Purnell*, 1992 U.S. App. LEXIS 24313, at *7-8.

[68] *Macon Telegraph*, 436 S.E.2d at 679.

[69] *Johnson*, 47 F.3d at 732 (citing Cox Broadcasting v. Cohn, 420 U.S. 469, 495 (1975)).

[70] *Purnell*, 1992 U.S. App. LEXIS 24313, at *8 (stating that allegations of racial discrimination are a matter of public interest); *Ayash*, 822 N.E.2d at 682-84.

[71] *Merlo*, 43 F.3d at 104 (quoting Prosser, LAW OF TORTS § 117 (5th ed. 1984)).

[72] *Berkeley Publishers*, 496 S.E.2d at 636.

[73] *Ayash*, 822 N.E.2d at 683.

[74] 2011 U.S. App. LEXIS 1461, No. 07-4535, at *17.

[75] *See, e.g.*, *Doe2*, 331 F.3d at 442; *Veilleux*, 206 F.3d at 107; *Cinel*, 15 F.3d at 1346 n.9 ("Because we find the broadcast of the materials a legitimate matter of public concern, we need not address whether the media is entitled to immunity from liability under the First Amendment for the public disclosure of lawfully obtained truthful facts."); *Cape Publ'ns, Inc.*, 549 So. 2d at 1379.

[76] *Veilleux*, 206 F.3d at 100-01 (quoting Cox Broad. v. Cohn, 420 U.S. 469, 491 (1975).

[77] *Id.* at 105. The majority wrote:

> We think defendants were entitled to illustrate their messages about highway safety and regulation with new information about the individual subject of their report. Simply reporting statistics about truckers who use drugs, or discussing the details of Kennedy's case without mentioning him by name, would have substantially less impact.

[78] *Haynes*, 8 F.3d at 1232.

[79] *Id.* at 1232.

[80] *Id.* at 1232-33.

[81] *E.g.*, *Steinbuch*, 518 F.3d at 591; *Anderson*, 499 F.3d at 1235-37; *Karraker*, 411 F.3d at 838; *Willan*, 280 F.3d at 1162; Phillips v. Grendahl, 312 F.3d

357, 371-72 (8th Cir. 2001); *Parry*, 236 F.3d at 313; *Roe*, 124 F.3d at 1236, *appeal after remand*, 127 F.3d 879 (10th Cir. 1999); *Thomas*, 998 F.2d at 452; *Lee*, 948 F.2d at 1165; *S.B.*, 959 So. 2d at 91-92; *Rosen*, 825 So.2d at 739; *Johnston*, 706 So.2d at 703; *Elliott*, 629 A.2d at 9; *Bodah*, 663 N.W.2d at 551-58; *Swerdlick*, 721 A.2d at 859; *Swinton*, 514 S.E.2d at 131-32; *Shattuck-Owen*, 16 P.3d at 558.

82 *See, e.g.*, *Showler*, 222 Fed. App'x at 764; *Baldwin*, 480 F.3d at 1308-09; *Merlo*, 43 F.3d at 104; *Haynes*, 8 F.3d at 1232-35; *S.B.*, 959 So. 2d at 92; *Steele*, 61 P. 3d at 607; *Svaldi*, 106 P.3d at 553; *G.D.*, 15 A.3d at 309-10; *Pontbriand*, 699 A.2d at 866.

83 *See infra* notes 137-183, 227-278, and accompanying text.

84 *Haw*, 2003 WL 21015134, at *3-4.

85 *Id.*

86 *See, e.g.*, *Coplin*, 111 F.3d at 1405-06.

87 *Haw*, 2003 WL at *2-3.

88 *Id.* at *2-3.

89 *Id.* at *6.

90 *Id.*

91 *Id.* Thomas Scanlon explained that principle by quoting Mill: "'The only purpose for which power can be rightfully exercised over any member of a civilized community, against his will, is to prevent *harm to others*.'" Thomas Scanlon, *A Theory of Freedom of Expression*, 1 PHIL. & PUB. AFF. 204, 213 (1972) (quoting JOHN STUART MILL, ON LIBERTY 13 (1956).

92 *Coplin*, 111 F.3d at 1405-06.

93 *Id.* at 1403.

94 *Id.* at 1404.

95 *Id.* at 1400-01.

96 *Id.* at 1405.

97 *Coplin*, 111 F.3d at 1405-06. Citing the U.S. Supreme Court's 1992 ruling in *R.A.V. v. City of St. Paul* in turn quoting *Chaplinsky v. New Hampshire*, the Eighth Circuit wrote, "'[O]ur society, like other free civilized societies, has permitted restrictions on the content of speech in a few limited areas, which are "of such slight social value as a step to truth that any benefit that may be derived from them is clearly outweighed by the social interest in order and morality."'" *Id.* at 1401-02 (citing *R.A.V.*, 505 U.S. at 382, quoting Chaplinsky v. New Hampshire, 315 U.S. 568, 572 (1942)).

98 *See, e.g.*, *Lowe*, 497 F.3d at 251-52; *Howell*, 106 F.3d at 220; *Reuber*, 925 F.2d at 719-21; *Young*, 572 So.2d at 384-85; *Svaldi*, 106 P.3d at 552-53.

99 497 F.3d at 251-52 (citing Cinel v. Connick, 15 F.3d 1338, 1346 (5th Cir. 1994)).

100 *Id.* at 251.

101 *Howell*, 106 F.3d at 220; *Reuber*, 925 F.2d at 719-21; *Young*, 572 So.2d at 384-85; *Svaldi*, 106 P.3d at 552-53.

[102] *Young*, 572 So.2d at 383-85. The court found that a qualified privilege defense, which indicates that employees with a mutual interest may share certain information without being liable for invasion of privacy, protected Jackson against liability for invasion of privacy.
[103] *Id.* at 382 (quoting Holmes, *The Path of Law*, 10 HARV. L. REV. 457, 466 (1897)).
[104] *Howell*, 106 F.3d at 220.
[105] *Id.* at 218.
[106] *Id.*
[107] *Id.* at 220-21.
[108] *Id.* at 221.
[109] *Id.*
[110] 925 F.2d 703, 719-21 (4th Cir. 1991).
[111] *Id.* at 706.
[112] *Id.* at 720-21.
[113] *Id.*
[114] *Id.* at 719-21.
[115] *See, e.g.*, *Doe2*, 331 F.3d at 421; *Gates*, 101 P.3d at 562-63; *Cape Publ'ns, Inc.*, 549 So. 2d at 1378-79; *Uranga*, 67 P.3d at 34-36.
[116] *See, e.g.*, *Gates*, 101 P.3d at 562-63; *Cape Publ'ns, Inc.*, 549 So. 2d at 1378-79 (citing Cox Broad. Corp. v. Cohn, 420 U.S. 469 (1975)); *Uranga*, 67 P.3d at 34-36.
[117] *Cox Broad. Corp.*, 420 U.S. at 491.
[118] *Id.* at 492.
[119] *See, e.g.*, *Gates*, 101 P.3d at 562-63; *Cape Publ'ns, Inc.*, 549 So. 2d at 1378-79; *Uranga*, 67 P.3d at 34-6.
[120] *Cape Publ'ns, Inc.*, 549 So. 2d at 1378-79.
[121] *Id.* at 1378.
[122] *Id.*
[123] *Id.*
[124] 492 F.3d 1210, 1219-21 (10th Cir. 2007).
[125] The court wrote, "An officer's alleged involvement in a sexual assault, even if off-duty, surely bears upon his or her qualifications and fitness to be a police officer." *Id.* at 1220.
[126] *Id.* at 1220-21.
[127] *Id.* at 1221.
[128] *See, e.g.*, *Alvarado*, 492 F.3d at 1219-21; *Howell*, 106 F.3d at 220; *Reuber*, 925 F.2d at 719-21; *Gates*, 101 P.3d at 562-63; *Cape Publ'ns, Inc.*, 549 So. 2d at 1378-79 (Fla. 1989); *Uranga*, 67 P.3d at 34-6; *Young*, 572 So.2d at 384-85; *Svaldi*, 106 P.3d at 552-53.
[129] *See, e.g.*, *Coplin*, 111 F.3d at 1405-06; *Haw*, 2003 WL 21015134, at *6-7.

[130] *Doe2*, 331 F.3d at 417-21; *Foncello*, 931 A.2d at 929; *Pontbriand*, 699 A.2d at 866; *Swinton*, 514 S.E.2d at 131-32.
[131] *Star-Telegram, Inc.*, 915 S.W.2d at 473 (quoting Warren & Brandeis, *Right To Privacy*, 4 HARV. L. REV. 193, 193 (1980)).
[132] *Doe 2*, 331 F.3d at 420; *Swinton*, 514 S.E.2d at 131-32.
[133] 822 N.E.2d 667, 681-82 (Mass. 2005).
[134] *Id.* at 682 (quoting RESTATEMENT (SECOND) TORTS § 652D cmt. b (1977)).
[135] *Id.* at 682-83.
[136] *Ayash*, 822 N.E.2d at 682-83; *Bodah*, 663 N.W.2d at 553-54; *Lake*, 582 N.W.2d at 235.
[137] *Bodah*, 663 N.W.2d at 553-54; *Lake*, 582 N.W.2d at 235.
[138] *Lake*, 582 N.W.2d at 235.
[139] *Id.*
[140] *Id.*
[141] 161 N.H. 483, 486, No. 2010-343 (N.H. 2011) (quoting *Karch*, 794 A.2d at 763).
[142] Id. 488.
[143] *Randolph*, 973 A. 2d at 711.
[144] *Id.* at 711-12.
[145] *Id.* at 711 (quoting Afro-American Pub. Co. v. Jaffe, 366 F.2d 649, 653 (D.C. Cir. 1966)).
[146] *Id.* (quoting *Peay v. Curtis Pub. Co.*, 78 F. Supp. 305, 309 (D.D.C. 1948)).
[147] *Id.* at 711 n. 12 (quoting D.C. CODE § 28-3852 (2009)).
[148] *See, e.g.*, *Young*, 572 So.2d at 382; *Swinton*, 514 S.E.2d at 131.
[149] *Swinton*, 514 S.E.2d at 131.
[150] *Young*, 572 So. 2d at 382.
[151] *See, e.g.*, *Taus*, 151 P.3d at 1207 (stating the court doubted the statements made about the plaintiff's destructive behavior "constitutes disclosure of the kind of sufficiently sensitive or intimate private fact 'which would be offensive and objectionable to the reasonable person.'"); *Ozer*, 940 P.2d at 378 ("The term 'highly offensive' has been construed to mean that the disclosure would cause emotional distress or embarrassment to a reasonable person."); *Pontbriand*, 699 A.2d at 864 (requiring that "the "fact which has been made public [is] one which would be offensive or objectionable to a reasonable man of ordinary sensibilities").
[152] *See, e.g.*, *Methodist Hosp.*, 690 N.E.2d at 686-87; *Burger*, 964 A.2d at 378-80.
[153] *Burger*, 964 A.2d at 378.
[154] *Id.* at 378.
[155] *Methodist Hosp.*, 690 N.E.2d at 681. Only two members of the five-member court joined in the plurality opinion. Two justices filed a separate opinion concurring in the result while one justice concurred in the result without opinion.

[156] *Id.* at 686.
[157] *Methodist Hosp.*, 690 N.E.2d at 691-92.
[158] *Id.* at 692.
[159] *Id.*
[160] *Swinton*, 514 S.E.2d at 131-33.
[161] *Id.* at 133 (citing Warren & Brandeis, *Right To Privacy*, 4 HARV. L. REV. 210-11 (1890)).
[162] *Id.* at 133n.14.
[163] *Methodist Hosp.*, 690 N.E.2d at 686.
[164] *Id.*
[165] *Id.*
[166] *Id.*
[167] *Reid*, 961 P.2d at 339-40.
[168] *Id.* at 341 (quoting Cowles Publ'g Co. v. State Patrol, 748 P.2d 597, 602 (Wash.1998)).
[169] *Id.* at 341-42.
[170] *Id.* at 342.
[171] *See, e.g.*, *Randolph*, 973 A. 2d at 711-12; *Baldwin*, 480 F.3d at 1308-09; *Doe2*, 331 F.3d at 417-21; *Taus*, 151 P.3d at 1207; *Ozer*, 940 P.2d at 378; *Foncello*, 931 A.2d at 929; *Ayash*, 822 N.E.2d at 682-83; *Bodah*, 663 N.W.2d at 553-54; *Lake*, 582 N.W.2d at 235; *Young*, 572 So.2d at 382; *Burger*, 964 A.2d at 378-80; *Pontbriand*, 699 A.2d at 866; *Swinton*, 514 S.E.2d at 131-32; *Star-Telegram, Inc.*, 915 S.W.2d at 473 (quoting Warren & Brandeis, *Right To Privacy*, 4 HARV. L. REV. 193, 193 (1980)).
[172] *See, e.g.*, *Coplin*, 111 F.3d at 1404.
[173] *Shulman*, 955 P.2d at 486; *Ozer*, 940 P.2d at 378; *Tatum*, 6 S.E.2d at 657; *Uranga* v. Federated Publ'ns, No. 27118, at *26-27 (LEXIS June 21, 2001) (unpublished), *superseded by Uranga*, 67 P.3d at 35.
[174] *Tatum*, 436 S.E.2d at 657.
[175] *Id.* at 658 (quoting Pavesich v. New England Life Ins. Co., 50 S.E. 68, 74 (1905)).
[176] *Id.* at 658 n.2. The footnote states the Constitution of the State of Georgia clearly identifies the freedom to speak, write, and publish as a "liberty" for each individual person or publisher. *Id.*
[177] *Id.* at 658.
[178] *Id.*
[179] *Star-Telegram, Inc.*, 915 S.W.2d at 472.
[180] *Id.* at 473-74. The court asserted that "the 'right to be let alone' is as much a part of personal liberty as the right to be free from physical restraint and the right to possess property."
[181] *Id.* at 474.
[182] *Id.*

[183] *Id.*

[184] *Id.* at 475.

[185] *Star-Telegram, Inc.*, 915 S.W.2d at 475. The court wrote: "[I]t would be impossible to require them to anticipate and take action to avoid every conceivable circumstance where a party might be subjected to the stress of some unpleasant or undesired notoriety without an unacceptable chilling effect on the media." *Id.*

[186] *Id.*

[187] *Ozer*, 940 P.2d at 378 (citing U.S. CONST. amend. I; COLO. CONST., art. II, §10.).

[188] *Id.* at 378 (citing Gilbert v. Medical Econs. Co., 665 F.2d 305, 308 (10th Cir. 1981) and Virgil v. Time, Inc., 527 F.2d 1122, 1129 (9th Cir. 1975)).

[189] *Id.* (quoting RESTATEMENT (SECOND) TORTS § 652D cmt. h (1976)).

[190] *Shulman*, 955 P.2d at 474 (citing Warren & Brandeis, *Right To Privacy*, 4 HARV. L. REV. 193, 214 (1890)).

[191] *Id.* (citing Warren & Brandeis, 4 HARV. L. REV. at 214).

[192] *Id.*

[193] *Id.* at 478.

[194] *Id.* at 486.

[195] *Shulman*, 955 P.2d at 479.

[196] *Id.* at 484.

[197] *Id.* at 484.

[198] *Id.* at 474. "Also clear is that the freedom of the press, protected by the supreme law of the First and Fourteenth Amendments to the United States Constitution, extends far beyond simple accounts of public proceedings and abstract commentary on well-known events." *Id.*

[199] *Uranga*, No. 27118, at *26-27 (LEXIS June 21, 2001) (unpublished), *superseded by Uranga*, 67 P.3d at 35. The court explained, "[C]onstruing the record liberally in favor of Uranga, and drawing all inferences in his favor, we find reasonable people could reach different conclusions from the evidence in determining whether Uranga has a legitimate expectation of privacy in a statement regarding his sexuality contained in a forty-year-old court file." The court concluded, "[W]e find the district court erred in granting summary judgment to the Statesman on Uranga's claims for invasion of privacy by publication of private facts . . . ."

[200] *Id.* at 29-31.

[201] *Id.* at 16-17.

[202] *Id.* at 31.

[203] *Id.*

[204] *Uranga*, 67 P.3d at 33.

[205] *Id.* at 35.

[206] 420 U.S. 469, 474-75 (1975).

[207] *Uranga*, 67 P.3d at 35 ("There is no indication that the First Amendment provides less protection to historians than to those reporting current events.").
[208] *Id.* at 34 (citing *Cox Broad.*, 420 U.S. at 496).
[209] *Id.* at 35 (citing *Cox Broad.*, 420 U.S. at 492).
[210] *Id.*
[211] *Id.*
[212] *Id.*
[213] *Id.* at 420-21.
[214] *Id.* at 422 (quoting *Berkeley Publ'rs*, 496 S.E.2d at 637).
[215] *Doe 2*, 331 F.3d at 421 ("'[O]ur criminal law tradition insists on public indictment, public trial, and public imposition of sentence. Transparency is essential to maintaining public respect for the criminal justice system, ensuring its integrity, and protecting the rights of the accused.'") (quoting Smith v. Doe, 538 U.S. 84, 99 (2003)).
[216] *Taus*, 151 P.3d at 1208 (citing *Shulman*, 955 P.2d at 479).
[217] *Id.*
[218] *Id.* at 1208-09.
[219] *Taus*, 151 P.3d at 1208-09.
[220] *Id.* at 1208.
[229] *See, e.g.*, *Doe 2*, 331 F.3d at 422; *Taus*, 151 P.3d at 1208; *Shulman*, 955 P.2d at 479; *Ozer*, 940 P.2d at 378; *Uranga*, 67 P.3d at 32-3; *Star-Telegram, Inc.*, 915 S.W.2d at 473-84.
[222] *See, e.g.*, *Doe 2*, 331 F.3d at 4203-21; *Taus*, 151 P.3d at 1208-09; *Shulman*, 955 P.2d at 479; *Ozer*, 940 P.2d at 378; *Uranga*, 67 P.3d at 32-3; *Star-Telegram, Inc.*, 915 S.W.2d at 473-84.
[223] *See, e.g.*, *Doe 2*, 331 F.3d at 420-21; *Taus*, 151 P.3d at 1208-09; *Shulman*, 955 P.2d at 474; *Ozer*, 940 P.2d at 378; *Tatum*, 436 S.E.2d at 657; *Uranga*, 67 P.3d at 34-5; *Star-Telegram, Inc.* 915 S.W.2d at 473-74.
[224] *See, e.g.*, *Doe 2*, 331 F.3d at 420-21; *Uranga*, 67 P.3d at 34-5; *Tatum*, 436 S.E. 2d at 657; *Star-Telegram*, 915 S.W.2d at 472.
[225] *Uranga*, No. 27118, at *26-27 (LEXIS June 21, 2001) (unpublished), *superseded by Uranga*, 67 P.3d at 35.
[226] *Id. See also Uranga*, 67 P.3d at 32-33.
[227] 67 P.3d 29, 34 (2003).
[228] *See, e.g.*, *Doe 2*, 331 F.3d at 420-21; *Taus*, 151 P.3d at 1208-09; *Shulman*, 955 P.2d at 474; *Ozer*, 940 P.2d at 378; *Tatum* 436 S.E. 2d at 657; *Uranga*, 67 P.3d at 34-5; *Star-Telegram, Inc.*, 915 S.W.2d at 473-74.
[229] Zimmerman, *Requiem for a Heavyweight*, 68 CORNELL L. REV. 291, 364 (1983).
[230] *Methodist Hosp.*, 690 N.E.2d at 691; *Howell*, 612 N.E.2d at 703.

[231] *See, e.g.*, *Ozer*, 940 P. 2d at 379; *Lake*, 582 N.W.2d at 235; *Karch*, 794 A.2d at 774; *Reid*, 961 P.2d at 341.
[232] *Coplin*, 111 F.3d at 1404; *Haynes*, 8 F.3d at 1232.
[233] *Coplin*, 111 F.3d at 1404 (quoting *Haynes*, 8 F.3d at 1232).
[234] *See, e.g.*, *Uranga*, No. 27118, at *26-27 (LEXIS June 21, 2001) (unpublished), *superseded by Uranga*, 67 P.3d at 35; *Hoskins*, 971 P.2d at 1142; *Lake*, 582 N.W.2d at 232; *Karch*, 794 A.2d at 774; *Reid*, 961 P.2d at 342.
[235] *Uranga*, No. 27118, at *26-27 (LEXIS June 21, 2001) (unpublished), *superseded by Uranga*, 67 P.3d at 35.
[236] *See, e.g.*, *Lowe*, 497 F.3d at 251-52; *Howell*, 106 F.3d at 220; *Coplin*, 111 F.3d at 1405-06; *Reuber*, 925 F.2d at 719-21; *Haw*, 2003 WL 21015134, at *2-3, 6; *Young*, 572 So.2d at 384-85; *Svaldi*,106 P.3d at 552-53.
[237] *See, e.g.*, *Lowe*, 497 F.3d at 251-52; *Doe 2*, 331 F.3d at 421; *Howell*, 106 F.3d at 220; *Reuber*, 925 F.2d at 719-21; *Cape Publ'ns, Inc.*, 549 So. 2d at 1378-79; *Uranga*, 67 P.3d at 34-6; *Young*, 572 So.2d at 384-85; *Svaldi*,106 P.3d at 552-53.
[238] *See, e.g.*, *Lowe*, 497 F.3d at 251-52; *Howell*, 106 F.3d at 220; *Reuber*, 925 F.2d at 719-21; *Young*, 572 So.2d at 384-85; *Svaldi*,106 P.3d at 552-53.
[239] *Coplin*, 111 F.3d at 1403; *Haw*, 2003 WL at *2-3.
[240] *See, e.g.*, *Doe 2*, 331 F.3d at 421; *Howell*, 106 F.3d at 220; *Coplin*, 111 F.3d at 140; *Reuber*, 925 F.2d at 719-21; *Gates*, 101 P.3d at 562-63; *Cape Publ'ns, Inc.*, 549 So. 2d at 1378-79; *Uranga*, 67 P.3d at 34-6; *Young*, 572 So.2d at 384-85; *Svaldi*, 106 P.3d at 552-53.
[241] *See, e.g.*, *Lowe*, 497 F.3d at 251-52 *(5th Cir. 2007)*; *Howell*, 106 F.3d at 220; *Coplin*, 111 F.3d at 1405-06; *Reuber*, 925 F.2d at 719-21; *Young*, 572 So.2d at 384-85; *Svaldi*, 106 P.3d at 552-53.
[242] *Haw*, 2003 WL 21015143, at *6.
[243] *Coplin*, 111 F.3d at 1404.
[244] *See, e.g.*, *Taus*, 151 P.3d at 1208-09; *Shulman*, 955 P.2d at 478-79.
[245] *Ozer*, 940 P.2d at 378-79 (quoting Gilbert v. Medical Econs. Co., 665 F.2d 305, 307 (10th Cir. 1981)).
[246] 376 U.S. 254, 298-99 (1964).
[247] *Young*, 572 So. 2d at 382.
[248] *Howell*, 106 F.3d at 220.
[249] *Reuber*, 925 F.2d at 720-21.
[250] *See supra* notes 1, 101, 116-28, 178-82, 201-10, and accompanying text.
[251] *Cox Broad. Corp.*, 420 U.S. at 491; *Gates*, 101 P.3d at 562-63; *Cape Publ'ns, Inc.*, 549 So. 2d at 1378-79; *Uranga*, 67 P.3d at 34-6.
[252] *Cape Publ'ns Inc.*, 549 So.2d at 1378-79.
[253] Alvarado, 492 F.3d at 1219-21.
[254] *Id.* at 1222.

---

[255] *See, e.g.*, *Randolph*, 973 A. 2d at 710-11; *Doe 2*, 331 F.3d at 417-20; *Taus*, 151 P.3d at 1207; *Ozer*, 940 P.2d at 378; *Methodist Hosp.*, 690 N.E.2d at 691; *Ayash*, 822 N.E.2d at 681-82; *Bodah*, 663 N.W.2d at 553-54; *Lake*, 582 N.W.2d at 235; *Young*, 572 So.2d at 382; *Burger*, 964 A.2d at 378; *Pontbriand*, 699 A.2d at 864; *Swinton*, 514 S.E.2d at 131; *Star-Telegram, Inc.*, 915 S.W.2d at 473; *Reid*, 961 P.2d at 339-40.

[256] *Methodist Hosp.*, 690 N.E.2d at 686; *Swinton Creek Nursery*, 514 S.E.2d at 131-33; *Reid*, 961 P.2d at 339-40.

[257] *Doe 2*, 331 F.3d at417-21; *Foncello*, 931 A.2d at 929; *Ayash*, 822 N.E.2d at 682-83; *Bodah*, 663 N.W.2d at 553-54; *Lake*, 582 N.W.2d at 235; *Pontbriand*, 699 A.2d at 866; *Swinton Creek Nursery*, 514 S.E.2d at 126); *Star-Telegram, Inc.*, 915 S.W.2d at 473.

[258] *Star-Telegram, Inc.*, 915 S.W.2d at 473 (citing Warren & Brandeis, *Right To Privacy*, 4 HARV. L. REV. 193, 193 (1980)).

[259] *See, e.g.*, *Ayash*, 822 N.E.2d at 682-83; *Bodah*, 663 N.W.2d at 553-54; *Lake*, 582 N.W.2d at 235.

[260] *Lake*, 582 N.W.2d at 235.

[261] *See, e.g.*, *Taus*, 151 P.3d at 1207; *Ozer*, 940 P.2d at 378; *Pontbriand*, 699 A.2d at 864.

[262] *Swinton*, 514 S.E.2d at 131.

[263] *Randolph*, 973 A. 2d at 711 n. 12.

[264] *Id.* (citing D.C. Code § 28-3852 (2009)).

[265] *Methodist Hosp.*, 690 N.E.2d at 686; *Reid*, 961 P.2d at 342.

[266] *Swinton*, 514 S.E.2d at 131-33.

[267] *Id.*

[268] *Reid*, 961 P.2d at 342.

[269] 491 U.S. 524 (1989).

[270] *Id.* at 533.

[271] 532 U.S. at 534 (2001).

[272] 420 U.S. 469, 491 (1975).

[273] *See, e.g.*, *Doe 2*, 331 F.3d at 420-21; *Taus*, 151 P.3d at 1208-09; *Shulman*, 955 P.2d at 474; *Ozer* 940 P.2d at 378; *Uranga*, 67 P.3d at 34-5; *Star-Telegram, Inc.*, 915 S.W.2d at 473-74.

[274] *See, e.g.*, *Doe 2*, 331 F.3d at 420-21; *Taus*, 151 P.3d at 1208-09; *Ozer*, 940 P.2d at 378; *Star-Telegram, Inc.*, 915 S.W.2d at 473-74.

[275] *See, e.g.*, *Alvarado*, 492 F.3d at 1219-20; *Doe 2*, 331 F.3d at 420-21; *Howell*, 106 F.3d at 220; *Reuber*, 925 F.2d at 719-21; *Gates*, 101 P.3d at 562-63; *Cape Publ'ns, Inc.*, 549 So. 2d at 1378-79; *Uranga*, 67 P.3d at 34-5; *Young*, 572 So.2d at 384-85; *Svaldi*, 106 P.3d at 552-53.

[276] *See, e.g.*, *Randolph*, 973 A. 2d at 710-12; *Baldwin*, 480 F.3d at 1308-09; *Doe 2*, 331 F.3d at 417-20; *Taus*, 151 P.3d at 1207; *Ozer*, 940 P.2d at, 378; *Foncello*, 931 A.2d at 929; *Methodist Hosp.*, 690 N.E.2d at 686; *Ayash*, 822

N.E.2d at 681-82; *Bodah*, 663 N.W.2d at 553-55; *Young*, 572 So. 2d at 382; *Burger*, 964 A.2d at 378-80; *Pontbriand*, 699 A.2d at 866; *Swinton*, 514 S.E.2d at 131; *Star-Telegram, Inc.*, 915 S.W.2d at 473; *Reid*, 961 P.2d at 339-40.

[277] *See, e.g.*, *Taus*, 151 P.3d at 1207; *Ozer*, 940 P.2d at 378; *Macon Telegraph*, 436 S.E.2d at 657; *Star-Telegram, Inc.*, 915 S.W.2d at 474.

[278] *See, e.g.*, *Taus*, 151 P.3d at 1207; *Shulman*, 955 P.2d at 474; *Cape Publ'ns, Inc.*, 549 So. 2d at 1378-79.

[279] *Lake*, 582 N.W.2d at 232; *Karch*, 794 A.2d at 774; *Reid*, 961 P.2d at 342.

[280] *Hoskins*, 971 P.2d at1142; *Lake*, 582 N.W.2d at 232; *Karch*, 794 A.2d at 774; *Reid*, 961 P.2d at 342.

[281] Lake v. Wal-Mart Stores, Inc., No. 14-C2-96-001324, ¶ 4-5 (Minn. Clay Cnty. Sept. 21, 1999).

[282] *Zaffuto*, 308 F.3d at 491 (affirming the award of $2 in compensatory damages and remanding for a new trial on punitive damages.).

[283] *See, e.g.*, *Coplin*, 111 F.3d at 1404.

CHAPTER 4

Recognizing Privacy Rights: Appropriation of Likeness

Appropriation, the first privacy tort, was recognized by state statute in 1903 in New York[1] and then under common law in 1905 in Georgia.[2] More than 60 years later, the U.S. Supreme Court first addressed the conflict between freedom of expression and privacy in a false light case filed under the New York privacy law, originally passed in 1903 to provide a remedy for appropriation but subsequently applied to false light claims.[3] Because that case, *Time, Inc. v. Hill*,[4] involved the claim that publication of non-defamatory falsehoods constituted an invasion of privacy, the opinion provided little guidance for courts attempting to reconcile conflicts between freedom of expression and the privacy interests affected by the commercial exploitation of one's name, image, or likeness.

The U.S. Supreme Court has ruled on only one case involving misappropriation of identity. In 1977 in *Zacchini v. Scripps-Howard Broadcasting Co.*, the Court held that the First Amendment did not protect a broadcast station from liability for appropriation when a newscast presented a human-cannon ball performer's entire act, which was protected by the right of publicity under Ohio law. A narrow majority of the Court focused on the individual's right of publicity, a property-based right related to economic harm, not a privacy-based right related to emotional harm. The Court described that right as "the right of the individual to reap the reward of his endeavors, and having little to do with protecting feelings or reputation."[5] This chapter does not address right of publicity cases unless they also involve invasion of privacy claims because the right of publicity is distinct from the right to privacy. As one legal scholar argued, the publicity-based tort of appropriation "has nothing to do with protecting personal privacy."[6]

In fact, the conflict between freedom of expression and the right to privacy was only implied in the *Zacchini* ruling by dissenting justices.[7] In one dissenting opinion, Justices Powell, Brennan, and Marshall criticized the majority for providing insufficient clarity and inappropriate "sensitivity to the First Amendment values at stake."[8] Those dissenting justices indicated that they would have granted greater deference to press freedom than was granted by the majority. Writing for all three, Justice Powell argued that the First Amendment should protect news media against an appropriation suit "absent a strong showing by the plaintiff that the news broadcast was a subterfuge or cover for private or commercial exploitation."[9] His rationale involved the right to privacy as well as the right of publicity, but he indicated that free expression rights are paramount. In the other *Zacchini* dissenting opinion, Justice Stevens suggested the majority did not show "proper sensitivity to First Amendment principles" because it focused on the "reach of the common-law tort" rather than the limits imposed by the First Amendment.[10]

Looking to Lower Courts

Since the U.S. Supreme Court decided *Florida Star v. B.J.F.* in June 1989, the starting point for this study, state high courts and federal circuit courts of appeals have discussed key freedom of expression and privacy values in a number of rulings involving privacy-based appropriation claims.[11] However, in only one case, in which an appellant claimed that the privacy-based appropriation tort violated the freedom of expression provisions of the First Amendment, did a court explicitly engage in ad hoc balancing of interests.[12] Also, only one post-1989 ruling identified by this study has hinted that a state might decline to recognize the appropriation tort. That ruling contained no discussion of privacy or free expression values, merely noting that the North Dakota Supreme Court had had opportunities to recognize the privacy torts but had failed to do so.[13]

In the cases examined by this study,[14] the highest courts in four states recognized the appropriation branch of invasion of privacy for the first time after June 1989.[15] In addition, in 1998, the Supreme Court of Washington clarified that the common law of its state recognizes the privacy tort of appropriation.[16] Three years later, the U.S. Fifth Circuit

Court of Appeals asserted that it expected Mississippi would recognize invasion of privacy by appropriation under the state's common law if a suitable case arose.[17]

State high court and federal circuit court of appeals rulings analyzed for this chapter primarily turned on the appellate courts' applications of the tort's elements, common law privileges, or constitutional defenses. Approximately one third of 52 relevant appropriation rulings evaluated whether summary judgment awards were properly granted.[18] Only one federal circuit court of appeals ruling reversed a summary judgment order for a news media defendant.[19] In that case, *Solano v. Playgirl, Inc.*, the Ninth Circuit Court of Appeals considered whether the First Amendment barred Solano's common law invasion of privacy by misappropriation claim against Playgirl, Inc..[20] Jose Solano, Jr., sued the corporation after his image was placed on the cover of the magazine and juxtaposed with headlines implying that issue included photographs of Solano wearing less than the swimsuit he wore when playing a lifeguard on Baywatch, a television program. The Court held that "the newsworthiness privileges do not apply where a defendant uses a plaintiff's name and likeness in a knowingly false manner to increase sales of the publication," and "There is enough disputed evidence to require a jury resolution."[21] Playgirl, Inc. sought a writ of certiorari from the U.S. Supreme Court, but the Court denied its request.[22] Other state high court and circuit courts of appeals rulings involving alleged tortious appropriations of names or likenesses by news media defendants were considered privileged uses because the uses of plaintiffs' identities were accurate representations of matters of public interest reported by the respective news outlet.[23]

Most post-*Florida Star* appellate rulings involving appropriation claims focused on whether the use of the plaintiff's name or likeness constituted an actionable invasion of privacy according to the elements of the tort.[24] Four decisions reversed summary judgment awards or a judgment notwithstanding verdict and remanded appropriation claims for trial.[25] Fourteen rulings upheld summary judgments because the alleged appropriation either was a privileged publication pertinent to a matter of public interest[26] or failed to satisfy the elements of the tort.[27] In four cases, the courts upheld jury awards for plaintiffs who claimed their names or likenesses were exploited.[28] And one court upheld a permanent injunction to prevent appropriation.[29] The rationales for some of the aforementioned rulings clearly tied the analyses of the facts to key individual privacy values—liberty, autonomy, and emotional health—one key communicator-based free expression value—autonomy—and key audience-based free expression values—the marketplace of ideas, self-governance, and the checking function.[30]

Elements of Appropriation and Key Defenses

Most states have adopted the invasion of privacy by appropriation tort.[31] Many states have recognized appropriation under the common law by adopting language from the *Restatement (Second) of Torts*.[32] A few states have appropriation statutes, often modeled on the New York Right of Privacy Law adopted in 1903.[33] All the states have recognized substantially similar elements and privileges for invasion of privacy under the appropriation theory. The *Restatement (Second) of Torts* states, "One who appropriates to his own use or benefit the name or likeness of another is subject to liability to the other for invasion of his privacy."[34] Similarly, statutory law in New York and Virginia allows liability to be assigned to anyone who uses "for advertising purposes or for the purposes of trade" the name, image, or likeness of a person "without having first obtained the written consent of such person."[35] Courts, however, have defined and applied each of the appropriation tort's three key elements — exploitative or commercial use; name, likeness, or identity; and lack of consent.

Exploitative or commercial use

In determining whether a particular use constitutes an exploitative or commercial use, some courts have used the concept of intentional exploitation.[36] In two of those cases, both involving Texas's invasion of privacy law, the U.S. Fifth Circuit considered whether the uses at issue constituted "excessive exploitation" that reduced the value of the plaintiff's "property rights in his name or likeness."[37] In another case, the Supreme Judicial Court of Massachusetts reasoned that an attorney did not exploit the identity of a Massachusetts Institute of Technology professor of toxicology when the attorney included the professor's name in a list of experts he expected to call as witnesses in a trial.[38] The court acknowledged that an expert's name might be used to provide an attorney with the perception of an advantage, but the court explained that the attorney's truthful response that he had consulted with the professor did not constitute an actionable exploitative use of the expert's name "for purposes of trade" to benefit the attorney.[39] That suggests an exploitative use must unfairly help an individual in his or her business or profession in an unreasonable manner.

In 2007 in *Zarrilli v. John Hancock Life Insurance Company*, the U.S. Third Circuit Court of Appeals found that James Zarrilli and his wife, Carol, did not have an actionable misappropriation claim against John Hancock Life Insurance Company because the exploitation was not intentional under New Jersey common law.[40] The Zarrillis claimed James's identity was used to the defendant's advantage when the company kept his voice mail message active and included his name in correspondence after his employment was terminated.[41] The court's unpublished, per curiam opinion stated, "[T]he Zarrillis presented no evidence that John Hancock acted with a commercial purpose or sought some other benefit from what it claimed had been a mistake."[42]

<u>Use of valuable identity</u>

Other courts have questioned whether analysis of an exploitative use should require a plaintiff to prove that his or her identity had value that could be exploited.[43] In 1991, the U.S. Sixth Circuit Court of Appeals found that Larry Lusby failed to demonstrate *Cincinnati Magazine* had appropriated his identity by publishing an article explaining he had been married and divorced six times.[44] The court ruled that summary judgment was properly granted for the magazine because the plaintiff's likeness was used in relation to a news article. The court reasoned that under Ohio law, Lusby failed to show "that the defendant appropriated something of value beyond the value each person places on his own name or likeness."[45] The court continued, "The only complaint Lusby can make is that the use of his wedding photograph with six paper doll brides damages his name and reputation . . . ."[46] Two years later, the Supreme Court of Alabama applied a similar rationale when it held that several individuals could not prevail on an appropriation claim because they failed to demonstrate their identities had unique qualities or values that would result in a commercial profit.[47]

Almost a decade later, however, the Supreme Court of Colorado rejected the idea that a plaintiff had to prove his or her identity had value in order to prevail in a privacy-based appropriation lawsuit, suggesting that a commercial value requirement was more appropriate when the claim was based on a right of publicity, an exploitation of a property value, rather than an invasion of privacy. [48] In *Joe Dickerson & Associates v. Dittmar*, the Colorado Supreme Court stated:

> It appears illogical to require the plaintiff to prove that her identity has value in order for her to recover for her personal damages. The market value of the plaintiff's identity is unrelated to the question of whether she suffered mental anguish as a result of the alleged wrongful appropriation.[49]

Rather than analyze whether a plaintiff's identity had value worth exploiting, some courts have focused more directly on what constitutes commercial purposes that would benefit a defendant.[50] In 2002, the Supreme Court of Virginia indicated that "a name is used 'for advertising purposes' when 'it appears in a publication which, taken in its entirety, was distributed for use in, or as part of, an advertisement or solicitation for patronage of a particular product or service.'"[51] Any such unauthorized use "'has almost uniformly been held actionable.'"[52] In *WJLA v. Levin*, the court found that use of Dr. Levin's name and image was not an unauthorized use for advertising purposes. Rather, his name and image were used in promotional announcements on "a newsworthy event and a matter of public interest."[53] That case involved a news station's use of a physician's name in advertisements for a news story reporting that several of Levin's patients alleged he performed unnecessary "inappropriate" vaginal procedures.[54]

Courts have found that using an individual's name and/or picture in various types of promotional materials for a non-news related business constitutes advertising purposes.[55] For example, in 1991 in *Beverley v. Choices Women's Medical Center*, the Court of Appeals of New York applied a test to determine whether the use of plaintiff's name and photo in a medical facility's calendar qualified as "advertising purposes."[56] The court explained that a person's identity "is used 'for advertising purposes' if it appears in a publication which, taken in its entirety, was distributed for use in, or as part of, an advertisement or solicitation for patronage of a particular product or service."[57] The court asserted that the medical center's calendar, which included the facility's name, logo, telephone number, and services provided, in addition to the plaintiff's image, "is an advertising medium and promotional publication."[58] The court reasoned that sending a targeted audience a calendar with "laudatory references" about the center was "plainly designed to preserve existing patronage and to educate and solicit new clients."[59] Thus, including the plaintiff's name and photograph in a product designed to solicit customers was an actionable use.[60]

In another case, the Supreme Court of Virginia considered whether a use could serve a public interest rather than solely serving the defendant's commercial interests.[61] In *Town & Country Properties, Inc. v. Riggins* the majority concluded that a former football star's name was used in a flier to promote a sale, not to benefit consumers.[62] Referring to the distinction between uses protected by the First Amendment and actionable uses for trade or advertising purposes, the court asserted that constitutional protection for speech "'is based on the informational function of advertising.'"[63] The majority wrote:

> [T]he plaintiff's name was used strictly in a promotional sense to generate interest in the sale of real estate. The use was not relevant to dissemination of information to consumers about the physical condition, architectural features, or quality of the home. Simply, this is not the type of commercial speech accorded constitutional protection.[64]

Accordingly, the Supreme Court of Virginia found the trial court properly had awarded damages to Riggins because the football star's name was used primarily to benefit Town & Country financially rather than to provide information beneficial to the public.[65]

Use of name or likeness

A few courts have focused on the second element of the appropriation tort, whether a plaintiff's identity was used.[66] The *Restatement (Second) of Torts* refers to this element as the use of a plaintiff's "name or likeness," which can mean different things in different jurisdictions.[67] For instance, using a plaintiff's first and last names without including other identifying attributes was not considered a use of identity in *Botts v. New York Times Company* in 2004 under New Jersey law.[68] The U.S. Third Circuit Court of Appeals found *The New York Times*, an advertising agency, and the United Negro College Fund did not appropriate the identity of Lawrence Botts III by using the name "Larry Botts" "as a generic placeholder for the prototypical underprivileged African-American youth" in an advertisement.[69] The court reasoned that using the identity of Lawrence Botts III, a "college-educated Caucasian," actually would have hindered the advertisement's effectiveness as a fundraising tool for the United Negro College Fund.[70] Thus, Botts's identity was not appropriated in the ad.[71]

However, courts have found that using a name or image with an individual's other readily identifiable characteristics could be sufficient to constitute use of identity.[72] In 1998, in *Newcombe v. Adolf Coors Co.*, the U.S. Ninth Circuit Court of Appeals concluded that a question of material fact remained about whether a beer advertisement featuring a sketch of a baseball pitcher had appropriated the identity of Donald Newcombe, who played major league baseball in the 1940s.[73] It reversed the trial court's grant of summary judgment for the defendant in favor of Newcombe.[74] The appeals court found that "it would not be unreasonable for a jury to conclude" that the advertisement used Newcombe's identity to sell beer.[75] The appeals court asserted a jury could reasonably find Newcombe's likeness was used because the sketch included a pitcher with a dark complexion, similar to Newcombe's complexion, who assumed Newcombe's pitching stance.[76] Although an artist drew another player's number on the pitcher's jersey, the combination of other unique attributes was sufficient for a jury reasonably to believe Newcombe was identified, the appeals court reasoned.[77]

Merely describing events from a person's life, however, may not constitute an actionable use of one's likeness, especially when the events are used in a book, movie, or other non-commercial venue.[78] The U.S. Fifth Circuit Court of Appeals has determined that describing "general incidents from a person's life" or life story does not appropriate the unique value associated with an individual's identity.[79] Applying Texas law, that court reasoned that the tort of appropriation is intended to protect unique values, such as reputation or prestige, associated with a plaintiff's identity.[80] The court wrote:

> The term "likeness" does not include general incidents from a person's life, especially when fictionalized. The narrative of an individual's life, standing alone, lacks the value of a name or likeness that the misappropriation tort protects. Unlike the goodwill associated with one's name or likeness, the facts of

> an individual's life possess no intrinsic value that will deteriorate with repeated use.[81]

When a similar question arose in a recent publicity-based appropriation claim, the Supreme Court of Florida indicated that a First Amendment privilege prevented the fictionalized use of an individual's life story in a book or movie from being considered an actionable appropriation of identity.[82] The Florida case involved a book and film that provided a dramatized story about members of a fishing vessel crew who died when their ship was lost at sea during a severe storm.[83]

<u>Lack of consent</u>

The final element commonly applied in privacy-based appropriation claims assesses whether the plaintiff's name or likeness was used without proper authorization.[84] Courts have found that individuals may waive the right to privacy associated with using their identities through implied consent or explicit consent.[85] For instance, in 1993, the Supreme Court of Alabama reasoned that individuals could not prevail on a privacy-based appropriation claim against a Greyhound Park for including a picture of the plaintiffs at the park in a promotional brochure.[86] The court suggested the individuals essentially consented to the use because the plaintiffs would have seen their picture being taken after hearing announcements that the park was taking photographs for a promotional brochure.[87] Similarly, the Supreme Court of Missouri found that a university's use of a researcher's name in a federal grant application was an authorized use because the researcher and plaintiff, Rama K. Nemani, worked for the university when the grant application was prepared.[88] The court overturned a $300,000 jury verdict for Nemani because the business relationship between the university and Nemani at that time constituted implied consent.[89]

Courts consistently have found that consent is a strong defense against a claim of misappropriation when the use does not exceed the scope of explicit consent granted in a contract or other written agreement.[90] Nebraska's privacy law states that any use that "does not differ materially in kind, extent, or duration from that authorized by the consent as fairly construed" is not actionable.[91] In a 1991 ruling in *Miller v. American Sports Co., Inc.*, the Supreme Court of Nebraska found that publishing a promotional brochure with the word sex above a photograph of a female model was not an actionable invasion of privacy because the model "agreed to the unremunerated and unrestricted use of her photographs to sell products."[92] On the other hand, a 2008 U.S. Eleventh Circuit Court of Appeals per curiam ruling in *Rivell v. Private Health Care Systems, Inc.* found that the existence of a contract between medical providers and a discount medical services network did not preempt an invasion of privacy by appropriation claim under Georgia law for the network's use of plaintiffs' identities for purposes not included in the contract.[93] Remanding the case for trial, the Eleventh Circuit asserted that courts in seven states had "recognized that a use outside the scope of the permission granted in a contract . . . gives rise to an action by the licensor for invasion of privacy."[94]

Privileged uses

Courts also have considered whether uses were exempt from liability because the alleged appropriation was privileged under a First Amendment, common law, or statutory exception for material that conveys a legitimate matter of public concern or interest.[95] This, of course, is closely related to the issue of whether the use qualifies as a commercial, trade or advertising use.

Courts have found uses of a plaintiff's name or likeness to be privileged when a real relationship exists between the use of that plaintiff's identity and a matter public interest or concern addressed by news media.[96] For instance, in 2007, applying Oklahoma law, the U.S. Tenth Circuit Court of Appeals found that *Harper's Magazine* did not violate the privacy of Sergeant Brinlee, who was killed while serving in Iraq in the Oklahoma National Guard, by publishing a photograph of him in an open coffin at his funeral.[97] The court explained that the soldier's death and funeral were a matter of public interest and clearly relevant to the photo essay on grieving deaths resulting from the U.S. military intervention in Iraq.[98] Thus, the use was privileged because a real relationship existed between Sergeant Brinlee's image and the matter of public interest represented in the photo essay.[99]

Courts also have used a real relationship test to determine whether the use of a plaintiff's identity was privileged even though it served both a commercial use and a non-commercial use.[100] For instance, the Supreme Court of Colorado indicated that a private investigation firm, Joe Dickerson & Associates, was not liable for using Rosanne

Dittmar's name in an article about her conviction of theft.[101] The article was published in a newsletter that explained financial fraud investigations conducted by the defendants, and the court acknowledged that the article at issue involved commercial purposes as well as informational purposes.[102] The court assessed "whether the character of the publication is primarily noncommercial" under Colorado law by reviewing whether the content primarily conveyed a commercial message or whether the content related to a matter of public concern.[103] Recognizing that the U.S. Supreme Court had established in *Cox Broadcasting v. Cohn* that information about the commission of and prosecution of crime are "matters of public concern," the Supreme Court of Colorado found that summary judgment had been properly awarded to the defendant because the business's use of Dittmar's name in association with her arrest and conviction was privileged.[104]

Courts also have found news organizations' uses of individuals' images in advertisements for news to be privileged on First Amendment grounds.[105] To determine whether a use of an individual's identity is privileged, some courts have assessed whether a use is "an advertisement in disguise," meaning a "real relationship" does not exist between the plaintiff's identity and the matter of public interest presented.[106] In 2002, in *WJLA v. Levin*, the Supreme Court of Virginia found a news station was not liable for appropriating a doctor's identity by including his image in two advertisements that encouraged viewers to tune in to learn about allegations that Dr. Levin performed unnecessary vaginal procedures on his patients.[107] The court reasoned, "[I]t cannot reasonably be disputed that the principal purpose of WJLA's announcements was to promote a report "of [a] newsworthy event[] or matter[] of public interest." It is a newsworthy event and a matter of public interest when a physician is accused by his patients of sexually assaulting them." [108] The Virginia Supreme Court reversed a $575,000 award for Dr. Levin and held that a reasonable relationship existed between the advertisement and the subject of the news report. The highest state courts in Rhode Island and New York and the U.S. Tenth and Sixth Circuit Courts of Appeals, applying Oklahoma and Ohio law respectively, also have found that a First Amendment privilege protects news outlets' use of individuals' images to illustrate content pertinent to matters of public interest.[109]

On the other hand, the Ninth Circuit ruling in *Solano v. Playgirl, Inc.*, clarified that using an individual's image in a knowingly false manner will not necessarily be protected by a loose connection to a news item. Using Solano's image and creative headlines hinting that the magazine included photographs of the actor wearing little to no clothing, a manner that mislead consumers about the content of news media was not protected by the First Amendment. The court wrote, "Even though the exceptions are to be broadly construed, the newsworthiness privileges do not apply where a defendant uses a plaintiff's name and likeness in a knowingly false manner to increase sales of the publication."[110] That suggests the privilege for use of a person's likeness is limited when the use intentionally takes advantage of the plaintiff as well as members of the public.

Summary

As indicated above, more than one-half of the post-1989, privacy-based appropriation claims identified by this study were found not actionable either because plaintiffs failed to support each element of the tort or because defendants demonstrated that the uses at issue were privileged as expression on matters of public interest or concern.[111] One important ruling, however, clarified that exploitative uses of likeness may not be protected when they intentionally mislead members of the public. The following sections explore if and how courts discussed free expression and privacy values when ruling on privacy-based appropriation claims.

Free Expression Values

Courts have mentioned free expression values primarily when issuing rulings that consider whether an alleged appropriation of a plaintiff's identity was protected under a First Amendment, common law, or statutory privilege for publishing matters of public interest.[112] Autonomy is the only communicator-based free expression value discussed in the rulings reviewed for this chapter.[113] When discussing free expression values, courts focused on audience-based values in eight cases.[114] Relevant rulings described at least one of three key audience-based values—the marketplace of ideas, self-governance, and the checking function—occasionally in tandem with the autonomy value underlying freedom of the press.[115] Much of the relevant discussion was found in cases involving state statutory torts, including the New York Right to Privacy Law and others modeled upon the New York law.[116]

Autonomy value

A few rulings that assessed whether a news outlet's use of a plaintiff's image or likeness was sufficiently newsworthy to merit First Amendment protection have discussed or suggested the autonomy value for freedom of expression.[117] For instance, in 1993 in *Howell v. New York Post Company*, the New York Court of Appeals indicated that courts in the state repeatedly had found that publishing matters of public interest would not be considered tortious in deference to the legislative intent for the right to privacy law and "constitutional values in the area of free speech and free press."[118] In that case, Pamela J. Howell sought a reversal of a summary judgment award for the defendant and support for her claim that the New York Post Company violated her privacy by publishing a photograph taken of Howell on the grounds of a private psychiatric hosptital where she was walking with Hedda Nussbaum, another patient who was "the "adoptive" mother of" a six-year old whose "death from child abuse generated intense public interest."[119] The photo was published in conjunction with an article about Nussbaum's recovery from being beaten almost a year earlier. Although Howell had not consented to the newspaper's use of her image, the court of appeals determined the First Amendment prevented the newspaper from being found liable for invasion of privacy when the newspaper published information clearly relevant to a matter of interest to the public.[120] The court reasoned that it had been "reluctant to intrude upon reasonable editorial judgments in determining whether there is a real relationship between an article and photograph."[121] The court's rationale involved the autonomy value for freedom of the press because it acknowledged the importance of allowing the individual news entity to decide what constitutes news.

Marketplace of ideas value

When courts have discussed the importance of allowing publishers or news outlets to provide an unfettered free flow of information, the courts' commentary has involved the communicator-based autonomy value and the audience-based marketplace of ideas value for freedom of expression.[122] For instance, in *Groden v. Random House Publishing*, the U.S. Second Circuit Court of Appeals found summary judgment was properly awarded to the defendant because the First Amendment protected the publisher's use of Robert J. Groden's likeness in an advertisement incidental to a book involving a matter of public interest.[123] Groden's name and photograph were published in an advertisement for *Case Closed*, Gerald Posner's book about the assassination of President Kennedy, a matter of public interest.[124] The court explained that the publication of Groden's name fell under the incidental use exception that recognizes a right for "'news disseminators to publicize, to make public, their own communications.'"[125] That ruling added that the New York privacy law was designed "to protect privacy without preventing publication of matters of public interest." [126] The court continued, "At least since *Time, Inc. v. Hill*, the New York courts have been vigilant in interpreting the right of privacy to permit the free flow of information."[127] The court's mention of a free flow of information relates generally to the audience-based marketplace of ideas value, implying the public has a right to receive and to discuss information.[128]

Five years later, a New York Court of Appeals per curiam ruling also implicated the marketplace of ideas value for freedom of expression when it discussed whether a magazine's alleged appropriation was a privileged publication of a matter of public interest.[129] In *Messenger v. Gruner + Jahr Printing*, the court found that the publishing corporation did not invade a 14-year-old's privacy when it used her photograph to illustrate its "Love Crisis" column in 1995.[130] Although a jury awarded Messenger $100,000 in damages because *YM*'s use of her image created the false implication that Messenger wrote the letter, the state high court asserted that the newsworthiness privilege extended to *YM*'s juxtaposition of Messenger's picture with a column about a young woman getting drunk and having sex with multiple partners.[131] The court reasoned:

> Consistent with the statutory—and constitutional—value of uninhibited discussion of newsworthy topics, we have time and again held that, where a plaintiff's picture is used to illustrate an article on a matter of public interest, there can be no liability under sections 50 and 51 unless the picture has no real relationship to the article or the article is an advertisement in disguise.[132]

Mentioning the "value of uninhibited discussion" connects the court's rationale to the audience-based marketplace of ideas value for freedom of speech and of the press.[133]

Self-governance and checking values

In 2004, the Supreme Court of Rhode Island ruling in *Leddy v. Narragansett Television, L.P.*, focused on the marketplace of ideas, self-governance, and checking values for freedom of expression when the court found the television station's use of Leddy's likeness was a privileged incidental use.[134] The appropriation claim arose from Channel 12's use of Gerald A. Leddy's name and image in promotions for a three-part investigative series on public employees who collected tax-free disability pensions from a city and paychecks from the state.[135] The court determined that the promotional uses were protected under the First Amendment.[136] The Rhode Island Supreme Court supported that conclusion with quotations from U.S. Supreme Court rulings that relate to the marketplace of ideas as well as the self-governance and checking values for freedom of the press.[137] Quoting *New York Times v. Sullivan*, a case involving defamation of a public official, the Supreme Court of Rhode Island tied First Amendment protection for free speech to the need for '"debate on public issues"' to '"be uninhibited, robust, and wide-open."'[138] Next, the court connected freedom of expression to the U.S. Supreme Court's '"recognition of the fundamental importance of the free-flow of ideas and opinions on matters of public interest and concern"' in *Hustler v. Falwell*, a case involving a claim for intentional infliction of emotional distress by a public figure.[139]

Although the Rhode Island Supreme Court recognized key First Amendment principles in *Leddy*, the court scolded Channel 12 for focusing its "attention on low-level government employees and others who do not deserve to bear the brunt of such base antics."[140] The court's ruling related the investigative series to the "disreputable aspects of 'ambush journalism'" even though the subject matter presented in the Channel 12 series related directly to the self-governance and checking values for freedom of expression.[141] The court affirmed summary judgment for the defendants, justifying its conclusion by stating, "[I]t is not our place to serve as the censors of journalistic discretion."[142] In a different context, that statement could suggest the importance of editorial autonomy rather than suggest the court's sensitivity to injuries Leddy sustained.

Summary

When courts discussed key free expression values they primarily found that summary judgment was awarded properly to defendants or that awards granted to plaintiffs should be reversed.[143] A few rulings tied press freedom to the communicator-based autonomy value when courts explained their reluctance to censor content involving a matter of public interest.[144] Courts more often tied freedom of speech or press to the audience-based marketplace of ideas, self-governance, and checking values.[145]

Privacy Values

In contrast to the tendency for state high courts and federal courts of appeals post-*Florida Star* appropriation rulings to implicate audience-based free expression values that generally benefit society,[146] state high courts and federal courts of appeals have discussed primarily individual, rather than societal, values for privacy.[147] Almost half the relevant rulings on privacy-based appropriation claims have implied that the appropriation tort provides redress for harm to the individual values of autonomy, liberty, or emotional health.[148] Only one ruling implicated the societal privacy value of forming and maintaining relationships.[149]

Autonomy value

When courts have discussed the elements of invasion of privacy by appropriation, some have mentioned the value of individual identity, or personality, associated with the autonomy value for privacy.[150] For instance, in *King v. PA Consulting Group, Inc.*, the U.S. Court of Appeals for the Tenth Circuit focused on the value of identity when it affirmed a trial court's denial of the consulting firm's request for a new trial. That ruling allowed a jury verdict, which awarded Michael King $57,672 for invasion of privacy by appropriation, to stand. After King resigned from the consulting firm to work for a competitor, the firm "continued to distribute promotional materials listing King as the contact person for PA's Wholesale Energy Markets Practice."[151] King alleged that PA employees changed a voicemail message "to indicate King was unavailable, but that the caller should leave a message."[152]

King also claimed that his replacement had all of King's email messages forwarded to King's replacement. King argued that the firm was using his name and identity to its commercial advantage. And the U.S. Court of Appeals for the Tenth Circuit found the firm's misuse of King's name constituted an invasion of privacy under Colorado law.[153] That finding involved the diminution of King's personal agency for his professional identity, which harmed personal autonomy.

Autonomy and liberty values

Similarly, when the Supreme Court of New Hampshire's ruling in *Remsburg v. Docusearch, Inc.* recognized the appropriation tort under the state's common law, the court suggested an autonomy value and liberty value for privacy.[154] Helen Remsburg, the administrator of the estate of Amy Lynn Boyer, filed the appropriation case after an information broker sold Boyer's address, Social Security number, and other personal information to the man who killed Boyer.[155] The court explained that the interest protected by the tort "'is the interest of the individual in the exclusive use of his own identity, in so far as it is represented by his name or likeness, and in so far as the use may be of benefit to him or to others.'"[156] That description relates to an individual's interest in controlling the use of his or her identity through which each person expresses individuality, the core of personal autonomy. Adding that appropriation is only actionable if the use at issue takes advantage of the individual's "'reputation, prestige or other value'" specifically associated with the plaintiff's identity, the court reasoned that the investigator sold the "information for the value of the information itself, not to take advantage of the person's reputation or prestige."[157] Thus, the Supreme Court of New Hampshire concluded that Boyer's privacy was not invaded because her identity was not exploited, and therefore, the autonomy and liberty interests at issue were not harmed.[158]

Three years later, the Supreme Court of New Hampshire's rationale in *Thompson v. C&C Research and Development* also related to the individual and liberty values for privacy.[159] In fact, the ruling in *Thompson* found that former Olympic gold medal-winning swimmer Jenny Thompson's privacy was not invaded because she had signed a contract that authorized the defendants' use of her identity. The court wrote:

> An individual has an interest in controlling the use of his or her own name or likeness insofar as a benefit may be derived from its use, but when the individual authorizes another and its licensee to use his or her name or likeness under the terms of a contract, such authorization precludes a finding that either the contractual party or its licensee is liable for misappropriation.[160]

Thus, the plaintiff's autonomy and liberty values for privacy were not harmed by the use of her identity.

Other rulings also have discussed the autonomy and liberty values for privacy.[161] For instance, when the Supreme Court of Minnesota first recognized the appropriation tort, as well as disclosure of private fact and intrusion, under the state's common law in 1998 in *Lake v. Wal-Mart Stores, Inc.*, the court stated, "Appropriation protects an individual's identity."[162] As mentioned previously, identity is related to individuality, personality, and thus, personal autonomy. In discussing its decision to recognize the three privacy torts, the Minnesota court added, "The heart of our liberty is choosing which parts of our lives shall become public and which parts we shall hold close."[163] Choosing which aspects of one's personal life to expose to others relates to the liberty value for privacy. The Minnesota Supreme Court reversed the lower courts' rulings dismissing the appropriation, disclosure and intrusion claims and remanded the case for trial.[164] Elli Lake and Melissa Weber had charged Wal-Mart Stores, Inc. with all four types of invasion of privacy for allowing at least one image of the women standing together naked in a shower to circulate after the film was taken to a Wal-Mart store for processing.[165] The court reasoned: "One's naked body is a very private part of one's person and generally known to others only by choice. This is a type of privacy interest worthy of protection."[166] While the Minnesota court was referring to the privacy torts in general, rather than specifically to appropriation, that rationale relates directly to an individual's sense of personal dignity and bodily integrity, or personal liberty, by suggesting the distribution of the photographs revoked the individuals' control over when and how others viewed their naked bodies. Losing that control harmed Lake's and Weber's liberty as well as their autonomy.

Two more rulings referred to the individual privacy values of liberty and autonomy when discussing appropriation as an exploitation of one's identity or personality that harms individuality and undermines one's freedom to control the flow of information about one's self.[167] In *Sloan v. South Carolina Department of Public Safety*, the Supreme Court of South Carolina in 2003 defined the right to privacy as "the right to be let alone; the right of a person to be free from unwarranted publicity."[168] Sloan claimed her privacy was invaded when the State of South Carolina sold her driver's license information to Image Data. The ruling included the South Carolina common law definition for the appropriation tort, a "wrongful appropriation of personality."[169] That definition relates to the liberty value that is harmed when an individual loses the agency to protect her personality from exploitation by others. The court's explanation of the tort also overlaps with the autonomy value, or the right to control one's individuality, or "personal identity."[170] After clarifying the parameters of the privacy-based appropriation tort, the South Carolina Supreme Court affirmed the lower court's award of summary judgment for the defendant because the plaintiff had not demonstrated the facts were actionable. The court explained that a 1997 act passed by the state's legislature allowed driver's license information to be sold. "Because the 1997 Act authorized the transaction between Image Data and DPS, Image Data did not misappropriate Sloan's driver's license information and photograph," the court said.[171]

Autonomy, liberty, and emotional health values

When the Supreme Court of Colorado recognized the appropriation tort under the common law of Colorado in *Joe Dickerson & Associates v. Dittmar* in 2001, the ruling described autonomy, liberty, and emotional well-being, and mental health values for privacy.[172] That case arose because Joe Dickerson's private investigation firm published an article in a newsletter stating that Rosanne Dittmar had been convicted after the firm investigated her involvement in the theft of bearer bonds from her place of employment.[173] Finding that Dittmar's privacy had not been invaded, the court quoted from the 1890 Harvard Law Review article "The Right To Privacy," stating that privacy law would protect the "'general immunity of the person—the right to one's personality'" and "'the individual's right 'to be let alone.'''[174] As personality relates directly to the autonomy value for privacy, the right "to be let alone" relates directly to the personal liberty value. In discussing the evolution of privacy law, the majority also mentioned a mental health value for privacy. The court explained that states have allowed individuals to "recover for personal injuries such as mental anguish and injured feelings,"[175] and the injury resulting from appropriation of identity "may be 'mental and subjective'—in the nature of humiliation, embarrassment, and outrage."[176] Although the Supreme Court of Colorado discussed those individual values for privacy, the majority concluded that the information at issue in Dittmar's claim was a privileged publication of a matter of public interest. In fact, a concurring opinion criticized for the majority for recognizing the tort when the facts at issue did not constitute a tortious invasion of privacy.[177]

Emotional well-being

Key literature has included both emotional release and protection from emotional injuries under the emotional well-being value, however state high courts and federal circuit courts of appeals have focused primarily on the privacy-based appropriation tort as a shield from emotional harm. One ruling in which a state court first recognized the privacy-based appropriation tort discussed an emotional health value for the right to privacy. [178] In that 1990 ruling, *Staruski v. Continental Telephone Company of Vermont*, the Supreme Court of Vermont reasoned that the plaintiff did not need to prove that her identity had "pecuniary value" in order to receive damages for the appropriation of her name.[179] Staruski sued her employer for using her name and photograph in an advertisement for the company even though she refused to participate in the company's advertising. The Vermont Supreme Court found that courts in other jurisdictions had awarded damages even when the "'injury suffered is mental anguish alone.'"[180] Upholding an award of damages for Staruski, the court wrote that Staruski "feared harassment" and Continental's management "showed 'a reckless or wanton disregard' of her rights" by ignoring her request not to include her name and photograph in an advertisement for the company.[181] That rationale, accordingly, relates to the individual mental health value as well as the individual liberty value for privacy.

Promoting civility and community

In addition to mentioning at least one individual privacy value, two rulings involved a societal value for privacy, promoting civility and community.[182] In 1998 in *Reid v. Pierce County*, the Supreme Court of Washington considered whether plaintiffs' privacy was invaded by county employees' unauthorized public displays of plaintiffs' relatives' autopsy photographs.[183] The court held "the immediate relatives of a decedent have a protectable privacy interest in the autopsy records of the decedent." [184] The court continued, "That protectable privacy interest is grounded in maintaining the dignity of the deceased."[185] Thus, the court's ruling that the Reid family's privacy could have been invaded by the county employees' exploitation of their deceased relative was undergirded by the autonomy of their deceased relative.[186] The court's rationale relates to the privacy value of civility and community because the county employees failed to extend a basic form of respect to the deceased and their relatives.[187] In *Showler v. Harper's Magazine, Inc.*, the U.S. Circuit Court of Appeals for the Tenth Circuit found that under Oklahoma law a news magazine's publication of photographs of an Oklahoma National Guard member in his coffin at a public funeral was different than the gruesome autopsy photographs at issue in *Reid.*[188] In *Showler*, the Tenth Circuit explained that the funeral photographs of Sergeant Brinlee clearly involved a matter of public interest and thus were not the type of images that could harm the privacy of Brinlee's relatives by offending community standards of decency.[189]

<u>Summary</u>

Relevant rulings primarily explored three individual values for privacy—the autonomy, liberty, and emotional health values.[190] References to liberty or autonomy typically arose when courts discussed the development of privacy torts or the right to control the use of one's identity.[191] And some discussion of the emotional health value resulted from plaintiffs' claimed injuries.[192] Although relevant rulings often mentioned one or more individual privacy values, especially when courts recognized an appropriation tort for the first time under state common law, only two rulings involved a societal privacy value, promoting civility and community.[193] The following section explores if and how courts have reconciled conflicts between freedom of expression and privacy values.

Reconciling Free Expression and Privacy Values

Few privacy-based appropriation rulings discussed both free expression values and privacy values,[194] and in only one case did the court explicitly attempt to balance free expression and privacy values.[195] In a couple of cases, courts allowed the elements of the tort or defenses to delineate the boundaries between free expression and privacy rights as if those boundaries prevented free expression and privacy values from conflicting, thus negating the need for ad hoc balancing.[196]

Balancing free expression and privacy values

In a 1994 case, *Doe v. Roe*, the Supreme Court of Alabama analyzed whether the use of plaintiff's adoptive children's identities was actionable under the appropriation tort or privileged under the free speech and free press provision of the Alabama Constitution.[197] John Roe filed the invasion of privacy claim on behalf of his children, alleging that Jane Doe would invade the privacy of the children if she distributed a novel based on the murder of the children's natural mother by their father. Roe argued that distributing the book would harm the children "by appropriating a tragic event in their lives for commercial gain."[198] The Alabama Supreme Court disagreed, holding that a trial court erred by issuing a temporary restraining order to prevent Doe from distributing the story.

The court held that Doe's novel did not violate the children's personality-based privacy interest, which literature has associated with autonomy, or society's privacy interest in promoting civility and community because the novel was "based on events of public interest."[199] The court explained, "Doe's novel possesses social worth and is a significant medium for the communication of her ideas about an event in which society has an interest."[200] That rationale recognized non-specific communicator-based and audience-based values for free expression, but it did not suggest that expression serving those values would always outweigh the values underlying the appropriation tort. The court implied that privacy interests might overcome free expression interests under different circumstances, stating that Doe "may not exercise" her free speech "right in a manner that will injure the children's right to privacy."[201] Distribution of the novel, however, did not violate those rights.[202] Distributing information that was already available to the public and was matter of public concern could not offend community standards of decency, associated with the social value of promoting civility and community, or a personal interest in agency, associated with the individual privacy values of autonomy and liberty.

No balancing of free expression and privacy values

During the past twenty-two years, ad hoc balancing was not used in states where privacy is recognized by statute.[203] The New York Court of Appeals said balancing free expression and privacy interests was not a job for the court because privacy is recognized by statute in the state.[204] The court wrote, "Balancing the competing policy concerns underlying tort recovery for invasion of privacy is best left to the Legislature . . . ."[205] The court explained that the statute only applies to uses for advertising or trade purposes and courts have held that uses for news purposes are exempt from liability. "This is both a matter of legislative intent and a reflection of constitutional values in the area of free speech and free press," the court wrote.[206] As mentioned previously, in *Howell v. New York Post, Inc.*, the court indicated that the *New York Post* had not invaded Pamela J. Howell's privacy by publishing a photograph of Howell walking with another patient at a private psychiatric hospital.[207] The court reasoned that the newspaper's use of the photograph was privileged because the photograph was related to the subject of an article about the other patient's recovery from being beaten by her lover, the man accused of killing the patient's six-year-old adoptive daughter. That reasoning was grounded by the court's previous interpretations of a newsworthiness exception that corresponds to constitutional concerns about penalizing the publication of truthful information.[208] Thus, the ruling reconciled the potential conflict between press freedom and privacy by applying the newsworthiness exception rather than by engaging in overt balancing of free expression or privacy values.

In a 1995 ruling in *Town & Country Properties, Inc. v. Riggins*, the Supreme Court of Virginia found no need to engage in ad hoc balancing because the speech at issue, a flier designed to sell the house where John Riggins once lived, primarily served the advertiser's interest in promoting a sale rather than the public's interest in receiving information that could benefit the public.[209] The court disagreed with the defendant's assertion that a trial court violated the free speech provisions of the First Amendment and the Virginia Constitution by awarding damages to the plaintiff for invasion of privacy by appropriation.[210] The court reasoned that the U.S. Supreme Court had tied First Amendment protection for commercial speech to the informational function that speech serves for message recipients.[211] Thus, the state court reasoned that Virginia's privacy law "is not constitutionally invalid" as applied to award the football star damages for appropriation because the published information did not serve the audience-based values that the Court has tied to the protection afforded to speech that promotes a product or sale.[212] That suggests the court did not need to weigh competing interests because the court defined the use of Riggins' name as expression unrelated to core constitutional values for freedom of expression.

Summary

Most courts did not engage in balancing free expression values and privacy values when attempting to reconcile conflicts between the right to publish and the right to privacy in the appropriation cases studied in this research. [213] The only ruling that did seek to balance free expression and privacy interests compared broad communicator and audience-based free expression values to the individual privacy values of autonomy and liberty.[214] While the Supreme Court of Alabama in *Doe v. Roe* suggested that privacy interests might overcome free expression interests under different circumstances, the court concluded that the alleged appropriation of the plaintiff's children's life stories did not invade the children's privacy.[215] The New York Court of Appeals in another case only mentioned balancing free expression and privacy values when it assigned the job of balancing competing policy interests to state legislators.[216] And the Virginia Supreme Court found no need to engage in balancing when it determined the use of a plaintiff's name for advertising purposes was not protected expression.

Protecting Individuals from Exploitation

Recognition of the common law invasion of privacy by appropriation tort has expanded during the past twenty years.[217] The highest courts in four states recognized the privacy-based appropriation tort for the first time after the U.S. Supreme Court suggested in 1989 in *Florida Star* that privacy and freedom of expression are both significant interests.[218] To date, more than half of the states have recognized an invasion of privacy by appropriation tort.[219] And only one ruling reviewed for this chapter has indicated that the invasion of privacy by appropriation tort might not be recognized under a state's law.[220] Most other rulings focused on whether the use was a privileged publication of newsworthy information or whether the plaintiff satisfied the three elements of the tort—commercial use of name or likeness without authorization.[221]

Commercial use and individual privacy values

Courts have discussed individual privacy values when considering the commercial use element. Several rulings implicated the liberty, autonomy, or emotional health privacy values when assessing whether a defendant exploited an individual's identity by using her name, image, or likeness for the purpose of advertising a product or service.[222] Courts have found that actionable uses for advertising purposes include publishing a former football star's name in a flier promoting the sale of a home and using a physician's name in a medical center's calendar sent to solicit patrons. Those uses harmed the plaintiffs' autonomy and liberty.[223] The court's consideration of whether the flier's use of the football player's name was actionable also related to the emotional health value because the player alleged he felt "humiliated" and "violated" by the exploitation of his name.[224] A Supreme Court of Massachusetts' ruling that defined a commercial use as an exploitative use for trade purposes related to the individual liberty value for privacy. The court reasoned that an attorney had not used a professor's name for trade purposes when he included the professor's name in a list of experts he expected to call as witnesses because the attorney had talked with the professor and considered using the professor as an expert witness.[225]

Use of identity and individual privacy values

Courts' discussion of the use of identity, name, or likeness primarily related to the individual privacy values of autonomy and liberty.[226] A few courts found that uses of individuals' life stories did not exploit their names or likenesses when those stories were already available to the public prior to the alleged appropriation.[227] The later use of material that was distributed in manners the plaintiff could not control did not undermine a plaintiff's autonomy or liberty. But the U.S. Ninth Circuit Court of Appeals' rationale in *Newcombe v. Adolf Coors Co.*, which found that using a pitcher's skin tone and unique stance in a beer advertisement might be an exploitative use of his identity under California law, related to the individual privacy values of autonomy, liberty, and emotional health because the plaintiff, a "known recovering alcoholic," would not have promoted beer.[228] The connection to emotional health arose because the plaintiff claimed he endured emotional distress from the association of his identity with beer.

Lack of consent and privacy values

One court's discussion of the final element, lack of authorization, related to all three individual privacy values and to the societal value of promoting civility and community when it focused on dignitary harms.[229] The Supreme Court of Washington's ruling related to autonomy and civility and community when it found that county employees' unauthorized displays of gruesome autopsy photographs at parties and other settings invaded the privacy of immediate relatives of the deceased because the employees failed to respect the deceased and their relatives.[230]

Privileged uses and societal privacy values

Community standards for decency, which undergird the social value of civility and community, also were mentioned in a U.S. Tenth Circuit Court of Appeals ruling that considered whether the publication of a national guard soldier's funeral photographs were privileged. Applying Oklahoma law in *Showler v. Harper's Magazine, Inc.*, the court found the magazine's publication of the photographs did not harm the decedent's family members' privacy because the photographs were closely related to the matter of public interest that they illustrated.[231] The court explained that publishing the photographs was not "so extreme and outrageous 'as to go beyond all possible bounds of decency, and to be regarded as atrocious, and utterly intolerable in a civilized community.'"[232]

Privileged uses and free expression values

Courts more often discussed the communicator-based autonomy value or the audience-based marketplace of ideas values for free expression when considering whether an alleged appropriation was a privileged publication of a matter of newsworthy information or an advertisement "in disguise."[233] When courts suggested that a public interest or newsworthiness exception relates to the communicator-based autonomy value, their rationales tied the importance of freedom from government censorship to the ability for expression to serve audience-based interests.[234] For instance, in 1993 the New York Court of Appeals mentioned courts' reluctance to inhibit press freedom by "intrud[ing] upon reasonable editorial judgments" in relation to a public interest privilege.[235] That ruling tied freedom of expression to the impact of the content on audiences. When rulings suggested that an alleged appropriation served a communal value for free expression, courts almost uniformly found the alleged appropriations were privileged, leaving no need to balance privacy and free expression interests.[236]

Audience-based free expression and individual privacy values

The only ruling that used balancing found that free expression values outweighed the privacy interests at issue.[237] The Supreme Court of Alabama found that the trial court erred by holding a prior restraint was necessary to prevent the distribution of a book from injuring children's privacy.[238] Reasoning that the novel pertained to a matter of public interest, the court wrote: "Thus, like most courts, faced with the competing interests of the right to privacy and the right to freedom of speech, this [c]ourt has held that the right to freedom of speech transcends the right to privacy so long as the speech pertains to a matter of public concern."[239] The Supreme Court of Alabama, however, indicated that liberty-based values for freedom of expression did not automatically outweigh privacy interests. The Alabama court stated that its constitution provides individuals with freedom to publish information but requires individuals to be "responsible for the abuse of that liberty."[240]

Favoring audience-based free expression values

Courts routinely ruled in favor of defendants when the courts' discussions of facts related to free expression values.[241] Courts only upheld awards for plaintiffs when uses of plaintiffs' identities were not clearly connected to matters of public interest,[242] which relate to the audience-based marketplace of ideas, self-governance, or checking function values. State and federal courts upheld awards of damages for plaintiffs whose names were used for unauthorized advertising purposes or exploitative purposes that received little, if any, constitutional protection and that harmed at least one of the individual privacy values—autonomy, liberty, or emotional health.[243] In one of the few mentions of societal privacy values, the Supreme Court of Washington remanded a case for trial on whether the unauthorized use of autopsy photographs was tortious because the "egregious" facts offended community standards for decency when audience-based free expression values were not served by the use of those photographs.[244] Those findings bode well for media defendants who publish individuals' names or images to illustrate news articles. Courts primarily found for defendants when their uses of plaintiffs' names were rationalized by relating protection for speech on matters of public interest to communicators' rights to publish information and audiences' rights to receive information.

If courts mentioned free expression values when finding a plaintiff's privacy was invaded under the appropriation theory, they tied constitutional protection for expression to audiences' rights to receive accurate information about advertised products or services.[245] The commercial speech doctrine supports those rationales because several rulings by the U.S. Supreme Court have tied protection for speech that promotes a product or service to audiences' rights to be informed, and thus have indicated that the First Amendment does not protect false or misleading commercial speech.[246] In several cases examined for this chapter, the unauthorized uses of plaintiffs' names to promote a product or service were misleading.[247] Some rulings focused on whether the primary benefit intended for the unauthorized use was informing the public or promoting the advertiser's products or services.[248]

Summary

State high courts' and circuit courts of appeals' rulings typically relied on the elements of the tort or the newsworthiness privilege to draw a definitional boundary between the uses that served free expression values and uses that exploited an individual's identity. The rulings have indicated that individuals who publish other persons' names, likenesses, or images in advertisements without obtaining proper authorization may be responsible for paying damages to plaintiffs whose identities are used in a manner that conflicts with key privacy values without serving key free expression values. But individuals who use persons' identities to illustrate a matter of public interest, a matter that serves communicator-based and audience-based free expression values generally will not be found liable for invasion of privacy.

Chapter 4 Notes

---

[1] N.Y. CIV. RIGHTS LAW §§ 50-51 (LEXIS 2010).

[2] Pavesich v. New England Life Ins. Co., 50 S.E. 68, 69-70 (Ga. 1905).

[3] *See, e.g.*, Spahn v. Julian Messner, Inc., 221 N.E.2d 543 (N.Y. 1966).

[4] 385 U.S. 374 (1967).

[5] 433 U.S. 562, 573 (1977).

[6] Andrew McClurg, *Bringing Privacy Law out of the Closet: A Tort Theory of Liability for Intrusions in Public Places*, 73 N.C.L. REV. 988, 1003 n.61 (1995).

[7] 433 U.S. at 579-80 (Powell, J., dissenting); *id.* at 583 (Stevens, J., dissenting).

[8] *Id.* at 579-80. It is worth noting that Justice Marshall wrote the majority opinion in *Florida Star v. B.J.F.*, which recognized that press freedom and privacy both are significant interests. 491 U.S. 524, 526 (1989).

[9] *Id.* at 581.

[10] Zacchini v. Scripps Howard Broad. Co., 433 U.S. 562, 581-83 (U.S. 1977) (Stevens, J., dissenting). ("I emphasize that this is a 'reappropriation' suit, rather than one of the other varieties of 'right of privacy' tort suits identified by Dean Prosser in his classic article.") (citing William Prosser, *Privacy*, 48 CALIF. L. REV. 383 (1960)).

[11] Searches for the key words of "privacy" and ("appropriation" or "use of name" or "use of image" or "use of likeness") in LexisNexis, Westlaw, and the Media Law Reporter found 331 court rulings from June 1989 through July 2011. Most of those rulings are not relevant to this study because they were handed down by state courts at the intermediate appellate level, only involved other invasion of privacy torts, only involved right of publicity claims, or only involved statutory claims unrelated to the appropriation tort. Only fifty-two post-*Florida Star* rulings involved privacy-based appropriation claims. The relevant rulings include: Spiegel v. Schulmann, 604 F.3d 72, 77-78 (2d. 2010) (per curiam); Dan Tana v. Dantanna's CNN Center, 611 F.3d 767, 783 (11th Cir. 2010); Rivell v. Private Health Care Sys., Inc., 520 F.3d 1308, 1310 (11th Cir., 2008) (per curiam); Christian Broad. Network, Inc. v. Busch, 254 Fed. App'x 957, 958 (4th Cir. 2007) (per curiam) (unpublished); Showler v. Harper's Magazine Found., 222 Fed. App'x 755, 759 (10th Cir. 2007) (unpublished); King v. PA Consulting Group, Inc., 485 F.3d 577, 593 (10th Cir. 2007); Zarrilli v. John Hancock Life Ins. Co., 231 Fed. App'x 122, 123-25 (3d Cir. 2007) (per curiam) (unpublished); Meadows v. Hartford life Ins. Co., 492 F.3d 634, 637 (5th Cir. 2007); Botts v. New York Times, 106 Fed. App'x, 109, 110 (3d. Cir., 2004) (unpublished); Solano v. Playgirl, Inc., 292 F.3d 1078, 1080-82 (9th Cir. 2002); Matthews v. Wozencraft, 15 F.3d 432, 436 (5th Cir. 1994); Am.

Guar. & Liability Ins. Co. v. 1906 Co., 273 F.3d 605, 608 (5th Cir. 2001); Brown v. Ames, 201 F.3d 654, 661-62 (5th Cir. 2000), *rehearing denied,* 2000 U.S. App. LEXIS 5632 (2000); Downing v. Abercrombie & Fitch, 256F.3d 994 (9th Cir. 2001); Williams v. Newsweek, No. 99-7243, 1999 U.S. App. LEXIS 347, at *1-2 (4th Cir. 1999) (per curiam), cert. denied, 530 U.S. 1279 (2000); Newcombe v. Adolf Coors Co., 157 F.3d 686, 693 (9th Cir. 1998); Groden v. Random House, Inc., 61 F.3d 1045, 1049 (2d. Cir. 1995); Matthews v. Wozencraft, 15 F.3d 432, 436 (5th Cir. 1994); Bowling v. Bowling, No. 91-5920, 1992 U.S. App. LEXIS 18505, at *2 (6th Cir. 1992)(unpublished) (per curiam); Puckett v. Am. Broad. Companies, 1990 U.S. App'x LEXIS 19761, at *7-8 (6th Cir. 1990) (unpublished); Lusby v. Cincinnati Magazine, No. 89-3854, 1990 U.S. App. LEXIS 9144, at *7 (6th Cir. 1990) (unpublished); Doe v. Roe, 638 So. 2d 826, 828-30 (Ala. 1994) (per curiam); Schifano v. Greene County Greyhound Park, Inc., 624 So. 2d 178, 179 (Ala. 1993); Baker v. State Farm General Insurance Co., 585 So. 2d. 804, 807-08 (Ala. 1991); Christoff v. Nestle USA, Inc., 213 P.3d 132, 133-36 (Cal. 2009); Joe Dickerson & Assoc. v. Dittmar, 34 P.3d 995, 997 (Colo. 2001) (en banc); Tyne v. Time Warner Ent. Co., 901 So.2d 802, 809-810 (Fla. 2005), *aff'd,* 425 F.3d 1363, 1364 (11th Cir. 2005) (per curiam); Felsher v. Univ. of Evansville, 755 N.E.2d 589, 599 (Ind. 2001); Tannenbaum v. Grady, 604 N.E.2d 16, 16 (Mass. 1992); Simpson v. Central Maine Motors, Inc., 669 A.2d 1324, 1326 (Me. 1996); Lake v. Wal-Mart Stores, Inc., 582 N.W.2d 231, 236 (Minn. 1998) (en banc); Nemani v. St. Louis Univ., 33 S.W.3d 184, 187 (Mo. 2000), *cert. denied,* 532 U.S. 981 (2001); Wilkinson v. Methodist, 612 N.W.2d 213, 216 (Neb. 2000); Miller v. Am. Sports Co., Inc., 467 N.W.2d 653, 656 (Neb. 1991); PETA v. Bobby Berosini, Ltd., 895 P.2d 1269, 1283-85 (Nev. 1995); Thompson v. C & C Research & Dev., 898 A.2d 495, 499-500 (N.H. 2006); Remsburg v. Docusearch, Inc., 816 A.2d 1001, 1009-10 (N.H. 2003); G.D. v. Kenny, 15 A.3d 300, 304 (N.J. 2011); Messenger v. Gruner + Jahr Printing, 727 N.E.2d 549, 552-54 (N.Y. 2000) (per curiam); Howell v. New York Post Co., Inc., 612 N.E.2d 699, 701(N.Y. 1993); Finger v. Omni Publ'ns Int'l, Ltd., 566 N.E.2d 141, 144 (N.Y. 1991); Beverley v. Choices Women's Med. Ctr, Inc., 587 N.E.2d 275, 279 (N.Y. 1991); Hougum v. Valley Memorial Homes, 574 N.W.2d 812 (N.D. 1998); Leddy v. Narragansett Television, L.P., 843 A.2d 481, 490-91 (R.I. 2004); Gignilliat v. Gignilliat, Savitz & Bettis, L.L.P., 684 S.E.2d 756 (S.C. 2009); Sloan v. South Carolina Dept. of Pub. Safety, 586 S.E.2d 108, 108 (S.C. 2003); PTS Corp. v. Buckman, 263 Va. 613, 621-22 (Va. 2002); WJLA v. Levin, 564 S.E.2d 383, 395-396 (Va. 2002); Town & Country Props., Inc., v. Riggins, 457 S.E.2d 356, 362-64 (Va. 1995); Staruski v. Cont'l Tel. Co. of Vermont, 581 A.2d 266, 269 (Vermont 1990); Reid v. Pierce County, 961 P.2d 333, 339 (Wash. 1998) (en banc).

[12] *Roe*, 638 So. 2d at 828-30.

[13] *Hougum*, 574 N.W.2d at 812.

[14] *Roe*, 638 So. 2d at 828-30; *Joe Dickerson & Assoc.*, 34 P.3d at 997; *Lake*, 582 N.W.2d at 236; *Remsburg*, 816 A.2d at 1009-10; *Hougum*, 574 N.W.2d at 812; *Staruski*, 581 A.2d at 269.

[15] *Joe Dickerson & Assoc.*, 34 P.3d at 997; *Lake*, 582 N.W.2d at 236; *Remsburg*, 816 A.2d at 1009-10; *Staruski*, 581 A.2d at 269.

[16] *Reid*, 961 P.2d at 339.

[17] *Am. Guar. & Liability Ins. Co.*, 273 F.3d at 608 (concluding that the Supreme Court of Mississippi would find that an employee of the 1906 Co. committed invasion of privacy by under the intrusion and appropriation torts by secretly recording women in the dressing room at a store owned by Hattiesburg Coca-Cola Bottling Company and the insurance company)

[18] *See, e.g.*, *G.D.*, 15 A.3d at 304; *Spiegel*, 604 F.3d at 77-78; *Showler*, 222 Fed. App'x at 759; *Zarrilli*, 231 Fed. App'x at 123-25; *Meadows*, 492 F.3d at 637; *Am. Guar. & Liability Ins. Co.*, 273 F.3d at 615; *Newcombe*, 157 F.3d at 693; *Matthews*, 15 F.3d at 436; *Puckett*, 1990 U.S. App'x LEXIS 19761, at *7-8; *Schifano*, 624 So. 2d at 179; *Joe Dickerson & Assoc.*, 34 P.3d at 997; *Felsher*, 755 N.E.2d at 599; *Tannenbaum*, 604 N.E.2d at 16; *Simpson*, 669 A.2d at 1326; *Lake*, 582 N.W.2d at 236; *Howell*, 612 N.E.2d at 701; *Beverley*, 587 N.E.2d at 279; *Leddy*, 843 A.2d at 490-91; *Sloan*, 586 S.E.2d at 108; *Staruski*, 581 A.2d at 273; *Reid*, 961 P.2d at 335.

[19] *Solano*, 292 F.3d at 1080-82.

[20] *Id.*

[21] *Id.* at 1089.

[22] 537 U.S. 1029, 1029 (2002).

[23] *See, e.g.*, *Showler*, 222 Fed. App'x at 759; *Botts*, 106 Fed. App'x, at 110; *Lusby*, No. 89-3854, 1990 U.S. App. LEXIS 9144, at *7; *Puckett*, 1990 U.S. App'x LEXIS at *7-8; *Messenger*, 727 N.E.2d at 552-54; *Howell*, 612 N.E.2d at 701; *Finger*, 566 N.E.2d at 144; *Leddy*, 843 A.2d at 490-91; *WJLA*, 564 S.E.2d at 387-88; *Lusby*, No. 89-3854, 1990 U.S. App. LEXIS 9144, at *7.

[24] *See, e.g.*, *Zarrilli*, 231 Fed. App'x at 123-25; *Am. Guar. & Liability Ins. Co.*, 273 F.3d at 608; *Tannenbaum*, 604 N.E.2d at 16; *Newcombe*, 157 F.3d at 689; *Schifano*, 624 So. 2d at 179; *Felsher*, 755 N.E.2d at 599; *Simpson*, 669 A.2d at 1326; *Sloan*, 586 S.E.2d at 108; *Staruski*, 581 A.2d at 273; *Reid*, 961 P.2d at 335.

[25] *Downing*, 256F.3d at 994; Newcombe, 157 F.3d at 694; *Lake*, 582 N.W.2d at 236; *Staruski*, 581 A.2d at 273-74.

[26] *Showler* 222 Fed. App'x at 759; *Matthews*, 15 F.3d at 436; *Lusby*, 1990 U.S. App. LEXIS 9144, at *7; *Joe Dickerson & Assoc.*, 34 P.3d at 997; *Howell*, 612 N.E.2d at 701; *Leddy*, 843 A.2d at 490-91; *Reid* 961 P.2d at 335.

[27] *See, e.g.*, 231 Fed. App'x at 123-25; *Meadows*, 492 F.3d at 637; *Am. Guar. & Liability Ins. Co.*, 273 F.3d at 615; *Schifano*, 624 So. 2d at 179; *Tannenbaum*, 604 N.E.2d at 16; *Simpson*, 669 A.2d at 1326; *Sloan*, 586 S.E.2d at 108; *Reid*, 961 P.2d at 335.

[28] *King*, 485 F.3d at 593 (affirming a judgment for King that included an award of damages in the amount of $57,672); *Brown*, 201 F.3d at 662 (finding the jury did not err in awarding $100,000 for misappropriation); *Bowling*, No. 91-5920, 1992 U.S. App. LEXIS 18505, at *2 (affirming a judgment for Bowling that included an award of $100 for the appropriation of his likeness); *Town & Country Props., Inc.*, , 457 S.E.2d at 362-64 (affirming a judgment for Riggins that included a $2 award of compensatory damages).

[29] *Felsher*, 755 N.E.2d at 599.

[30] *See, e.g.*, *Showler*, 222 Fed. App'x at 759; *Solano*, 292 F.3d at 1081; *Matthews*, 15 F.3d at 436; *Joe Dickerson & Assoc.*, 34 P.3d at 997; *Felsher*, 755 at 593; *Lake*, 582 N.W.2d at 234-35; *Howell*, 612 N.E.2d at 704; *Beverley*, 587 N.E.2d at 279; *Leddy*, 843 A.2d at 490-91; *Sloan*, 586 S.E.2d at 110-11; *Staruski*, 581 A.2d 269-70; *WJLA*, 564 S.E.2d at 395.

[31] *Joe Dickerson & Assoc.*, 34 P.3d at 999.

[32] *See, e.g.*, *Matthews*, 15 F.3d at 437; *Schifano*, 624 So. 2d at 181; *Dickerson*, 34 P.3d at 999; *Felsher*, 755 N.E.2d at 593; *Simpson* v, 669 A.2d at 1326; *Nemani*, 33 S.E.3d at 187; *Remsburg*, 816 A.2d at 1009-10; *Staruski*, 581 A.2d at 269.

[33] *See, e.g.*, CAL. CIV. CODE § 3344 (Deering 1995); FLA. STAT. § 540.08 (1998); MASS. ANN. LAWS. Ch. 214 § 3A (LexisNexis 2009); NEB. REV. ST. § 20-201 (1943) (West 2006); N.Y. CIV. RIGHTS §§ 50-51 (LexisNexis 2010); OKLA. STAT. ANN. tit. 21, § 839.1 (West 2002); R.I. GEN. LAWS. § 9-1-28.1 (1956); VA. CODE. ANN. § 8.01-40A (LexisNexis 2009); WIS STAT. § 895.50 (1997).

[34] RESTATEMENT (SECOND) OF TORTS § 652C (1977).

[35] N.Y. CIV. RIGHTS LAW § 50-51 (LexisNexis 2010); VA. CODE ANN. § 8.01-40A (LexisNexis 2009)

[36] *Dan Tana*, 611 F.3d at 783; *Zarrilli*, 231 Fed. App'x at 123-25; *Meadows*, 492 F.3d at 639; *Matthews*, 15 F.3d at 437-38; *Schifano*, 624 So.2d at 179-181; *Tannenbaum*, 604 N.E.2d at 17; *Wilkinson*, 612 N.W.2d at 216.

[37] *Meadows*, 492 F.3d at 639; *Matthews*, 15 F.3d at 438-39.

[38] *Tannenbaum*, 604 N.E.2d at 17.

[39] *Id.*

[40] *Zarrilli*, 231 Fed.App'x at 125.

[41] *Id.*

[42] *Id.*

[43] *See, e.g.*, *Brown*, 201 F.3d at 661-62; *Matthews*, 15 F.3d at 437; *Schifano*, 624 So.2d at181; *Remsburg*, 816 A.2d at 1009-10; *Lusby*, 1990 U.S. App. LEXIS 9144, at *7.

[44] *Lusby*, 1990 U.S. App. LEXIS at *7.

[45] *Id.*

[46] *Id.*

[47] *Schifano*, 624 So.2d at 179-81.

[48] *Joe Dickerson & Assoc.*, 34 P.3d at 1002.

[49] *Id.*

[50] *See, e.g.*, *King*, 485 F.3d at 592-93; *Puckett*, 1990 U.S. App'x LEXIS 19761, at *7-8; *Beverley*, 587 N.E.2d at 276-77; *WJLA*, 564 S.E.2d at 388; *Riggins*, 457 S.E.2d at 362.

[51] *WJLA*, 564 S.E.2d at 388 (quoting VA. CODE § 8.01-40A)).

[52] *Id.* at 395 (citing *Riggins*, 457 S.E.2d at 362).

[53] *WJLA*, 564 S.E.2d at 388.

[54] *Id.* at 387.

[55] *See, e.g.*, *King*, 485 F.3d at 592-93; *Beverley*, 587 N.E.2d at 276-77.

[56] *Beverley*, 587 N.E.2d at 276-77.

[57] *Id.* at 278.

[58] *Id.*

[59] *Id.*

[60] *Id.*

[61] *See, e.g.*, *Beverley*, 587 N.E.2d at 278-79; *Riggins*, 457 S.E.2d at 362-64.

[62] *Town & Country Props., Inc.*, 457 S.E.2d at 362-64.

[63] *Id.* at 362-63 (quoting Central Hudson Gas & Elec. Corp. v. Pub. Serv. Comm'n of New York, 447 U.S. 557, 563 (1980)).

[64] *Id.*

[65] *Id.*

---

[66] *See, e.g.*, *Newcombe*, 157 F.3d at 692-93; *Matthews*, 15 F.3d at 437-38; *Simpson*, 669 A.2d at 1326; *Botts*, 106 Fed. App'x, at 110.

[67] RESTATEMENT (SECOND) OF TORTS § 652C (1977). *See also Newcombe*, 157 F.3d at 690; *Matthews*, 15 F.3d at 437; *Simpson*, 669 A.2d at 1326; *Botts*, 106 Fed. App'x at 110.

[68] *Botts*, 106 Fed. App'x at 110.

[69] *Id.*

[70] *Id.*

[71] *Id.*

[72] *See, e.g.*, *Staruski*, 581 A.2d at 273 (holding that a telephone company appropriated plaintiff's identity when it published a photograph of her, which was accompanied by her name, job description, and an endorsement of her employer).

[73] 157 F.3d 686, 693-94 (9th Cir. 1998).

[74] *Id.* at 694.

[75] *Id.*

[76] *Id.* at 693.

[77] *Id.*

[78] *See, e.g.*, *Matthews*, 15 F.3d at 437; *Tyne*, 901 So.2d at 809-810, *aff'd*, 425 F.3d 1363, 1364 (11th Cir. 2005) (per curiam).

[79] *Matthews*, 15 F.3d at 437 (affirming the district court's grant of summary judgment for Wozencraft "because Texas law does not recognize a cause of action for appropriation of one's life story and because if it did, there would be an exception for biographies and 'fictionalized biographies.'").

[80] *Id.* at 437 (referring to RESTATEMENT (SECOND) OF TORTS § 652C, cmt. d (1977)).

[81] *Id.* at 438.

[82] *Tyne*, 901 So.2d at 809-810, *conformed to*, *Tyne*, 425 F.3d at 1363.

[83] *Id.*

[84] RESTATEMENT (SECOND) OF TORTS § 652C (1977).

[85] *Rivell*, 520 F.3d at 1310; *Christian Broad. Network, Inc.*, 254 Fed. App'x at 958; *Schifano*, 624 So.2d at 179; *Nemani*, 33 S.W.3d at 187, *cert. denied*, 532 U.S. 981 (2001); *Miller*, 467 N.W.2d at 656.

[86] *Schifano*, 624 So.2d at 179-181.

[87] *Id.*

[88] *Nemani*, 33 S.W.3d at 187.

---

[89] *Id.*

[90] *See, e.g., Id. Christian Broad. Network, Inc.*, 254 Fed. App'x at 958.

[91] NEB. REV. STAT. § 20-202 (Reissue 1987); *Miller*, 467 N.W.2d at 656.

[92] *Miller*, 467 N.W.2d at 656.

[93] *Rivell*, 520 F.3d at 1310.

[94] *Id.* at 1310 (stating that courts in Georgia, New York, California, Massachusetts, Connecticut, Ohio, and Illinois all have recognized that standard of law.).

[95] *See, e.g., Showler*, 222 Fed. App'x at 761; *Groden*, 61 F.3d at 1049; *Joe Dickerson & Assoc.*, 34 P.3d at 1004; *Tyne*, 901 So.2d at 809-810, aff'd by 425 F.3d at 1364; *Messenger*, 727 N.E.2d at 552-54; *Leddy*, 843 A.2d at 490; *Beverley*, 587 N.E.2d at 278-79; *Finger*, 566 N.E.2d at 144; *WJLA*, 564 S.E.2d at 387-88.

[96] *Showler*, 222 Fed. App'x at 763-64; *Tyne*, 901 So.2d at 809-810; *Groden*, 61 F.3d at 1049; *Joe Dickerson & Assoc.*, 34 P.3d at 1004; *Messenger*, 727 N.E.2d at 552-54; *Leddy*, 843 A.2d at 490; *Beverley*, 587 N.E.2d at 278-79; *Finger*, 566 N.E.2d at 144; *WJLA*, 564 S.E.2d at 387-88.

[97] *Showler*, 222 Fed. App'x at 763-64.

[98] *Id.*

[99] *Id.*

[100] *Joe Dickerson & Assoc.*, 34 P.3d at 1003; *Howell*, 612 N.E.2d at 703-04; *Beverley*, 587 N.E.2d at 278-79.

[101] *Joe Dickerson & Assoc.*, 34 P.3d at 1003 ("[T]he defendant's use of the plaintiff's name and likeness in the context of an article related to her crime and conviction is newsworthy and, therefore, privileged.").

[102] *Id.* at 1003.

[103] *Id.* at 999.

[104] *Id.* at 1004 (citing Cox Broad. Corp. v. Cohn, 420 U.S. 469, 492 (1975)).

[105] *See, e.g., Messenger*, 727 N.E.2d at 544-46, 448; *Leddy*, 843 A.2d at 490-91; *WJLA*, 564 S.E.2d at 387-88.

[106] *Showler*, 222 Fed. App'x at 763-64; *Joe Dickerson & Assoc.*, 34 P.3d at 1003-04; *Beverley*, 587 N.E.2d at 752; *Leddy*, 843 A.2d at 490-91; *WJLA*, 564 S.E.2d at 387-88.

[107] *WJLA*, 564 S.E.2d at 395.

[108] *Id.* (quoting *Messenger*, 727 N.E.2d at 552).

[109] *Showler*, 222 Fed. App'x at 763-64; *Lusby*, No. 89-3854, 1990 U.S. App. LEXIS 9144, *7; *Messenger*, 727 N.E.2d at 551-54; *Howell*, 612 N.E.2d at 703-05; *Finger*, 566 N.E.2d at 144; *Leddy*, 843 A.2d at, 488-89.

[110] *Solano*, 292 F.3d at 1089.

[111] *See, e.g., Rivell*, 520 F.3d at 1310; *Meadows*, 492 F.3d at 638-39; *Christian Broad. Network, Inc.*, 254 Fed. App'x at 958; *Zarrilli*, 231 Fed. App'x at 125; *Botts*, 106 Fed. App'x at 110; *Matthews*, 15 F.3d at 437; *Schifano*, 624 So.2d at 179; *Tannenbaum*, 604 N.E.2d at 17; *Simpson*, 669 A.2d at 1326; *Nemani*, 33 S.W.3d at 186; *Wilkinson*, 612 N.W.2d at 217; *Miller*, 467 N.W.2d at 656; *Sloan*, 586 S.E.2d at 108; *Town & Country Props., Inc.*, 457 S.E.2d at 356; *Staruski*, 581 A.2d at 273.

[112] *Showler*, 222 Fed. App'x at 759; *Tyne*, 901 So.2d at 809-810; *Lusby*, 1990 U.S. App. LEXIS 9144 at *7; *Joe Dickerson & Assoc., LLC*, 34 P.3d at 998-1001; *Messenger*, 727 N.E.2d at 559-61; *Howell*, 612 N.E.2d at 703; *Beverley*, 587 N.E.2d at 279; *Leddy*, 843 A.2d at 490-91; *WJLA*, 564 S.E.2d at 490-91; *Town & Country Props., Inc.*, 457 S.E.2d at 361-62.

[113] *Groden*, 61 F.3d at 1051; *Joe Dickerson & Assoc., LLC*, 34 P.3d at 998-1001; *Messenger*, 727 N.E.2d at 552-54; *Howell*, 612 N.E.2d at 703; *Finger*, 566 N.E.2d at 143 (N.Y. 1991); *Leddy*, 843 A.2d at 490-91.

[114] *See, e.g., Showler*, 222 Fed. App'x at 759; *Tyne*, 901 So.2d at 809-810; *Lusby*, 1990 U.S. App. LEXIS 9144 at *7; *Joe Dickerson & Assoc., LLC*, 34 P.3d at 998-1001; *Howell*, 612 N.E.2d at 704; *Leddy*, 843 A.2d at 491; *WJLA*, 564 S.E.2d at 395; *Town & Country Props., Inc.*, 457 S.E.2d at 361-62.

[115] *Lusby*, 1990 U.S. App. LEXIS 9144 at *7; *Joe Dickerson & Assoc., LLC*, 34 P.3d at 998-1001; *Messenger*, 727 N.E.2d at 552-53; *Howell*, 612 N.E.2d at 703-04; *Finger*, 566 N.E.2d at 143; *Leddy*, 843 A.2d at 490-91; *WJLA*, 564 S.E.2d at 395; *Town & Country Props., Inc.*, 457 S.E.2d at 361-62.

[116] *See, e.g., Messenger*, 727 N.E.2d at 552-54; *Howell*, 612 N.E.2d at 703; *Finger*, 566 N.E.2d at 143-44.

[117] *Howell*, 612 N.E.2d at 703; *Finger*, 566 N.E.2d at 143-44; *Leddy*, 843 A.2d at 490-91.

[118] *Howell*, 612 N.E.2d at 703 (citing Finger v. Omni Publ'ns Int'l, Ltd., 566 N.E.2d at 143-44).

[119] *Id.*

[120] *Id.* at 704.

[121] *Id.*

[122] *See, e.g.*, *Groden*, 61 F.3d at 1051; *Howell*, 612 N.E.2d at 703; *Finger*, 566 N.E.2d at 143-44; *Leddy*, 843 A.2d at 491.

[123] *Groden*, 61 F.3d at 1050-51.

[124] *Id.*

[125] *Id.* at 1051.

[126] *Id.*

[127] *Id.* (citing Time, Inc. v. Hill, 385 U.S. 374 (1967); Arrington v. New York Times Co., 434 N.E.2d 1319 (N.Y. 1982)).

[128] *Id.*

[129] *Messenger*, 727 N.E.2d at 550-51.

[130] *Id.*

[131] *Id.*

[132] *Id.* at 553.

[133] *Id.*

[134] 843 A.2d 481, 490-91 (R.I. 2004).

[135] *Id.* at 484-85.

[136] *Id.* at 490-91.

[137] *Id.* (quoting New York Times v. Sullivan, 376 U.S. 254, 270 (1964); Hustler v. Falwell, 485 U.S. 46, 50 (1988)).

[138] *Id.* at 490 (quoting *New York Times*, 376 U.S. at 270).

[139] *Id.* at 491 (quoting *Hustler*, 485 U.S. at 50).

[140] *Leddy*, 843 A.2d at 490-91.

[141] *Id.*

[142] *Id.*

[143] *See, e.g.*, *Showler*, 222 Fed. App'x at 759; *Matthews*, 15 F.3d at 440; *Lusby*, No. 89-3854, 1990 U.S. App. LEXIS 9144, at *7; *Joe Dickerson & Assoc.*, 34 P.3d at 998-1001; *Messenger*, 727 N.E.2d at 559-61; *Howell*, 612 N.E.2d at 699; *Beverley*, 587 N.E.2d at 279; *Leddy*, 843 A.2d at 490-91; *WJLA*, 564 S.E.2d at 395; *Town & Country Props., Inc.*, 457 S.E.2d at 361-62.

[144] *Howell*, 612 N.E.2d at 703 (N.Y. 1993); *Finger*, 566 N.E.2d at 143-44; *WJLA*, 564 S.E.2d at 395.

[145] *See, e.g.*, *Showler*, 222 Fed. App'x at 764; *Groden*, 61 F.3d at 1051; *Joe Dickerson & Assoc.*, 34 P.3d at 998-1001; *Messenger*, 727 N.E.2d at 552-54; *Lusby*, No. 89-3854, 1990 U.S. App. LEXIS 9144, at *7); *Howell, Inc.*, 612 N.E.2d at 703; *Beverley*, 587 N.E.2d at 279; *Finger*, 566 N.E.2d at 143-44; *Leddy*, 843 A.2d at 491; *Town & Country Props., Inc.*, 457 S.E.2d at 361-62.

[146] *See, e.g.*, *Showler*, 222 Fed. App'x at 759; *Groden*, 61 F.3d at 1051; *Joe Dickerson & Assoc*, 34 P.3d at 998-1001; *Messenger*, 727 N.E.2d at 552-54; *Lusby*, No. 89-3854, 1990 U.S. App. LEXIS 9144, at *7; *Howell, Inc.*, 612 N.E.2d at 703; *Beverley*, 587 N.E.2d at 279; *Finger*, 566 N.E.2d at 143-44; *Leddy*, 843 A.2d at 491; *Leddy*, 843 A.2d at 491; *WJLA*, 564 S.E.2d at 394-95; *Town & Country Props., Inc.*, 457 S.E.2d at 361-62.

[147] *King.*, 485 F.3d at 591-92; *Brown*, 201 F.3d at 658; *Bowling*, No. 91-5920, 1992 U.S. App. LEXIS 18505, at *2; *Felsher*, 755 N.E.2d at 600-01; *Miller*, 467 N.W.2d at 679-80; *Reid*, 961 P.2d at 342.

[148] *See, e.g.*, *Brown*, 201 F.3d at 658; *King*, 485 F.3d at 591-92; *Bowling*, No. 91-5920, 1992 U.S. App. LEXIS 18505 at *2,; *Schifano*, 624 So. 2d at 181; *Joe Dickerson & Assoc.*, 34 P.3d at 1000; *Felsher*, 755 N.E.2d at 600-01; *Lake*, 582 N.W.2d at 233; *Miller*, 467 N.W.2d 653, 679-80 (Neb. 1991); *Thompson*, 898 A.2d at 499-500; *Remsburg*, 816 A.2d at 1009-1010; *Sloan*, 586 S.E.2d at 110-11; *Reid*, 961 P.2d at 342.

[149] *Reid*, 961 P.2d at 341.

[150] *Brown*, 201 F.3d at 658; *King*, 485 F.3d at 591-92; *Bowling*, 1992 U.S. App. LEXIS 18505; *Schifano*, 624 So. 2d at 181; *Felsher*, 755 N.E.2d at 600-01; *Lake*, 582 N.W.2d at 233; *Miller*, 467 N.W.2d at 679-80; *Reid*, 961 P.2d at 342.

[151] *King*, 485 F.3d at 591-92.

[152] *King*, 485 F.3d at 591-92.

[153] *Id.*

[154] *Remsburg*, 816 A.2d at 1009-1010.

[155] *Id.* at 1006.

[156] *Id.* at 1009 (quoting RESTATEMENT (SECOND) OF TORTS § 652C cmt. b (1977)).

[157] *Id.* at 1009-10 (quoting RESTATEMENT (SECOND) OF TORTS § 652C cmt. d (1977)).

[158] *Id.* Three years later, the Supreme Court of New Hampshire's rationale in *Thompson v. C&C Research and Development*, 898 A.2d at 499-500, also related to the individual and liberty values for privacy. In fact, the ruling in *Thompson* found Thompson's privacy was not invaded because she had signed a contract that authorized the defendants' use of her identity. Thus, the plaintiff's autonomy and liberty values for privacy were not harmed under the facts of that case.

[159] 898 A.2d at 499-500 (N.H. 2006).

[160] *Id.* at 500.

[161] *Schifano*, 624 So. 2d at 181; *Lake*, 582 N.W.2d at 233.

[162] *Lake*, 582 N.W.2d at 233.

[163] *Id.* at 235. The Minnesota Supreme Court, however, declined to recognize the false light invasion of privacy tort. *Id.* at 236.

[164] *Id.* at 235.

[165] *Id.* at 233.

[166] *Id.* at 235.

[167] *Felsher*, 755 N.E.2d at 593-99, 601; *Sloan*, 586 S.E.2d at 110-11.

[168] 586 S.E.2d at 110-11.

[169] *Id.* at 110.

[170] *See id.* at 110-11 (citing Snakenberg v. Hartford Casualty Ins. Co., 299 S.C. 164, 383 S.E.2d 2 (Ct. App. 1989)).

[171] *Id.* at 110.

[172] *See* 34 P.3d 995, 1000 (Colo. 2001).

[173] *Id.* at 998.

[174] *Id.* at 999 (quoting Samuel D. Warren & Louis D. Brandeis, *The Right to Privacy*, 4 HARV. L. REV. 193, 200-01, 207 (1890)).

[175] *Id.* at 999 (citing Reed v. Real Detective Publ'g Co., 63 Ariz. 294, 162 P.2d 133, 139 (1945); Fairfield v. Am. Photocopy Equip. Co., 138 Cal. App. 2d 82, 291 P.2d 194, 197 (1955); Annerino v. Dell Publ'g Co., 17 Ill. App. 2d 205, 149 N.E.2d 761, 762 (1958); J. THOMAS MCCARTHY, THE RIGHTS OF PUBLICITY AND PRIVACY, § 1:7 (2d ed. 2000)).

[176] *Joe Dickerson & Aossc.*, 4 P.3d at 1002.

[177] *Id.* at 1005 (Coats, J., concurring).

[178] *Staruski*, 581 A.2d at 270.

[179] *Id.* at 269.

[180] *Id.* (citing Faber v. Condecor, Inc., 195 N.J. Super. 81, 90-91, 477 A.2d 1289, 1294-95 (App.Div.1984)).

[181] *Id.* at 273.

[182] *Showler*, 222 Fed. App'x at 763-74; *Reid*, 961 P.2d at 342.

[183] *Showler*, 222 Fed. App'x at 763-74; *Reid*, 961 P.2d at 342.

[184] *Reid*, 961 P.2d at 342.

[185] *Id.*

[186] *Id.* at 335-37.

[187] *See* Robert C. Post, *The Social Foundations of Privacy: Community and Self in the Common Law Tort*, 77 CALIF. L. REV. 957, 962-64 (1989).

[188] *Showler*, 222 Fed. App'x at 761-62.

[189] *Id.* at 763.

[190] *See, e.g.*, *Id.* at 763-74; *Brown*, 201 F.3d at 658; *King*, 485 F.3d at 591-92; *Bowling, No. 91-5920*, 1992 U.S. App. LEXIS at 18505; *Schifano*, 624 So. 2d at 181; *Joe Dickerson & Assoc.*, 34 P.3d at 1000; *Felsher*, 755 N.E.2d at 600-01; *Lake*, 582 N.W.2d at 233; *Miller*, 467 N.W.2d at 679-80; *Thompson* v. 898 A.2d at 499-500; *Remsburg*, 816 A.2d at 1009-1010; Howell v. New York Post Co., Inc., 612 N.E.2d 699, 701-02 (N.Y. 1993); *Sloan*, 586 S.E.2d at 110-11; *PTS Corp.*, 263 Va. at 621-22; *WJLA*, 564 S.E.2d at 395-396; *Staruski*, 581 A.2d at 269-70; *Reid*, 961 P.2d at 342.

[191] *See, e.g.*, *Brown*, 201 F.3d at 658; *King*, 485 F.3d at 591-92; *Bowling*, 1992 U.S. App. LEXIS at 18505; *Schifano*, 624 So. 2d at 191; *Joe Dickerson & Assoc.*, 34 P.3d at 999; *Felsher*, 755 N.E.2d at 600-01; *Lake*, 582 N.W.2d at 233; *Miller*, 467 N.W.2d at 679-80; *Thompson*, 898 A.2d at 499-500; *Remsburg*, 816 A.2d at 1009-10; *Howell*, 612 N.E.2d at 701-02; *Sloan*, 586 S.E.2d at 1001-11; *PTS Corp.*, 263 Va. at 621-22; *WJLA*, 564 S.E.2d at 396; *Staruski*, 581 A.2d at 269; *Reid*, 961 P.2d at 342.

[192] *See, e.g.*, *Joe Dickerson & Assoc.*, 34 P.3d at 999; *PETA*, 895 P.2d at 1283-84; *Howell*, 612 N.E.2d at 701-02; *PTS Corp.*, 263 Va. at 621-22; *WJLA*, 564 S.E.2d at 396; *Staruski*, 581 A.2d at 269.

[193] *See, e.g.*, *Showler*, 222 Fed. App'x at 763-74; *Reid*, 961 P.2d at 342.

[194] *Roe*, 638 So. 2d at 829-30; *Howell*, 612 N.E.2d at 703-05; *Town & Country Props., Inc.*, 457 S.E.2d at 363-64.

[195] *Roe*, 638 So. 2d at 829-30.

[196] *Town & Country Props., Inc.*, 457 S.E.2d at 363-64.

[197] *Roe*, 638 So. 2d at 827 (citing ALA. CONST. art. 1, § 4).

[198] *Id.* at 829.

[199] *See id.* at 829-30.

[200] *Roe*, 638 So. 2d at 829.

[201] *Id.* at 830.

[202] *Id.* at 830.

[203] *See, e.g.*, *Tannenbaum*, 604 N.E.2d at 17; *Wilkinson*, 612 N.W.2d at 216; *Messenger*, 727 N.E.2d at 553-54; *Howell*, 612 N.E.2d at 700, 703-05; *Beverley*, 587 N.E.2d at 278-80; *Finger*, 566 N.E.2d at 143-45; *PTS Corp.*, 263 Va. at 623-24; *WJLA*, 564 S.E.2d at 396; *Town & Country Props., Inc.*, 457 S.E.2d at 363-64.

[204] *Messenger*, 727 N.E.2d at 553-54; *Howell*, 612 N.E.2d at 703-05; *Beverley*, 587 N.E.2d at 278-80; *Finger*, 566 N.E.2d at 143-45.

[205] *Howell*, 612 N.E.2d at 703.

[206] *Id.* at 704-05.

[207] *Id.* at 703-05.

[208] *Id.*

[209] *Town & Country Props., Inc.*, 457 S.E.2d at 363-64.

[210] *Id.*

[211] *Id.*

[212] *Id.* at 395 to 96 (quoting Central Hudson Gas & Elec. Corp. v. Public Serv. Comm'n of New York, 447 U.S. 557, 563 (1980); Ohralik v. Ohio State Bar Ass'n, 436 U.S. 447, 455-56 (1978); Bates v. State Bar of Arizona, 433 U.S. 350, 384, (1997)).

[213] *See, e.g.*, *Rivell*, 520 F.3d at 1310; *Zarrilli*, 231 Fed. App'x at 125; *Christian Broad. Network, Inc.*, 254 Fed. App'x at 958; *Meadows*, 492 F.3d at 637; *Showler*, 222 Fed. App'x at 759; *King*, 485 F.3d at 593; *Solano*, 292 F.3d at 1081; *Am. Guar. & Liab. Ins. Co.*, 273 F.3d at 615; *Brown*, 201 F.3d at 658, 661; *Newcombe*, 157 F.3d at 693; *Matthews*, 15 F.3d at 436; *Schifano*, 624 So.2d at 179-181; *Joe Dickerson & Assoc.*, 34 P.3d at 998-1001; *Felsher*, 755 N.E.2d at 593-94; *Tannenbaum*, 604 N.E.2d at 16; *Simpson*, 669 A.2d at 1326;

Nemani, 33 S.W.3d at 187; *Lake*, 582 N.W.2d at 222-33; *Thompson*, LLC, 898 A.2d at 500; *Remsburg*, 816 A.2d at 1009-10; *Messenger*, 727 N.E.2d at 553-54; *Howell*, 612 N.E.2d at 703-05; *Beverley*, 587 N.E.2d at 278-80; *Finger*, 566 N.E.2d at 143-45; *Leddy*, 843 A.2d at 490-91; *Sloan*, 586 S.E.2d at 108; *PTS Corp.*, 263 Va. at 623-24; *WJLA*, 564 S.E.2d at 396; *Town & Country Props., Inc.*, 457 S.E.2d at 363; *Staruski*, 581 A.2d at 268; *Reid*, 961 P.2d at 339.

[214] *Roe*, 638 So. 2d at 829-30.

[215] *Id.*

[216] *Messenger*, 727 N.E.2d at 553-54; *Howell*, 612 N.E.2d at 703-05; *Beverley*, 587 N.E.2d at 278-80; Finger, 566 N.E.2d at 143-45.

[217] *Joe Dickerson & Assoc.*, 34 P.3d at 997; *Lake*, 582 N.W.2d at 236; *Remsburg*, 816 A.2d at 1009-10; *Staruski*, 581 A.2d at 268; *Reid*, 961 P.2d at 339.

[218] Florida Star v. B.J.F., 491 U.S. 524, 530 (U.S. 1989); *Joe Dickerson & Assoc., LLC*, 34 P.3d at 997; *Lake*, 582 N.W.2d at 236; *Remsburg*, 816 A.2d at 1009-10; *Staruski*, 581 A.2d at 268.

[219] *Joe Dickerson & Assoc.*, 34 P.3d at 999.

[220] Nelson v. J.C. Penney Co., Inc., 75 F.3d 343, 347 ((8th Cir. 1996) "[A]lthough it has been given a number of opportunities to hold that some types of invasion of privacy are actionable, the Supreme Court of North Dakota has consistently refused to do so. . . . this studied reluctance does not bode well for the acceptance of this kind of action in North Dakota in the future.").

[221] RESTATEMENT (SECOND) OF TORTS § 652C (1977).

[222] *See supra* notes 172–181 and accompanying text.

[223] *Beverley*, 587 N.E.2d at 276; *Town & Country Props., Inc.*, 457 S.E.2d at 358.

[224] *Town & Country Props., Inc.*, 457 S.E.2d at 361.

[225] *Tannenbaum*, 604 N.E.2d at 17.

[226] *See supra* notes 150–181 and accompanying text.

[227] *Matthews*, 15 F.3d at 437; *Tyne*, 901 So.2d at 809-810; *Roe*, 638 So. 2d at 829-30.

[228] *Newcombe*, 157 F.3d at 689.

[229] *Showler*, 222 Fed. App'x at 763-74; *Reid*, 961 P.2d at 342.

[230] *See* Robert C. Post, *The Social Foundations of Privacy: Community and Self in the Common Law Tort*, 77 CALIF. L. REV. 957, 962-64 (1989).

[231] *Showler*, 222 Fed. App'x at 763.

[232] *Id.* at 760.

[233] *Messenger*, 727 N.E.2d at 552-54; *Howell*, 612 N.E.2d at 703; *Finger*, 566 N.E.2d at 143; *Leddy*, 843 A.2d at 491; *WJLA*, 564 S.E.2d at 387-88.

[234] *Messenger*, 727 N.E.2d at 552-54; *Howell*, 612 N.E.2d at 703; *Beverley*, 587 N.E.2d at 278-79; *Finger*, 566 N.E.2d at 144; *Leddy*, 843 A.2d at 490; *WJLA*, 564 S.E.2d at 387-88; *Town & Country Props., Inc.*, 457 S.E.2d at 361-62.

[235] *Howell*, 612 N.E.2d at 704.

[236] *See, e.g.*, *Showler*, 222 Fed. App'x at 764; *Groden*, 61 F.3d at 1051; *Joe Dickerson & Assoc.*, 34 P.3d at 998-1001; *Messenger*, 727 N.E.2d at 552-54; *Lusby*, 1990 U.S. App. LEXIS 9144, at *7; *Howell, Inc.*, 612 N.E.2d at 703;

Beverley, 587 N.E.2d at 279; *Finger*, 566 N.E.2d at 143-44; *Leddy*, 843 A.2d at 491; *Town & Country Props., Inc.*, 457 S.E.2d at 361-62.

[237] *Roe*, 638 So. 2d at 829.

[238] *Id.* at 827.

[239] *Id.* at 828.

[240] *Id.*

[241] *See supra* notes 122–142 and accompanying text.

[242] *King*, 485 F.3d at 593; *Brown*, 201 F.3d at 662; *Bowling, No. 91-5920*, 1992 U.S. App. LEXIS 18505, at *2; *Felsher*, 755 N.E.2d at 599; *Town & Country Props., Inc.*, 457 S.E.2d at 362-64.

[243] *See, e.g., King*, 485 F.3d at 593 (affirming a judgment for King, including $57,672 for damages); *Brown*, 201 F.3d at 662 (finding the jury did not err in awarding $100,000 for misappropriation); *Bowling*, No. 91-5920, 1992 U.S. App. LEXIS 18505, at *2 (affirming a judgment for Bowling, including $100 for the appropriation of his likeness); *Town & Country Props., Inc.*, , 457 S.E.2d at 362-64 (affirming a judgment for Riggins, including $2 for compensatory damages).

[244] *Reid*, 961 P.2d at 342.

[245] *See, e.g., King*, 485 F.3d at 593; *Town & Country Props., Inc.*, 457 S.E.2d at 363-64.

[246] *See, e.g.*, Central Hudson Gas & Elec. Corp. v. Public Serv. Comm'n of New York, 447 U.S. 557, 563 (1980); Ohralik v. Ohio State Bar Ass'n, 436 U.S. 447, 455-56 (1978); Bates v. State Bar of Arizona, 433 U.S. 350, 384, (1997); *Town & Country Props., Inc.*, 457 S.E.2d at 363-64.

[247] *See, e.g., King*, 485 F.3d at 591-92; *Beverley*, 587 N.E.2d at 276-77.

[248] *See supra* notes 35-65 and accompanying text.

CHAPTER 5

Reconciling Future Conflicts

The highest courts in four states have recognized the disclosure of private facts or appropriation tort for the first time since June 1989,[1] when Justice White's dissenting opinion in *Florida Star v. B.J.F.* warned that the majority ruling could "obliterate one of the most noteworthy legal inventions of the 20th century: the tort of the publication of private facts." [2] Contrary to that prediction, state high court and federal circuit courts of appeals rulings have identified merit for freedom of expression as well as the privacy rights recognized by both privacy torts. During that period, approximately half the state high courts and federal circuit courts of appeals' post-*Florida Star* rulings involving disclosure of private facts[3] or appropriation[4] have discussed or implied at least one fundamental democratic value undergirding either freedom of expression or privacy rights, suggesting that some courts recognize both sets of values are important for American society.[5]

Some post-*Florida Star* state high courts and federal circuit courts of appeals rulings have acknowledged tensions between freedom of expression and privacy, as the majority ruling in *Florida Star* acknowledged.[6] However, the lower court rulings involving the First Amendment privilege established by *Florida Star*, which exempts disclosure of private facts defndants from liability for the truthful publication of lawfully obtained information on matters of public significance, include little explicit discussion of how to reconcile clashes between free expression and privacy interests.[7] Rulings involving that privilege or the common law defense of newsworthiness protecting matters of public interest more often have focused on the editorial autonomy of the press or the rights for members of the public to receive information, giving little or no attention to specific privacy interests for plaintiffs. Perhaps not surprisingly, the broad swath of protection woven by the constitutional privilege and the common law defense has shielded news media defendants from liability in almost every disclosure of private facts or appropriation of name or likeness ruling by a state high court or federal circuit court of appeals during the past twenty-two years.[8]

Although most post-*Florida Star* disclosure of private facts and appropriation rulings have favored free expression interests, a few rulings have clarified that individual and news media defendants may be held liable for invasion of privacy when the publicity at issue fails to serve a public interest often associated with audience-based free expression values. Connecting protection for freedom of speech and press to audiences' rights to receive specific types of information ultimately emphasizes societal values undergirding freedom of expression, such as self-governance, which could place media defendants at greater risk for liability if societal concerns about invasions of privacy continue to grow.[9] Such results could lead to greater consideration for privacy and reduce the appearance of favoritism for freedom of expression. But simply shifting the balance toward privacy rather than press freedom leaves essential questions unanswered. Rather than allow this area of law to remain "somewhat uncharted," as it was described by Justice Thurgood Marshall in the *Florida Star* majority opinion, the current study indicates that certain trends in post-*Florida Star* jurisprudence may chart an effective way for media professionals and courts to reconcile conflicts between freedom of expression and privacy rights.

Free Expression and Privacy Values in Disclosure Cases

As indicated in chapter three, post-*Florida Star* state high courts and federal circuit courts of appeals' rulings primarily focused on the elements of the disclosure tort or the public interest privilege. A number of rulings identified a liberty-based autonomy value for freedom of expression or at least one audience-based value for freedom of expression—marketplace of ideas, self-governance, or checking function—when discussing whether the information at issue related to the matter of public interest privilege or newsworthiness defense.[10] Some rulings implicated at least one individual privacy value—liberty, autonomy, or emotional health—or a societal privacy value—

promoting civility and community or forming and maintaining relationships—when examining whether a case involved widespread publicity of private information.[11] Few disclosure of private facts rulings, however, used balancing to reconcile conflicts between the key democratic values undergirding freedom of expression and privacy.[12]

Focus on the elements

Almost half the state high courts and federal circuit courts of appeals' rulings in disclosure cases focused on whether the plaintiffs' claims were able to satisfy the elements of the tort as matter of law.[13] In seventeen cases, courts determined the defendants had not given widespread publicity to private information.[14] Three rulings turned on plaintiffs' failure to prove the disclosed information was true.[15] Sixteen rulings scrutinized whether the information at issue was private, meaning the information was not widely available and was so intimate, intensely personal, or embarrassing that the disclosure would cause shame or humiliation.[16] Three other rulings used reasonableness tests to determine whether plaintiffs expected the information at issue to remain private and whether community members agreed that expectation was reasonable.[17] In almost one-third of the rulings, courts used the fourth element, whether the disclosed information was a matter of legitimate public concern, to distinguish tortious disclosures of private facts from privileged disclosures of newsworthy information.[18]

Implicating free expression values

Courts typically implicated the liberty-based free expression value of editorial autonomy as well as audience-based free expression values when discussing the legitimate public concern element. For instance, in *Shulman v. Group W. Productions*, the Supreme Court of California found that a television production team could not be liable for disclosure of private facts for recording and broadcasting a medical team's treatment of car collision victims. The Court suggested that members of the press deserve the degree of editorial autonomy necessary to serve audiences' general right to receive information of interest to their community:

> [I]t has long been apparent that the desire for privacy must at many points give way before our right to know, and the news

> media's right to investigate and relate, facts about the events and individuals of our time. Brandeis and Warren were themselves aware that recognition of the right to privacy requires a line to be drawn between properly private events, words and actions and those of "public and general interest" with which the community has a "legitimate concern."[19]

That explanation could limit editorial autonomy by connecting the right to publish to subjective community-based standards likely to vary with time. Fortunately, the court added that press freedom "extends far beyond simple accounts of public proceedings and abstract commentary on well-known events."[20] That implies the First Amendment values limiting privacy claims may include matters pertinent to self-governance and the watchdog function as well as matters that promote a marketplace of ideas. The latter value broadens the sphere of protected material beyond reports on crime, courts, community events, and public administration to include material that promotes discussion and debate. Connecting the protection for disclosures to those free expression values may provide a more consistent standard for separating protected and unprotected disclosures than a common law standard that connects common law protection for disclosing matters of public interest to subjective community standards likely to evolve over time.

The marketplace of ideas and self-governance values undergirding freedom of expression relate to Seventh Circuit Court of Appeals Chief Judge Posner's clarification of the line separating private and public matters. In *Haynes v. Alfred Knopf Publishing,* he wrote:

> An individual, and more pertinently perhaps the community, is most offended by the publication of intimate personal facts when the community has no interest in them beyond the voyeuristic thrill of penetrating the wall of privacy that surrounds a stranger. The reader of a book about the black migration to the North would have no legitimate interest in the details of Luther Haynes's sex life; but no such details are disclosed. Such a reader does have a legitimate interest in the aspects of Luther's conduct that the book reveals.

Judge Posner added that no details in the book, which Haynes claimed had invaded his privacy, are "not germane to the story that the author wanted to tell, a story not only of legitimate but of transcendent public interest." That assertion relates the newsworthiness of the book at issue to the audience-based marketplace of ideas and checking values. Four circuit courts of appeals' decisions have since cited that rationale from Posner's opinion in *Haynes v. Knopf*, also connecting protection for freedom of expression to the audience model for free expression.[21]

Other rulings that related protection for free expression to the self-governance and checking values for freedom of expression cited the U.S. Supreme Court's rationale from *Cox Broadcasting Corp. v. Cohn*, connecting the public's right to receive information to "the beneficial effects of public scrutiny of the administration of justice."[22] That rationale provides a much narrower scope of protection for freedom of expression by limiting the privileged matters of public interest to those that shed light on government and the official acts of government employees. Such limitations could allow courts to protect disclosures of embarrassing, intimate information not contained in court records, related to the administration of justice, or pertinent to self-governance. In fact, rulings favoring freedom of expression have focused primarily on public interest served by disclosures of information related to criminal judgment or self-governance without balancing those interests against the potentially harmful impact of disclosures on privacy.

Privacy values

Several courts discussed individual values for privacy—liberty, autonomy, or emotional health—when examining the elements of the tort or when determining whether to recognize the disclosure tort under state common law.[23] Some of those rulings implicated the liberty value for privacy when quoting Warren and Brandeis's definition of privacy as a right "to be let alone."[24] Another ruling related privacy to aspects of the individual autonomy value for privacy.[25]

Courts most often discussed the emotional health value for privacy, mentioning individuals' desires to prevent emotional harm, such as shame or humiliation.[26] For instance, the Supreme Court of Alabama focused strictly on the elements of the disclosure tort in a ruling involving the distribution of young females' nude, lewd photographs. Alabama's highest court found the females involved in *S. B. v. St. James School* had "failed to establish a prima facie case of giving publicity to a private matter."[27] Under common law, Alabama's definition of an invasion of privacy as an intentional and wrongful act that would "outrage or cause mental suffering, shame, or humiliation to a person of ordinary sensibilities," relates to the emotional health value for privacy.[28] Although the distribution of those photographs to other students undoubtedly was embarrassing, information about those explicit pictures was not considered "private" at the time school officials disclosed information that could have identified the females in those photographs. By that time, the court reasoned that "[t]he explicit photographs, which meet the definition of child pornography under Alabama law," had been disseminated widely throughout the school community and had become a matter of legitimate public concern. The personal emotional health value individual plaintiffs sought to protect was superseded by the public interest in learning about criminal activity and educators' handling of such sensitive materials.

Courts' references to societal values for privacy, however, were rare. The only references to the value of forming and maintaining relationships appeared in disclosure of private facts cases that also implicated the individual liberty and emotional health values for privacy.[29] The Supreme Court of Washington's 1998 ruling in *Reid v. Pierce County* involved the aforementioned societal values as well as individual values. Quoting a 1988 ruling in which the state's highest court recognized privacy under common law, the court wrote:

> Every individual has some phases of his life and his activities and some facts about himself that he does not expose to the public eye, but keeps entirely to himself or at most reveals only to his family or to close personal friends. Sexual relations, for example, are normally entirely private matters, as are family quarrels, many unpleasant or disgraceful or humiliating illnesses, most intimate personal letters, most details of a man's life in his home, and some of his past history that he would rather forget. When these intimate details of his life are spread before the public gaze in a manner highly offensive to the ordinary reasonable man, there is an actionable invasion of his privacy, unless the matter is one of legitimate public interest.[30]

The Court held that the autopsy photographs of the plaintiffs' loved ones were the type of intimate details that people "do not wish exposed" to the public when the images are disclosed to individuals without a genuine public interest. Such unauthorized disclosures of deeply personal information clearly could undermine the societal privacy values of fostering relationships and maintaining civility and community as well as the individual values of autonomy, liberty, and emotional health.

Notably, state high court rulings that overturned summary judgment awards originally granted to defendants implicated more than one privacy value without implicating any audience-based free expression values.[31] For instance, the Supreme Court of Minnesota explicitly connected privacy to personal liberty when it chose to recognize the disclosure of private facts tort in 1998.[32] That ruling also implied that privacy served personal autonomy, which is associated with personal agency and personal identity.[33] In that case, *Lake v. Wal-Mart Stores, Inc.*, the court wrote, "The right to privacy is an integral part of our humanity; one has a public persona, exposed and active, and a private persona, guarded and preserved. The heart of our liberty is choosing which parts of our lives shall become public and which parts we shall hold close."[34] *Lake v. Wal-Mart* assessed whether the corporation was liable for a clerk's unauthorized disclosure of photographs portraying two young, nude women showering together. The Court reasoned, "One's naked body is a very private part of one's person and generally known to others only by choice. This is a type of privacy interest worthy of protection."[35] That ruling assigns special importance to an individual's ability to determine if and how deeply intimate information about one's body is exposed to others, when knowledge of that information would not serve a legitimate public interest.

Acknowledging tensions

If courts mentioned conflicts,[36] clashes,[37] or tensions between freedom of expression and privacy[38] and attempted to reconcile those clashes, they typically applied a form of definitional balancing. Through that approach, they sought to identify a boundary between categories of privileged disclosures and categories of tortious disclosures to determine whether the facts at issue fell into the category of privileged publications or into the category of invasions of privacy.[39] Nine of those cases discussed values undergirding freedom of expression and values undergirding privacy.[40]

Applying the *Florida Star* First Amendment privilege in 2005, the Third Circuit Court of Appeals stated, "There no doubt exists a tension between the First Amendment right to a free press and an individual's statutory and common law right to privacy."[41] The privacy rights asserted in that case, *Bowley v. City of Uniontown Police Department*, pertained to a juvenile arrested on charges he allegedly raped a 7-year-old girl. Bowley argued that the state law required law enforcement officials to keep the identities of juvenile defendants confidential. Regardless of that requirement acknowledging the sensitive and embarrassing nature of such disclosures, the court held that the First Amendment privilege shielded the newspaper from liability for disclosure of private facts. Reports of violent crimes are matters of public importance, thus the audience-based interests in learning about the criminal justice system outweighed the asserted privacy interests of a youngster accused of committing a violent crime.

Rather than engaging in an explicit balancing approach that weighed competing interests, a few courts claimed to balance press freedom and privacy by applying a newsworthiness test that assesses the relevance of disclosed information to "a topic of legitimate public concern."[42] Notably, most rulings that applied a test to assess whether the information at issue was newsworthy, or related to a matter of public interest, found that the liberty-based editorial autonomy value for freedom of expression and audience-based marketplace of ideas and checking function values for freedom of expression could trump any privacy interests at issue.[43] In 1993 when the Georgia Supreme Court asserted that clashes between press freedom and privacy require courts to weigh individuals' privacy rights against the press's right to provide audiences with information,[44] the court indicated that a 1905 Georgia Supreme Court ruling had defined somewhat of an absolute balancing scheme by recognizing privacy was limited by free expression rights.[45]

In 1995, however, the Supreme Court of Texas suggested that information deemed newsworthy by editors was not necessarily protected free expression that audiences have a right to know. Based on the facts of that case, *Star-Telegram, Inc. v. Doe*, the court ruled that a newspaper could not be held liable for invading the privacy of a woman the paper identified as a sexual assault victim in a report on the crime. The court suggested that the public had a right to receive information about the reported commission of that crime,[46] which implied that report served at least one audience-based value for freedom of expression. But the court suggested in dicta that the media have a moral obligation to "take precautions" to ensure they do not reveal sensitive information about crime victims. [47] That court refrained from establishing that legal obligation, however, because such a limitation could chill press freedom.

Disclosure of private facts plaintiffs rarely prevail

Only two rulings in disclosure of private facts cases upheld lower court rulings that found a plaintiff could receive damages for invasion of privacy.[48] One of those opinions was vacated by the same state high court that issued it and was superseded on rehearing by a decision reaching the opposite conclusion.[49] In the other decision, *Zaffuto v. City of Hammond,* the Fifth Circuit Court of Appeals upheld $2 in compensatory damages and remanded the case for a new trial on the amount of punitive damages. [50] In that case, the court weighed the privacy interest of the plaintiff against the defendant's interest in disclosing information and concluded the defendant disclosed information for the purpose of shaming Zaffuto, harming the emotional health that privacy is intended to protect, without serving individual- or audience-based values for freedom of expression.[51] While those rulings did not require defendants to pay steep awards of monetary damages, litigating those rulings required a considerable amount of time and resources.

Summary

Since June 1989, federal circuit courts of appeals' and state high courts' rulings have recognized significant individual and societal values for freedom of expression and for privacy.[52] When courts have acknowledged the potential for freedom of expression and privacy to clash, though, they typically have found the published information was protected under constitutional or common law privileges for matters of public interest associated with audience-based marketplace of ideas, self-governance, or checking function values.[53] Only two opinions, one of which was vacated and superseded, have suggested that free expression interests might yield to individual privacy interests in circumstances that undermine the emotional health and liberty values for privacy without serving a liberty-based or audience-based value for freedom of expression.[54]

Free Expression and Privacy Values in Appropriation Cases

Four state high courts recognized appropriation for the first time during the past twenty years.[55] Although Dean Smolla asserted in 2002 that appropriation is the only area of privacy that "has been a ripping success for plaintiffs,"[56] state high courts and federal circuit courts of appeals only upheld four lower court rulings for appropriation plaintiffs in the invasion of privacy cases identified in this study.[57] Courts also remanded seven cases for further proceedings.[58] One of the rulings remanded for further proceedings involved a news media defendant.[59] In most other cases, however, appellate courts found lower courts had not erred by entering summary judgment orders for defendants or by dismissing plaintiffs' appropriation claims.[60]

Focus on the elements

Almost half the appropriation rulings analyzed in this study turned on the court's determination that a plaintiff failed to satisfy the elements of the tort—commercial use of identity or likeness without proper consent—as a matter of law.[61] Courts found that using a plaintiff's name or photograph in a brochure,[62] flyer,[63] or voicemail message without the plaintiff's implied or explicit consent constitutes an actionable use of identity for trade or advertising purposes.[64] Appellate courts only affirmed lower court awards of damages to plaintiffs when the use at issue promoted a product or service without serving a newsworthy purpose tied to at least one audience-based free expression value.[65]

Implicating free expression values

When examining whether a use of an individual's identity related to a matter of public interest and was, therefore, not a tortious commercial use, courts primarily discussed at least one audience-based free expression value—marketplace of ideas, self-governance, or checking function—or a combination of those values.[66] For instance, the marketplace of ideas, self-governance, and checking values relate to the Supreme Court of New Jersey's rationale that a political campaign flyer's use of the name and image of a man employed by a rival candidate was not an invasion of privacy. In that 2011 ruling in *G.D. v.*

Kenny, the court wrote: "The campaign flyers represented political speech attacking the judgment of a candidate running for public office. This is the type of speech that is at the heart of First Amendment guarantees."[67] The information at issue in that case also related to a public interest because it involved details of G.D.'s criminal conviction revealed in a court of law and open court records before G.D.'s conviction record was expunged.

A few rulings implicated the liberty-based autonomy value for freedom of the press when courts indicated that members of the press must decide what is newsworthy without judicial censorship or second-guessing.[68] For instance, the Supreme Court of Rhode Island's 2004 ruling in *Leddy v. Narragansett Television, L.P.*, tied the protection for the television station's promotion of an investigative news series to the audience-based self-governance and checking values as well as to the liberty-based autonomy value. Finding the television station's use of Leddy's likeness was a privileged incidental use, the court wrote:

> [I]n light of the free-speech considerations at issue in this case, we consider the legal questions raised "against the background of a profound national commitment to the principle that debate on-public issues should be uninhibited, robust, and wide-open." "At the heart of the First Amendment — is the recognition of the fundamental importance of the free flow of ideas and opinions on matters of public interest and concern." And even though we carry no brief for the disreputable aspects of "ambush journalism" — especially when the media focus their attention on relatively low-level government employees and others who do not deserve to bear the brunt of such base antics — it is not our place to serve as the censors of journalistic discretion, so long as the media do not overstep those broad — constitutional lines between which they are allowed considerable room to maneuver.[69]

That rationale relates to several values undergirding free expression that could be perceived as providing the limits of press freedom considering the court's warning that the First Amendment does not provide the press with absolute freedom. That New Jersey Supreme Court ruling scolded the press for challenging societal expectations for the right to be let alone, as did the 1995 Texas Supreme Court ruling involving the disclosure of private facts tort in *Star-Telegram, Inc. v. Doe.*[70]

Implicating privacy values

Appropriation rulings generally implicated the individual privacy values of autonomy, liberty, or emotional health when courts discussed the elements of the tort.[71] Some discussion of plaintiffs' injuries related to the emotional harm factor of the emotional health value.[72] For example, the Colorado Supreme Court ruling in *Dickerson and Associates v. Dittmar* connected the appropriation tort to the autonomy, liberty, and emotional health values for privacy. That was the first Colorado high court ruling to recognize the appropriation tort, thus, the en banc ruling traced the history of the tort back to the landmark Warren and Brandeis article.

> Warren and Brandeis suggested that increased abuses by the press required a remedy that would protect private individuals from mental distress and anguish. They proposed that the right of privacy would protect a person's rights in their appearance, sayings, acts, and personal relations. To Warren and Brandeis, the right of privacy did not involve property so much as the "more general immunity of the person --the right to one's personality." In short, they desired to protect the individual's right "to be let alone."[73]

Looking at other states' acceptance of the tort, the Supreme Court of Colorado stated "it has always been clear that a plaintiff could recover for personal injuries such as mental anguish and injured feelings resulting from an appropriation."[74]

Only two appropriation rulings implied a societal value underlies privacy, the forming and maintaining relationships value.[75] In *Showler v. Harper's Magazine Foundation*, the U.S. Tenth Circuit Court of Appeals stated that images of a deceased soldier at issue in *Showler* involved a magazine photographer's depictions of "the image seen by those who attended his funeral to pay their respects." The court distinguished those images from the types of images at issue when courts have acknowledged a family's privacy rights related to "death-scene images."[76] Autopsy photographs were at issue in the other appropriation ruling that implicated a relational value for privacy. That

1998 Washington Supreme Court ruling in *Reid v. Pierce County* reiterated that the state's common law recognition for the appropriation tort. The court held that "the immediate relatives of a decedent have a protectable privacy interest in the autopsy records of the decedent. That protectable privacy interest is grounded in maintaining the dignity of the deceased."[77] Noting the "egregious" nature of the exploitative use of the autopsy photographs and other death scene images at issue in cases considered invasions of relatives' privacy rights suggests that courts have limited the types of actionable appropriations that harm the societal value of maintaining relationships to extreme cases.[78] Those "egregious," actionable uses exploit a sensitive image in a manner that fails to serve a public interest.

<u>Using definitional boundaries rather than ad hoc balancing</u>

Courts rarely discussed freedom of expression as well as privacy values or engaged in an explicit balancing of interests.[79] A few courts followed the New York Court of Appeals' tendency to treat the public interest privilege or newsworthiness defense as the definitional boundary between freedom of expression rights and privacy rights.[80] Those rulings typically focused on whether the use was a newsworthy one related to a matter of public interest or was "an advertisement in disguise."[81] In *Finger v. Omni Publications International*, The Court of Appeals of New York defined newsworthiness broadly, stating the exception applies "to reports of political happenings and social trends" as well as "to news stories and articles of consumer interest such as developments in the fashion world" and "to matters of scientific and biological interest."[82] In most of cases involving newsworthiness or a public interest, courts suggested that uses of plaintiffs' identities served an informative purpose related to the marketplace of ideas, self-governance, and/or checking function values, and thus the courts did not need to weigh the values undergirding freedom of expression against the values undergirding privacy.[83]

One ruling suggested that privacy rights could limit free speech and press rights provided under different circumstances than those presented by the case.[84] In that per curiam ruling, *Doe v. Roe*, the Supreme Court of Alabama identified general communicator-based and audience-based values for free expression and implied that appropriations that harm individual privacy values, such as liberty and emotional health, could be punished without violating state-based free expression rights if children's identities are used in an exploitative manner unrelated to matters of public interest.

> The court erred in enjoining the distribution of defendant Doe's novel. Doe's freedom of speech is guaranteed by Article I, § 4, of the Alabama Constitution. Although she may not exercise that right in a manner that will injure the children's right to privacy, we do not find that the distribution of this novel, based on events of public interest, will violate that right of the children.[85]

The court concluded that the information at issue was based on details available from records available to the public. Adding that society's interest in the events related to the murder of the children's mother was a matter of public interest, the court stated, "this Court has held that the right to freedom of speech transcends the right to privacy so long as the speech pertains to a matter of public concern."[86]

After *Florida Star*, two state high court rulings indicated that a plaintiff's privacy was invaded by the unauthorized use of his or her identity for advertising purposes when the exploitative uses did not provide information that served a public interest.[87] Those rulings applied a definitional boundary to assess whether the plaintiff's identity was appropriated in a manner that harmed individual liberty, autonomy, or emotional health without benefiting society by contributing to an audience's right to receive information that facilitates discussion or debate of public issues, contributes to self-governance, or checks abuses of power.

Summary

Appropriation rulings primarily have recognized individual values for privacy—liberty, autonomy, and emotional health—and audience-based values for freedom of expression—marketplace of ideas, self-governance, or checking function values.[88] When a use of a person's identity implicated an audience-based value by providing information of a public interest, courts found that use fell on the privileged side of the definitional boundary associated with the newsworthiness exception.[89] Courts ruled in favor of plaintiffs only when the uses of their identities harmed individual privacy values without promoting free-expression values associated with audiences' rights to receive information on matters of public interest.[90]

Reconciling Conflicts between Free Expression and Privacy Values

Since the majority ruling in *Florida Star* asserted that free expression and privacy interests are important,[91] few state high courts and federal circuit courts of appeals have explicitly balanced privacy and free expression values.[92] Rather, courts consistently have focused on the privileges for publishing matters of legitimate concern or interest to the public and the elements of the disclosure of private facts tort or appropriation tort.[93] That tendency suggests that courts have assumed that the decades of precedent that defined common law and constitutional principles law as mechanisms that strike a proper balance between the right to publish and the right to privacy,[94] both of which are undergirded by fundamental democratic values. During the past twenty-two years, however, courts have conceptualized the boundaries for free expression and privacy in a manner that has allowed the constitutional right to publish to trump common law privacy rights in most appeals involving the invasion of privacy under a disclosure or appropriation theory.[95]

<u>Identifying a boundary in disclosure cases</u>

In disclosure of private facts cases, courts relied almost exclusively on whether the disclosed information related to a matter of public concern or significance, making the disclosure privileged under the First Amendment standards created by the Supreme Court's rulings in *Cox Broadcasting v. Cohn* and *Florida Star.*[96] For instance, in 2003, the Supreme Court of Idaho reasoned that a newspaper's publication of a document found in a twenty-year old court record was privileged because the First Amendment prohibited a state from sanctioning a media defendant for publishing information found in a record available to the public.

In fact, some rulings that determined the disclosed information related to a public concern did not even discuss the elements of the tort, much less the values undergirding the tort. Those rulings suggested the First Amendment privileges have provided a categorical boundary for constitutional rights that necessarily supersede privacy rights. That tendency supports legal scholars' assertions that lower courts could use the *Florida Star* ruling to focus on free expression rights and negate privacy rights.[97]

Notably, the only post-*Florida Star* award of damages to a disclosure of private facts plaintiff upheld on appeal did not apply the constitutional privilege nor did it apply the element of the tort some states have recognized that exempts disclosures of legitimate matters of public concern from liability. In *Zaffuto v. City of Hammond*, the Fifth Circuit Court of Appeals applied a balancing test recognized under Louisiana's disclosure tort.[98] The court found an assistant police chief invaded the privacy of a police sergeant and the sergeant's wife by recording and replaying one of the couple's private telephone conversations about the police sergeant's approval of "a controversial department restructuring."[99] In some contexts, commentary on the restructuring of a police department could be connected to the self-governance, checking value, or marketplace of ideas values for free expression. That ruling, however, was limited to considering whether a lower court erred in its application of Louisiana's reasonableness test, which assesses "the reasonableness of the defendant's conduct [] by balancing the plaintiff's interest in protecting his privacy from serious invasions with the defendant's interest in pursuing his course of conduct."[100] Reasoning that the defendant had no legitimate interest in disclosing that information other than to benefit the defendant, the court upheld a $2 award of compensatory damages and remanded the case for trial on punitive damages. That ruling focused on the intentional nature of the tort, examining whether a defendant's motivation for the disclosure could justify harming the plaintiff's privacy interests.[101] The rationale, which focuses on audience-based free expression values, shifts traditional conceptions of speech freedom that focused on benefits to the communicator as well as to message recipients.

Identifying a boundary in appropriation claims

Not surprisingly, state high courts and federal circuit courts awarded damages more often in appropriation cases involving commercial speech than in disclosure of private facts cases.[102] The U.S. Supreme Court established in a 1976 ruling in *Virginia Board of Pharmacy v. Virginia Consumer Council* that commercial speech, which does no more than promote the sale of a product or service and is true and not misleading, receives limited First Amendment protection,[103] less than would be extended to the truthful publication of news. Whereas the constitutional protection for publications of matters of public interest is grounded in the audience-based model's acknowledgement of benefits to information recipients and the liberty-based model's acknowledgement of benefits for communicators and audiences,[104] the constitutional protection for commercial speech is tied to the audience-based model.[105] Restricting that protection to the ability of information to benefit audiences has allowed courts to exclude false or misleading communications from the scope of constitutional protection. Thus, when unauthorized uses of plaintiffs' identities mislead audiences by inaccurately implying that plaintiffs are promoting a product or service, those uses fall outside the scope of constitutional protection.[106]

Courts often focused on the primary purpose for any use of a plaintiff's identity when determining whether an alleged appropriation was privileged.[107] If the purpose for using a plaintiff's name or likeness related to a matter of public interest, those uses were protected under common law or constitutional privileges.[108] The rulings that were not privileged, however, were considered exploitative uses or uses that primarily were intended to benefit the communicator in a manner that provided minimal, if any, benefit to others.[109] Those rulings, accordingly, respected the boundaries for constitutional protection in a manner that prevented defendants from paying damages for accidental, or unintended, uses of others' names or identities.

Not all appropriation claims, however, involve protected commercial speech that receives less First Amendment protection than political or newsworthy publications receive. To limit successful claims to those involving a knowingly exploitative unauthorized use of a plaintiff's identity, courts should consider adding a provision to the unauthorized use element that assess whether a defendant intentionally used a name or likeness for a purpose that benefits the defendant while providing little or no benefit to the plaintiff or the public. That requirement would parallel the recklessness element that the Supreme Court of Colorado adopted for the disclosure tort in 1997.[110]

Summary

Courts consistently have used the elements of the disclosure and appropriation torts and the newsworthiness defenses or public interest privileges to identify definitional boundaries between publicity associated with the right to publish and abuses of that right.[111] On one hand, those legal principles indicate that the right to publish and the right to privacy are both important for a democratic society. On the other, the tendency for courts to focus frequently on newsworthiness or the public interest served by a disclosure or use could threaten to develop tunnel vision that prevents courts from seeing potential mechanisms for reconciling future conflicts between press and privacy rights.

Suggestions for Reconciling Future Conflicts

Combining key principles from the individual-based liberty model and the audience-based model for free expression may provide courts with a viable mechanism for reconciling future conflicts. Slight modifications of the "Millian principle" from the liberty model ought to guide courts' future attempts to reconcile clashes among free expression interests and either individual or societal privacy interests.[112]

The "Millian principle" 3.0

As mentioned in chapter two, nineteenth century philosopher John Stuart Mill argued that "'[t]he only purpose for which power can be rightfully exercised over any member of a civilized community, against his will, is to prevent *harm to others*.'"[113] That approach focuses on personal autonomy. Thomas Scanlon, a legal philosopher, narrowed that premise when he proposed a "Millian principle" for an individual liberty model of freedom of expression that emphasized the agency of individuals.[114] Scanlon's principle indicates that restrictions on expression cannot be justified when the restrictions provide redress for harm to an injured individual whose own actions or beliefs contributed to the harm. That principle focuses on the autonomy of the injured party — a step that ought to be added to the autonomy-based approach taken by some courts.

A couple of courts that associated speech and privacy rights with liberty indicated that individuals' freedom to express themselves may end at the point that the expression intentionally would seriously harm an individual's privacy.[115] Their rationales focus on the agency of a communicator, limiting courts' ability to uphold an award of damages for an appropriation plaintiff to cases in which the intentionally exploitative use of the plaintiff's name or likeness fell outside the scope of protected expression.[116] Similarly, the agency of a communicator undergirds the recklessness element the Supreme Court of Colorado added to the disclosure tort to limit successful disclosure of facts claims to those in which a plaintiff can demonstrate a defendant's knowing disclosure of private facts.[117] That element parallels the element of intentionally exploitation required for appropriation claims.[118] Courts in each state recognizing the disclosure or appropriation tort should add those elements to ensure the torts respect the autonomy of a defendant as well as the autonomy of a plaintiff. Protecting the autonomy of both parties is necessary when applying a modified liberty-based approach to ensure freedom of expression is not unduly limited.

The audience-based model for free expression

Many post-*Florida Star* rulings have emphasized the free expression values associated with informing audiences.[119] Their approaches suggested that publishing information that serves First Amendment values could outweigh privacy values.[120] Some courts have indicated that defendants' disclosures of information about plaintiffs or defendants' uses of plaintiffs' identities were privileged because the publicized information encouraged a free flow of information or provided audiences with details that would foster discussion and debate, self-governance, and checking the power of government.[121] Those rulings primarily focus on a democratic society's need for information that serves as a check on government, enables self-governance, or improves the free flow of information imperative for a vital marketplace of ideas.

This study found that post-*Florida Star* state high courts and federal circuit courts of appeals rulings only upheld awards of damages for plaintiffs when publicity was given to sensitive information and when uses of identity conflicted with individual privacy values—liberty, autonomy, or emotional health—but did not serve any audience-based First Amendment values.[122] Although those rulings suggest that the audience-based values of self-governance, marketplace of ideas, and checking-function values can provide strong audience-based justification for publicizing certain information, some information currently publicized by the press or individuals does not relate to those values. Connecting freedom of expression to specific audience-based needs or desires ultimately could justify limits for freedom of expression, especially at a time when technology allows individuals to disseminate information to mass audiences in a manner that can meet the threshold element of publicity.

Applying a modified Millian approach

Freedom of expression ultimately may receive stronger protection from the First Amendment if courts focus on a modified Millian principle for freedom of expression rather than the potential for expression to serve at least one audience-based value.[123] Focusing on the liberty or autonomy of a communicator would not prevent courts from sanctioning abuses of freedom of expression in which information was publicized to knowingly harm a plaintiff or exploit a plaintiff's identity. Such an approach, however, could limit successful disclosure of private facts and appropriation cases to extreme cases in which an individual or institution knowingly harmed the plaintiff's autonomy, liberty, or emotional well-being. Accepting that limitation on freedom of speech and press would require courts to acknowledge harm to privacy in a manner that does not chill freedom of expression.

Some rulings in this study suggest a strong need exists for a clear, realistic boundary between the rights of privacy plaintiffs and the rights of media defendants. Those rulings reflect growing societal concerns about threats to privacy posed by unauthorized disclosures of intimate details regarding adults' medical conditions,[124] photographs of naked teenagers,[125] reports on individuals' sexual activity,[126] and uses of individuals' identities.[127] Such extreme cases typically involve publicity provided by individuals rather than traditional media defendants, but recent technological innovations have allowed individuals to disclose those intimate details to mass audiences, as the press primarily was able to do when Samuel D. Warren and Louis D. Brandeis called for greater legal protection for privacy in 1890.[128] As Warren and Brandeis sought to draw legal and moral distinctions among publications that were newsworthy and publications that defied standards of ordinary decency, the approach proposed by the current study suggests judges and communicators could distinguish between publicity provided in a manner that might serve at least one personal liberty-based or audience-based free expression value and publicity knowingly provided to harm privacy that intentionally undermines the liberty, autonomy, or emotional well-being of an identified individual.

Suggestions for the press

The modified Millian approach emphasizes personal agency and autonomy. The findings of this study accordingly suggest that publishers might benefit from asking several questions before they share communications with multiple recipients. First, a communicator should ask whether a communication is likely to benefit intended message recipients less than the sender. If the communication primarily will benefit the sender without benefiting recipients by serving an audience-based value for free expression—marketplace of ideas, self-governance, or checking function—the communication might fall outside the scope of constitutional protection from liability in an invasion of privacy claim. Second, the communicator should ask whether the communication is likely to harm any person identified in the communication. If the communication is likely to cause harm that conflicts with individual values for privacy—liberty, autonomy, or emotional health—or social values for privacy—forming relationships or promoting community and civility—the communication might lead to a successful invasion of privacy claim. Third, the communicator should ask whether the intent of the communication is closely tied to harming a person identified in the communication. Intentional wrongdoing could increase the likelihood that the communication would lead to a successful invasion of privacy claim, especially if the communication exposes a person identified in the communication to emotional harm or undermines that person's sense of autonomy, dignity, or liberty. Providing affirmative answers to at least two of those inquiries will indicate a communication may lead to a successful invasion of privacy claim under the standards applied during the past twenty-two years.

Suggestions for the nation's highest court

The U.S. Supreme Court also should consider taking action to provide greater clarity in this area. Now that individual communicators instantly can transmit information to mass audiences, individuals may more easily give widespread publicity to another's private information or use another's name or likeness to their own benefit. The Court's rulings involving disclosure of private facts and appropriation provide little guidance for individuals who widely publicize information because the rulings focus on news media's rights to disseminate information related to the audience-based self-governance and checking function values. *Cox Broadcasting* and *Florida Star*, however, do not clearly extend First Amendment protection to communications that serve a marketplace of ideas value or to individual free expression values without serving the self-governance and checking function values.[129]

State high courts and federal circuit courts of appeals rulings analyzed for this study have demonstrated a willingness to protect communications that serve a marketplace of ideas or an editorial autonomy value for free expression.[130] This study found that plaintiffs rarely win on appeal. The courts only ruled in favor of plaintiffs in cases involving non-media defendants who publicized matters not considered to be of public interest—matters that could relate to the marketplace of ideas or editorial autonomy values for free expression as well as the self-governance and checking function values.[131]

Those findings suggest the U.S. Supreme Court should accept an invasion of privacy case involving a non-media defendant and a matter of public or general interest. In that case, the Court could establish a clear constitutional privilege for individuals and for news media to freely publicize matters of public interest, a privilege undergirded by the individual autonomy value and the audience-based marketplace of ideas, self-governance, and checking-function values. Courts across the nation, then, would have to apply that broad constitutional privilege to strike a proper balance between the right to publish and the right to privacy.

As that privilege will appear to broaden the scope of protection for free expression, the Court should clarify that the disclosure of private facts and appropriation torts are not facially unconstitutional. The Court may justify the constitutionality of those torts by requiring disclosure and appropriation plaintiffs to satisfy a constitutional fault level similar to the actual malice fault level required for defamation cases involving media defendants.[132] In *Zaffuto v. City of Hammond*, the Fifth Circuit Court of Appeals focused on the intentional and unreasonable nature of an assistant police chief's disclosure of a phone conversation, which Terry Zaffuto and his wife assumed was private.[133] In *Town & Country Properties, Inc. v. Riggins*, the Supreme Court of Virginia indicated that a former professional football player's name was used in a manner intended to benefit an advertiser without providing message recipients with information that would help them make a decision about whether to purchase the advertised product.[134] Both of those rulings indicated that a plaintiff could prevail when a defendant intended to use another's sensitive, personal information or identity in a manner that would benefit the communicator without providing message recipients with information a reasonable person would relate to public health, public safety, public policies, or social awareness or with information that would help recipients make decisions related to the disclosed subject matter.

Under the new privilege, a plaintiff can only satisfy the recommended constitutional level of fault by proving that the defendant: 1) intentionally used another's sensitive, personal information or identity; 2) solely to the benefit of the defendant; 3) because the use did not benefit message recipients by providing information related to public health, public safety, public policies, or social awareness or providing accurate information that would help recipients make at least one decision about the advertised or publicized subject matter. A Supreme Court ruling adopting that privilege could clarify how lower courts must conceptualize the boundaries between the right to publish and the right to privacy in a manner that protects fundamental democratic values undergirding freedom of expression as well as privacy. The need for such a ruling likely will increase in a digital age when individuals can publish messages for mass audiences once only reached by news media.

Summary

This study found minimal balancing in state high courts' and federal circuit courts of appeals' rulings in disclosure and appropriation cases during the past twenty-two years.[135] Some courts indicated that they balanced free expression and privacy by applying newsworthiness tests.[136] Most cases implied that elements of the torts and the newsworthiness defense struck an appropriate balance between the right to publish and the right to privacy.[137] And some rulings discussed free expression values—autonomy, marketplace of ideas, self-governance, and checking function—in relation to the newsworthiness defense.[138]

The rationales from some rulings focused on respecting the constitutional boundaries for protection of freedom of expression.[139] In an unpublished ruling, the Supreme Court of Idaho indicated that taking another approach would limit speech and "shackle the First Amendment."[140] Other courts indicated that defendants' disclosures of information about plaintiffs or defendants' uses of plaintiffs' identities were privileged because the publicized information encouraged a free flow of information or provided audiences with details that would foster discussion and debate, self-governance, and checking the power of government.[141] Their approaches suggested that publishing information that served First Amendment values could outweigh potential harm to privacy values.[142] Indeed, courts rarely upheld awards of damages for plaintiffs. Awards of damages only were upheld when publicity was given to extremely sensitive information and when uses of identity conflicted with individual privacy values—liberty, autonomy, or emotional health—without serving any audience-based First Amendment values.[143]

Courts' conceptualization of boundaries between free expression and privacy rights has demonstrated the supremacy of constitutional law over common law. During the past twenty-two years, state high court and federal circuit court of appeals rulings only upheld awards of damages for common law invasions of privacy when claims involved an abuse of constitutional rights or a lack of constitutional rights.[144] That tendency has allowed few plaintiffs to recover for invasion of privacy. Still, invasion of privacy claims may chill freedom of expression if the area of law lacks further clarity. The U.S. Supreme Court should accept an invasion of private facts and an appropriation case involving a non-news media defendant to establish a constitutional privilege that clearly applies to media as well as to non-media defendants' publication of matters of public or general interest. In that ruling, the Court should adopt a constitutional fault level that limits successful disclosure of private facts and appropriation claims to those involving abuses of free expression rights that knowingly or intentionally harm the plaintiff in a manner that undermines key individual or societal values for privacy.

Chapter 5 Notes

---

[1] 491 U.S. 524 (1989). *See, e.g.*, Joe Dickerson & Assoc. v. Dittmar, 34 P.3d 995, 997 (Colo. 2001) (en banc); Ozer v. Borquez, 940 P.2d 371, 379 (Colo. 1997) (en banc); Lake v. Wal-Mart Stores, Inc., 582 N.W.2d 231, 235 (Minn. 1998) (en banc); Remsburg v. Docusearch, Inc., 816 A.2d 1001, 1009-10 (N.H. 2003); Karch v. Baybank, 794 A.2d 763, 774 (N.H. 2002); Staruski v. Cont'l Tel. Co. of Vermont, 581 A.2d 266, 269 (Vermont 1990).

[2] 491 U.S. 524 (1989).

[3] *See, e.g.*, Spilfogel v. Cox Broad. Co., No. 10-12507, *4 (11th Cir. July 5, 2011); Equal Employment Opportunity Comm'n v. C.R. England, Inc., 2011 U.S. App. LEXIS 8971, No. 09-4207, at *72 (10th Cir. 2011); Boring v. Google Inc., 362 Fed. App'x. 273, 278-80 (3d Cir. 2010); Alvarado v. KOB-TV, 492 F.3d 1210, 1219-21 (10th Cir. 2007); Anderson v. Suiters, 499 F.3d 1228, 1235-37 (10th Cir. 2007); Baldwin v. Blue Cross/Blue Shield of Alabama, 480 F.3d 1287, 1308-09 (11th. Cir. 2007); Lowe v. Hearst Newspapers P'ship L.P., 497 F.3d 246, 251-52 (5th Cir. 2007); Karraker v. Rent-A-Center, Inc., 411 F.3d 831, 838 (7th Cir. 2005); Doe 2 v. Associated Press, 331 F.3d 417, 421 (4th Cir. 2003); Dasey v. Anderson, 304 F.3d 148 (1st Cir. 2002) (citing Mass.Gen.Laws ch. 214 § 1B); Green v. CBS Inc., 286 F.3d 281, 283 (5th Cir. 2002); Willan v. Columbia Cnty, 280 F.3d 1160, 1162 (7th Cir. 2002); Zaffuto v. City of Hammond, 308 F.3d 485, 491 (5th Cir. 2002); Phillips v. Grendahl, 312 F.3d 357, 371-72 (8th Cir. 2001); Campbell v. Lyon, 26 Fed. App'x 183, 186 (4th Cir. 2001)(unpublished per curiam); Parry v. Mohawk Motors of Mich., Inc., 236 F.3d 299, 313 (6th Cir. 2000); Veilleux v. Nat'l Broad. Co., 206 F.3d 92, 107 (1st Cir. 2000); Dickinson v. Chitwood, No. 98-1446, 1998 U.S. App'x LEXIS 32569, at *6-7 (1st Cir. 1998); Coplin v. Fairfield Pub. Access Television Comm., 111 F.3d 1395, 1405-06 (8th Cir. 1997); Roe v. Cheyenne Mountain Conference Resort, Inc., 124 F.3d 1221, 1236 (10th Cir. 1997), *appeal after remand*, 127 F.3d 879 (10th Cir. 1999); Howell v. Tribune Entm't Co., 106 F.3d 215, 220 (7th Cir. 1997); McNewmar v. Disney Store, Inc., 91 F.3d 610, 622 (3d Cir. 1996); Johnson v. Sawyer, 47 F.3d 716, 731-33 (5th Cir. 1995)(en banc); Cinel v. Connick, 15 F.3d 1338, 1346 (5th Cir. 1994); Merlo v. United Way of Am., 43 F.3d 96, 104 (4th Cir. 1994); Tichenor v. Roman Catholic Church, 32 F.3d 953, 963 (5th Cir. 1994); Haynes v. Alfred A. Knopf, Inc., 8 F.3d 1222, 1232-35 (7th Cir. 1993); Thomas v. Pearl, 998 F.2d 447, 452 (7th Cir. 1993); Lee v. Calhoun, 948 F.2d 1162, 1165 (10th Cir. 1991); S.B. v. St. James Sch., 959 So. 2d 72, 91-92 (Ala. 2006); Rosen v. Montgomery Surgical Ctr., 825 So.2d 735, 739 (Ala. 2001); *Ex parte* The Birmingham News, Inc., 778 So.2d 814, 818-19 (Ala. 2000); Finebaum v. Coulter, 854 So. 1120, 1129 (Ala. 2003); Johnston v. Fuller, 706 So.2d 700, 703 (Ala. 1997); Milam v. Bank of Cabot, 937 S.E.3d 653 (Ark. 1997); Taus v. Loftus, 151 P.3d 1185, 1208-09 (Cal. 2007); Gates v. Discovery Commc'ns, Inc.,

101 P.3d 553, 562-63 (Cal. 2005); Barker v. Huang, 610 A.2d 1341, 1350 (Del. 1991); *Ozer*, 940 P.2d at 377; Elliott v. Healthcare Corp., 629 A.2d 6, 9 (D.C. 1993); Cape Publ'ns, Inc. v. Hitchner, 549 So. 2d 1374, 1378-79 (Fla. 1989); Macon Telegraph v. Tatum, 6 S.E.2d 655, 657 (Ga. 1993); Nation v. State of Idaho Dept. of Corrections, 158 P.3d 953, 967 (Idaho 2007); Doe v. Haw, 2003 WL 21015143, at *6 (Idaho Feb, 5 2003)(unpublished); Uranga v. Federated Publ'ns, No. 27118, at *26-27 (2001 LEXIS) (Idaho June 21, 2001) (unpublished), *superseded by* Uranga v. Federated Publ'ns, Inc. v. Idaho Statesman, 67 P.3d 29, 35 (Idaho 2003); Hoskins v. Howard, 971 P.2d 1135, 1142 (Idaho 1998); Doe v. Methodist Hosp., 690 N.E.2d 681, 691 (Ind. 1997) (plurality); Loe v. Town of Thomaston, 600 A.2d 1090, 1093 (Me. 1991); Ayash v. Dana-Farber Cancer Inst., 822 N.E.2d 667, 682-84 (Mass. 2005); Mulgrew v. City of Taunton, 574 N.E.2d 389, 393 (Mass. 1991); Warner-Lambert Co. v. Execuquest Corp., 691 N.E.2d 545, 548 (Mass. 1998) (stating that a corporation does not have a right to privacy); Gauthier v. Police Comm'r of Boston, 557 N.E.2d 1374, 1376 (Mass. 1990); Bodah v. Lakeville Motor Express, Inc., 663 N.W.2d 550, 551-58 (Minn. 2003); *Lake*, 582 N.W.2d at 235; Young v. Jackson, 572 So.2d 378, 384-85 (Miss. 1990); Nazeri v. Missouri Valley Coll., 860 S.W.2d 303, 303 (Mo. 1993); Svaldi v. Anaconda-Deer Lodge County, 106 P.3d 548, 553 (Mont. 2005); Lovejoy v. Linehan, 161 N.H. 483, 486, No. 2010-343 (N.H. 2011); Karch v. Baybank, 794 A.2d 763, 774 (N.H. 2002); G.D. v. Kenny, 15 A.3d 300, 309-10 (N.J. 2011); Howell v. New York Post Co., Inc., 612 N.E.2d 699, 703 (N.Y. 1993); Hadnot v. Shaw, 826 P.2d 978, 986 (Okla. 1992); Burger v. Blair, 964 A.2d 374, 380 (Pa. 2009); Lamarque v. Centreville Savings Bank, No. 2010-67, 2011 R.I. LEXIS 86, at *11(R.I. 2011); Swerdlick v. Koch, 721 A.2d 849, 859 (R.I. 1998); Pontbriand v. Sundlun, 699 A.2d 856, 864 (R.I. 1997); Swinton Creek Nursery v. Edisto Farm Credit, 514 S.E.2d 126, 131-32 (S.C. 1999); Doe v. Berkeley Publishers, 496 S.E.2d 636, 637 (S.C. 1998); Shattuck-Owen v. Snowbird Corp., 16 P.3d 555, 558 (Utah, 2000).

[4] *See, e.g.*, Spiegel v. Schulmann, 604 F.3d 72, 77-78 (2d. 2010) (per curiam); Dan Tana v. Dantanna's CNN Center, 611 F.3d 767, 783 (11th Cir. 2010); Rivell v. Private Health Care Sys., Inc., 520 F.3d 1308, 1310 (11th Cir., 2008) (per curiam); Christian Broad. Network, Inc. v. Busch, 254 Fed. App'x 957, 958 (4th Cir. 2007) (per curiam) (unpublished); Showler v. Harper's Magazine Found., 222 Fed. App'x 755, 759 (10th Cir. 2007) (unpublished); King v. PA Consulting Group, Inc., 485 F.3d 577, 593 (10th Cir. 2007); Zarrilli v. John Hancock Life Ins. Co., 231 Fed. App'x 122, 123-25 (3d Cir. 2007) (per curiam) (unpublished); Meadows v. Hartford life Ins. Co., 492 F.3d 634, 637 (5th Cir. 2007); Botts v. New York Times, 106 Fed. App'x, 109, 110 (3d. Cir., 2004) (unpublished); Solano v. Playgirl, Inc., 292 F.3d 1078, 1080-82 (9th Cir. 2002); Matthews v. Wozencraft, 15 F.3d 432,

436 (5th Cir. 1994); Am. Guar. & Liability Ins. Co. v. 1906 Co., 273 F.3d 605, 608 (5th Cir. 2001); Brown v. Ames, 201 F.3d 654, 661-62 (5th Cir. 2000), *rehearing denied,* 2000 U.S. App. LEXIS 5632 (2000); Downing v. Abercrombie & Fitch, 256F.3d 994 (9th Cir. 2001); Williams v. Newsweek, No. 99-7243, 1999 U.S. App. LEXIS 347, at *1-2 (4th Cir. 1999) (per curiam), cert. denied, 530 U.S. 1279 (2000); Newcombe v. Adolf Coors Co., 157 F.3d 686, 693 (9th Cir. 1998); Groden v. Random House, Inc., 61 F.3d 1045, 1049 (2d. Cir. 1995); Matthews v. Wozencraft, 15 F.3d 432, 436 (5th Cir. 1994); Bowling v. Bowling, No. 91-5920, 1992 U.S. App. LEXIS 18505, at *2 (6th Cir. 1992)(unpublished) (per curiam); Puckett v. Am. Broad. Companies, 1990 U.S. App'x LEXIS 19761, at *7-8 (6th Cir. 1990) (unpublished); Lusby v. Cincinnati Magazine, No. 89-3854, 1990 U.S. App. LEXIS 9144, at *7 (6th Cir. 1990) (unpublished); Doe v. Roe, 638 So. 2d 826, 828-30 (Ala. 1994) (per curiam); Schifano v. Greene County Greyhound Park, Inc., 624 So. 2d 178, 179 (Ala. 1993); Baker v. State Farm General Insurance Co., 585 So. 2d. 804, 807-08 (Ala. 1991); Christoff v. Nestle USA, Inc., 213 P.3d 132, 133-36 (Cal. 2009); *Joe Dickerson & Assoc.*, 34 P.3d at 997; Tyne v. Time Warner Ent. Co., 901 So.2d 802, 809-810 (Fla. 2005), *aff'd,* 425 F.3d 1363, 1364 (11th Cir. 2005) (per curiam); Felsher v. Univ. of Evansville, 755 N.E.2d 589, 599 (Ind. 2001); Tannenbaum v. Grady, 604 N.E.2d 16, 16 (Mass. 1992); Simpson v. Central Maine Motors, Inc., 669 A.2d 1324, 1326 (Me. 1996); *Lake*, 582 N.W.2d at 236; Nemani v. St. Louis Univ., 33 S.W.3d 184, 187 (Mo. 2000), *cert. denied*, 532 U.S. 981 (2001); Wilkinson v. Methodist, 612 N.W.2d 213, 216 (Neb. 2000); Miller v. Am. Sports Co., Inc., 467 N.W.2d 653, 656 (Neb. 1991); PETA v. Bobby Berosini, Ltd., 895 P.2d 1269, 1283-85 (Nev. 1995); Thompson v. C & C Research & Dev., 898 A.2d 495, 499-500 (N.H. 2006); *Remsburg*, 816 A.2d at 1009-10; *G.D.*, 15 A.3d at 304; Messenger v. Gruner + Jahr Printing, 727 N.E.2d 549, 552-54 (N.Y. 2000) (per curiam); Howell v. New York Post Co., Inc., 612 N.E.2d 699, 701(N.Y. 1993); Finger v. Omni Publ'ns Int'l, Ltd., 566 N.E.2d 141, 144 (N.Y. 1991); Beverley v. Choices Women's Med. Ctr, Inc., 587 N.E.2d 275, 279 (N.Y. 1991); Hougum v. Valley Memorial Homes, 574 N.W.2d 812 (N.D. 1998); Leddy v. Narragansett Television, L.P., 843 A.2d 481, 490-91 (R.I. 2004); Gignilliat v. Gignilliat, Savitz & Bettis, L.L.P., 684 S.E.2d 756 (S.C. 2009); Sloan v. South Carolina Dept. of Pub. Safety, 586 S.E.2d 108, 108 (S.C. 2003); PTS Corp. v. Buckman, 263 Va. 613, 621-22 (Va. 2002); WJLA v. Levin, 564 S.E.2d 383, 395-396 (Va. 2002); Town & Country Props., Inc., v. Riggins, 457 S.E.2d 356, 362-64 (Va. 1995); *Staruski*, 581 A.2d at 269; Reid v. Pierce County, 961 P.2d 333, 339 (Wash. 1998) (en banc).

[5] *See, e.g.*, Showler v. Harper's Magazine Found., 222 Fed. App'x 755, 759-64 (10th Cir. 2007); King v. PA Consulting Group, Inc., 485 F.3d 577, 591-92 (10th Cir. 2007); Alvarado v. KOB-TV, 492 F.3d 1210, 1219-21 (10th Cir. 2007); Lowe v. Hearst Newspapers P'ship L.P., 497 F.3d 246, 251-52 (5th

Cir. 2007); Bowley v. City of Uniontown Police Dep't., 404 F.3d 783, at 787-88 (3d Cir. 2005); Doe 2 v. Associated Press, 331 F.3d 417, 421 (4th Cir. 2003); Willan v. Columbia County, 280 F.3d 1160, 1163 (7th Cir. 2002); Brown v. Ames, 201 F.3d 654, 658 (5th Cir. 2000); Howell v. Tribune Entm't Co., 106 F.3d 215, 220 (7th Cir. 1997); Coplin v. Fairfield Pub. Access, 111 F.3d 1395, 1404 (8th Cir. 1997); Groden v. Random House, Inc., 61 F.3d 1045, 1051 (2d Cir. 1995); *Matthews*, 15 F.3d at 440; Reuber v. Food Chem. News, Inc., 925 F.2d 703, 719-21 (4th Cir. 1991); Lusby v. Cincinnati Magazine, No. 89-3854, 1990 U.S. App. LEXIS 9144, *7 (6th Cir. 1990) (unpublished); Taus v. Loftus, 151 P.3d 1185, 1208-09 (Cal. 2007); Gates v. Discovery Commc'ns, Inc., 101 P.3d 553, 562-63 (Cal. 2005); Shulman v. Group W. Prod., Inc., 955 P.2d 469, 486 (Cal. 1998) (plurality); Dickerson & Assoc., LLC v. Dittmar, 34 P.3d 995, 998-1001 (Colo. 2001); Ozer v. Borquez, 940 P.2d 371, 378 (Colo. 1997) (en banc); Cape Publ'ns, Inc. v. Hitchner, 549 So. 2d 1374, 1378-79 (Fla. 1989); Macon Telegraph v. Tatum, 6 S.E.2d 655, 657 (Ga. 1993); Uranga v. Federated Publ'ns, Inc., 67 P.3d 29, 34-6 (Idaho 2003); Felsher v. Univ. of Evansville, 755 N.E.2d 589, 600-01 (Ind. 2001); Young v. Jackson, 572 So.2d 378, 384-85 (Miss. 1990); Svaldi v. Anaconda-Deer Lodge County, 106 P.3d 548, 552-53 (Mont. 2005); Messenger v. Gruner + Jahr Printing, 727 N.E.2d 549, 552-54 (N.Y. 2000) (per curiam); Howell v. New York Post Co., Inc., 612 N.E.2d 699 (N.Y. 1993); Finger v. Omni Pub. Int'l, Ltd., 566 N.E.2d 141, 143 (N.Y. 1991); Beverley v. Choices Women's Med. Ctr, Inc., 587 N.E.2d 275, 279 (N.Y. 1991); Leddy v. Naragansett Television, L.P., 843 A.2d 481, 490-91 (R.I. 2004); WJLA v. Levin, 564 S.E.2d 383, 395 (Va. 2002); Town & Country Props., Inc. v. Riggins, 457 S.E.2d 356, 361-62 (Va. 1995).

[6] 491 U.S. at 532.

[7] *Id.* at 532.

[8] *See, e.g., Shulman*, 955 P.2d at 486; *Dickerson & Assoc.*, 34 P.3d at 998-1000; *Ozer*, 940 P.2d at 378; *Macon Telegraph*, 6 S.E.2d at 657-58; *Messenger*, 727 N.E.2d at 552-54; *Howell*, 612 N.E.2d at 703. *See also*, Rodney A. Smolla, *Accounting for the Slow Growth of American Privacy Law*, 27 NOVA L. REV. 289, 289 (2002).

[9] *See generally*, Edward J. Bloustein, *The First Amendment and Privacy: The Supreme Court Justice and the Philosopher*, 28 RUTGERS L. REV. 41 (1974).

[10] *See, e.g., Lowe*, 497 F.3d at 251-52; *Doe 2*, 331 F.3d at 421; *Willan*, 280 F.3d at 1163; *Howell*, 106 F.3d at 220; *Coplin*, 111 F.3d at 1404; *Reuber*, 925 F.2d at 719-21; *Gates*, 101 P.3d at 562-63; *Cape Publ'ns, Inc.*, 549 So. 2d at 1378-79; *Uranga*, 67 P.3d at 34-6; *Doe*, 2003 WL at 21015134.

[11] *See, e.g., Doe 2*, 331 F.3d at 417-21; Amorossi, 931 A.2d at 929; *Ayash*, 822 N.E.2d at 682-83; *Bodah*, 663 N.W.2d at 553-54; *Lake*, 582 N.W.2d at 235;

Pontbriand, 699 A.2d at 866; *Swinton Creek Nursery*, 514 S.E.2d at 126); *Star-Telegram, Inc.*, 915 S.W.2d at 473.

[12] *Shulman*, 955 P.2d at 486; *Ozer*, 940 P.2d at 378; *Macon Telegraph*, 6 S.E.2d at 657; Uranga v. Federated Publ'ns, No. 27118, 2001 Ida. LEXIS 71, *26-27 (June 21) (unpublished), *vacated and superseded on rehearing by* 67 P.3d 29, 35 (Idaho 2003).

[13] *See, e.g.*, *Steinbuch*, 518 F.3d at 591; *Karraker*, 411 F.3d at 838; *Willan*, 280 F.3d at 1162; *Veilleux*, 206 F.3d at 132-33; *Parry*, 236 F.3d at 313; *Roe*, 124 F.3d at 1236; *McNewmar*, 91 F.3d at 622; *Cinel*, 15 F.3d at 1346; *Thomas*, 998 F.2d at 452; *Haynes*, 8 F.3d at 1232-35; *Reuber*, 925 F.2d at 703; *Lee*, 948 F.2d at 1165; *S.B.*, 959 So. 2d at 91-92; *Rosen*, 825 So. 2d at 739; *Johnston*, 706 So. 2d at 703; *Taus*, 151 P.3d at 1207-08; *Elliott*, 629 A.2d at 9; *Ayash*, 822 N.E.2d at 682-84; *Mulgrew*, 574 N.E.2d at 393; *Gauthier*, 557 N.E.2d at 1376; *Loe*, 600 A.2d at 1093; *Bodah*, 663 N.W.2d at 551-58; *Hadnot*, 826 P.2d at 986; *Burger*, 964 A.2d at 380; *Swerdlick*, 721 A.2d at 859.

[14] *Steinbuch*, 518 F.3d at 591; *Karraker*, 411 F.3d at 838; *Willan*, 280 F.3d at 1162; *Phillips*, 312 F.3d at 371-72; *Veilleux*, 206 F.3d at 132-33; *Parry*, 236 F.3d at 313; *Roe*, 124 F.3d at 1236; *Cinel*, 15 F.3d at 1346; *Thomas*, 998 F.2d at 452; *Lee*, 948 F.2d at 1165; *S.B.*, 959 So. 2d at 91-92; *Rosen*, 825 So.2d at 739; *Ex parte* The Birmingham News, Inc., 778 So.2d at 818-19; *Johnston*, 706 So.2d at 703; *Ozer*, 940 P.2d at 379; *Bodah*, 663 N.W.2d at 551-58; *Swinton Creek Nursery*, 514 S.E.2d at 131-32; *Shattuck-Owen*, 16 P.3d at 558.

[15] *Campbell*, 26 Fed. App'x at 186; *Barker*, 610 A.2d at 1350; *Nazeri*, 860 S.W.2d at 303.

[16] *See, e.g.*, *G.D.*, 15 A.3d at 309-10; *Boring*, 362 Fed. App'x at 273; *Good*, 296 Fed. App'x at 676; *Showler*, 222 Fed. App'x at 764; *Raiser*, 211 Fed. App'x at 808-09; *Dasey*, 304 F.3d at 148; *Green*, 286 F.3d at 286; *Dickinson*, No. 98-1446, 1998 U.S. App'x LEXIS 32569, at *6-7; *Johnson*, 47 F.3d at 731-33; *Merlo*, 43 F.3d at 104; *Haynes*, 8 F.3d at 1232-35; *Reuber*, 925 F.2d at 719; *Puckett*, No. 89-6589, 1990 U.S. App. LEXIS 19761, at *6; *S.B.*, 959 So. 2d at 92; *Taus*, 151 P.3d at 1208-09; *Steele*, 61 P. 3d at 607; *Svaldi*, 106 P.3d at 553.

[17] *Baldwin*, 480 F.3d at 1308-09; *Zaffuto*, 308 F.3d at 491; *Pontbriand*, 699 A.2d at 864.

[18] *See, e.g.*, *G.D.*, 15 A.3d at 309-10; *Anderson*, 499 F.3d at 1235-37; *Bowley*, 404 F. 3d at 787-88; *Doe 2*, 331 F.3d at 417; *Hatch*, 311 F.3d at 83; *Veilleux*, 206 F.3d at 132-33, *Cinel*, 15 F.3d at 1346; *Thomas*, 998 F.2d at 452; *Haynes*, 8 F.3d at 1232-35; *Purnell*, No. 92-2053, 1992 U.S. App. LEXIS 24313, at *7-8; *Reuber*, 925 F.2d at 703; *Lee*, 948 F.2d at 1165; *Taus*, 151 P.3d at 1207-08; *Gates*, 101 P.3d at 562-63; *Cape Publ'ns, Inc.*, 549 So. 2d at 1379; *Macon Telegraph*, 436 S.E.2d at 679; *Ayash*, 822 N.E.2d at 682-84; *Mulgrew*, 574 N.E.2d at 393; *Gauthier*, 557 N.E.2d at 1376; *Loe*, 600 A.2d

at 1093; *Swerdlick*, 721 A.2d at 859; *Edward A. Sherman Pub'g. Co.*, 593 A.2d at 459; *Berkeley Publishers*, 496 S.E.2d at 637; *Star-Telegram, Inc.*, 915 S.W.2d at 473-74.

[19] 955 P.2d 469, 474 (Cal. 19

[20] *Id.*

[21] *Willan*, 280 F.3d at 1163; *Veilleux*, 206 F.3d at 104; *Howell*, 106 F.3d at 220; *Coplin*, 111 F.3d at 1404.

[22] *Cox Broad. Corp.*, 420 U.S. at 491; *Gates*, 101 P.3d at 562-63; *Cape Publ'ns, Inc.*, 549 So. 2d at 1378-79; *Uranga*, 67 P.3d at 34-36.

[23] *Doe 2*, 331 F.3d at 417-21; *Foncello*, 931 A.2d at 929; *Pontbriand*, 699 A.2d at 866; *Swinton Creek Nursery*, 514 S.E.2d at 131-32.

[24] *See, e.g.*, *Star-Telegram, Inc.*, 915 S.W.2d at 473.

[25] *Randolph*, 973 A. 2d at 711.

[26] *See, e.g.*, *Baldwin*, 480 F.3d at 1308-09; *Randolph*, 973 A. 2d at 711; *Young*, 572 So.2d at 382; *Swinton Creek Nursery*, 514 S.E.2d at 131.

[27] *S.B.*, 959 So. 2d at 92

[28] *Id.* at 90 (quoting *Rosen v. Montgomery Surgical Ctr.*, 825 So. 2d 735, 737 (Ala. 2001), quoting *Carter v. Innisfree Hotel, Inc.*, 661 So. 2d 1174, 1178 (Ala. 1995)).

[29] *Methodist Hosp.*, 690 N.E.2d at 686; *Swinton Creek Nursery*, 514 S.E.2d at 131-33; *Reid*, 961 P.2d 342.

[30] *Reid*, 961 P.2d at 333.

[31] *See, e.g.*, *Id.*; *Lake*, 582 N.W.2d at 235.

[32] *Lake*, 582 N.W.2d at 235.

[33] *Id.*

[34] *Id.*

[35] *Id.*

[36] *Uranga*, 67 P.3d at 33.

[37] *Shulman*, 955 P.2d at 479.

[38] *See, e.g.*, *Coplin*, 111 F.3d at 1404.

[39] *Doe 2*, 331 F.3d at 422; *Coplin*, 111 F.3d at 1405-06; *Haynes*, 8 F.3d at 1232; *Taus*, 151 P.3d at 1208-09; *Gates*, 101 P.3d at 562-63; *Shulman*, 955 P.2d at 486; *Ozer*, 940 P.2d at 378; *Macon Telegraph*, 6 S.E.2d at 657-58; *Uranga*, No. 27118, 2001 Ida. LEXIS 71, at *26-27; *Ayash*, 822 N.E.2d at 683; *Gauthier*, 557 N.E.2d at 1376; *Star-Telegram, Inc.*, 915 S.W.2d at 473-74.

[40] *Doe 2*, 331 F.3d at 422; *Coplin*, 111 F.3d at 1405-06; *Haynes*, 8 F.3d at 1232; *Taus*, 151 P.3d at 1208; *Shulman*, 955 P.2d at 479; *Ozer*, 940 P.2d at 378; *Uranga*, 67 P.3d at 32-3; *Ayash*, 822 N.E.2d at 683; *Star-Telegram, Inc.*, 915 S.W.2d at 473-84.

[41] *Bowley*, 404 F. 3d at 787-88.

[42] *Shulman*, 955 P.2d at 486. *Also see*, *Ozer*, 940 P.2d at 378 (citing Gilbert v. Medical Econs. Co., 665 F.2d 305, 308 (10th Cir. 1981) and Virgil v. Time,

Inc., 527 F.2d 1122, 1129 (9th Cir. 1975)); *Star-Telegram, Inc.*, 915 S.W.2d at 474.

[43] *See, e.g.*, *Macon Telegraph*, 6 S.E.2d at 657; *Star-Telegram, Inc.*, 915 S.W.2d at 474.

[44] *Macon Telegraph*, 6 S.E.2d at 657.

[45] *Id.* at 658 (quoting Pavesich v. New England Life Ins. Co., 50 S.E. 68, 74 (Ga. 1905)).

[46] *Star-Telegram, Inc.*, 915 S.W.2d at 472.

[47] *Id.* at 475.

[48] *Zaffuto*, 308 F.3d at 486-91; *Uranga*, No. 27118, 2001 Ida. LEXIS 71, at *26-27.

[49] *See, e.g., Uranga*, 2001 Ida. LEXIS at *26-27.

[50] *Zaffuto*, 308 F.3d at 486-491.

[51] *Zaffuto*, 308 F.3d at 491 (affirming the award of $2 in compensatory damages and remanding for a new trial on punitive damages).

[52] *See supra* notes 10 to 35 and accompanying text.

[53] *See supra* notes 36 to 50 and accompanying text.

[54] *Zaffuto*, 308 F.3d at 491; *Star-Telegram, Inc.*, 915 S.W.2d at 475.

[55] *Dickerson*, 34 P.3d at 997; *Lake*, 582 N.W.2d at 236; *Remsburg*, 816 A.2d at 1009-10; *Staruski*, 581 A.2d at 268-69.

[56] Smolla, *supra* note 8, at 289.

[57] *King*, 485 F.3d at 593; *Brown*, 201 F.3d at 662; *Bowling*, No. 91-5920, 1992 U.S. App. LEXIS 18505, at *2; *Town & Country Properties, Inc.*, 457 S.E.2d at 365.

[58] *Rivell*, 520 F.3d at 1310-11; *Solano*, 292 F.3d at 1080-82; *Am. Guarantee & Life Ins.*, 273 F.3d at 605; *Newcombe*, 157 F.3d at 693-94; *Joe Dickerson & Assoc.*; *Lake*, 582 N.W.2d at 231; *Staruski*, 581 A.2d at 273-74.

[59] *Solano*, 292 F.3d at 1080-82.

[60] *See, e.g.*, *Spiegel*, 604 F.3d at 72; *Showler*, 222 Fed. App'x at 759; *Zarilli*, 231 Fed. App'x at 123-25; *Meadows*, 492 F.3d at 637; *Am. Guar. & Liability Ins. Co.*, 273 F.3d at 608; *Newcombe*, 157 F.3d at 693; *Matthews*, 15 F.3d at 436; *Schifano*, 624 So. 2d at 179; *Baker*, 585 So. 2d at 807; *Dickerson & Assoc. v. Dittmar*, 34 P.3d at 997; *Felsher*, 755 N.E.2d at 599; *Tannenbaum*, 604 N.E.2d at 16; *Simpson*, 669 A.2d at 1326; *Lake*, 582 N.W.2d at 236; *Howell*, 612 N.E.2d at 701; *Beverley*, 587 N.E.2d at 279; *Leddy*, 843 A.2d at 490-91; *Sloan*, 586 S.E.2d at 108; *Staruski*, 581 A.2d at 273; *Reid*, 961 P.2d at 335.

[61] *See, e.g.*, *Howell*, 612 N.E.2d at 703; *Finger*, 566 N.E.2d at 143-44; *Leddy*, 843 A.2d at 490-91.

[62] *Bowling*, No. 91-5920, 1992 U.S. App. LEXIS 18505, at *2.

[63] *Town & Country Properties, Inc.*, 457 S.E.2d at 365.

[64] *King*, 485 F.3d at 593.

[65] *Id.*; *Brown*, 201 F.3d at 662; *Bowling*, 1992 U.S. App. LEXIS at *2; *Beverley*, 587 N.E.2d at 279-80; *Town & Country Properties, Inc.*, 457 S.E.2d at 365.

[66] *See, e.g.*, *Messenger*, 727 N.E.2d at 552-54; *Howell*, 612 N.E.2d at 703; *Beverley*, 587 N.E.2d at 278-79; *Finger*, 566 N.E.2d at 144; *Leddy*, 843 A.2d at 490; *WJLA*, 564 S.E.2d at 387-88; *Town & Country Props., Inc.*, 457 S.E.2d at 361-62.

[67] 15 A.3d 300, 311-12 (N.J. 2011).

[68] *Groden*, 61 F.3d at 1051; *Dickerson & Assoc.*, 34 P.3d at 998; *Showler*, 222 Fed. App'x at 763-74; *Messenger*, 727 N.E.2d at 552-54; *Howell*, 612 N.E.2d at 704; *Finger*, 566 N.E.2d at 143; *Leddy*, 843 A.2d at 490-91.

[69] *Leddy*, 843 A.2d at 490-91.

[70] *Star-Telegram, Inc.*, 915 S.W.2d at 473-74.

[71] *See, e.g.*, *King*, 485 F.3d at 591-92; *Bowling*, 1992 U.S. App. LEXIS 18505, at * 12-13; *Felsher*, 755 N.E.2d at 600-01; *Miller*, 467 N.W.2d at 679-80; *Reid*, 961 P.2d at 342.

[72] *See, e.g.*, *Dickerson & Assoc.*, 34 P.3d at 1005 (Coates, concurrence); *Staruski*, 581 A.2d at 269.

[73] *Dickerson & Assoc.*, 34 P.3d at 999 (quoting Samuel D. Warren & Louis D. Brandeis, *The Right To Privacy*, 4 HARV. L. REV. 193, 200-01, 205, 207 (1890)).

[74] *Id.*

[75] *Showler*, 222 Fed. App'x at 763-74; *Reid*, 961 P.2d at 342.

[76] *Id.*

[77] *Reid*, at 212-13.

[78] *Id.* at 212.

[79] *See, e.g.*, *Schifano*, 624 So.2d at 179; *Miller*, 467 N.W.2d at 656; *Sloan*, 586 S.E.2d at 108; *Staruski*, 581 A.2d at 273.

[80] *Showler*, 222 Fed. App'x at 763-64; *Dickerson & Assoc.*, 34 P.3d at 1003-04; *Messenger*, 727 N.E.2d at 552-54; *Howell*, 612 N.E.2d at 703; *Beverley*, 587 N.E.2d at 278-79; *Finger*, 566 N.E.2d at 144; *Leddy*, 843 A.2d at 490; WJLA, 564 S.E.2d at 387-88; *Town & Country Props., Inc.*, 457 S.E.2d at 361-62.

[81] *Showler*, 222 Fed. App'x at 763-64; *Dickerson & Assoc.*, 34 P.3d at 1003-04; *Messenger*, 727 N.E.2d 553; *Howell*, 612 N.E.2d at 703; *Beverley*, 587 N.E.2d at 278-79; *Leddy*, 843 A.2d at 490-91; *WJLA*, 564 S.E.2d at 387-88.

[82] *Finger*, 566 N.E.2d at 144.

[83] *But see*, *Town & Country Props., Inc.*, 457 S.E.2d at 361-62.

[84] *Roe*, 638 So. 2d at 829-30.

[85] *Id.*

[86] *Id.* at 828.

[87] *Beverley*, 587 N.E.2d at 279-80; *Town & Country Props., Inc.*, 457 S.E.2d at 365.

---

[88] *See supra* notes 55-78, and accompanying text.

[89] *See supra* notes 66-60, and accompanying text.

[90] *King*, 485 F.3d at 591-92; *Zaffuto*, 308 F.3d at 486-91; *Bowling*, No. 91-5920, 1992 U.S. App. LEXIS 18505, at * 12-13; *Uranga*, No. 27118, 2001 Ida. LEXIS 71, at *26-27, *vacated and superseded on rehearing by* Uranga v. Federated Publ'ns, Inc. v. Idaho Statesman, 67 P.3d 29, 32-33 (Idaho 2003); *Felsher*, 755 N.E.2d at 600-01.

[91] *Florida Star*, 491 U.S. at 530.

[92] *See, e.g., supra* notes 12, 36-50, and accompanying text.

[93] *Florida Star*, 491 U.S. at 532. *See supra* notes 13-21, 61-67 and accompanying text.

[94] The privilege for matters of public or general interest first was recognized in the now famous 1890 article by Samuel Warren and Louis Brandeis. Samuel Warren & Louis Brandeis, *The Right to Privacy*, 4 HARV. L.REV. 193 (1890). The Supreme Court connected that privilege to a constitutional privilege in *Time, Inc.v. Hill.*, 385 U.S. 374, 388 (1967). Eight years later, the Court identified a narrower category of protection in *Cox Broadcasting* by stating that press freedom protected reporting on the prosecution of criminals and judicial proceedings, which were matters of public concern. Cox Broad. v. Cohn, 420 U.S. 469, 492 (1975). In 1989, the Court established another narrow category of privileged information for matters of public significance in *Florida Star*. 492 U.S. at 532.

[95] *See supra* notes 42-51, 79-87, and accompanying text.

[96] *Florida Star*, 491 U.S. at 532. *See supra* notes 13-21, 61-67, and accompanying text.

[97] *See, e.g.*, 491 U.S. 524, 530 (1989).

[98] *Zaffuto*, 308 F.3d at 491.

[99] *Id.*

[100] *Id.* at 491.

[101] *Zaffuto*, 308 F.3d at, 491.

[102] Ultimately, one state high court upheld an award of damages in a disclosure of private facts case. *Zaffuto*, 308 F.3d at 491. State high courts and federal circuit courts of appeals upheld awards of damages in four appropriation cases. *King*, 485 F.3d at 593; *Brown*, 201 F.3d at 662; *Bowling*, No. 91-5920, 1992 U.S. App. LEXIS 18505, at *2; *Town & Country Props., Inc.*, 457 S.E.2d at 362-64.

[103] 425 U.S. 748, 759-65 (1976).

[104] *See, e.g.*, C. Edwin Baker, *Scope of the First Amendment Freedom of Speech*, 25 UCLA L. REV. 964, 990-92 (1977); FREDERICK SCHAUER, FREE SPEECH PRINCIPLE 71 (1982).

[105] *See, generally*, Gerald J. Baldasty & Roger A. Simpson, *The Deceptive 'Right to Know': How Pessimism Rewrote the First Amendment*, 56 WASH. L. REV. 365 (1981); Thomas I. Emerson, *The First Amendment and the Right to Know*, 1976 WASH. U. L.Q. 1; James C. Goodale, *Legal Pitfalls in the*

Right to Know, 1976 WASH. U. L.Q. 29; Michael J. Hayes, *What Ever Happened to 'the Right to Know'?: Access to Government-Controlled Information Since Richmond Newspapers*, 73 VA. L. REV. 1111 (2007); William E. Lee, *The Supreme Court and the Right to Receive Expression*, 1987 SUP. CT. REV. 303; David M. Obrien, *The First Amendment and the Public's 'Right to Know'*, 7 HASTINGS CONST. L.Q. 579 (1979).

[106] *See, e.g.*, *Town & Country Props, Inc.*, 457 S.E.2d at 365 (Va. 1995).

[107] *See supra* note 61-64, 78, and accompanying text.

[108] *See, e.g.*, *Showler*, 222 Fed. App'x at 763-64; *Dickerson & Assoc.*, 34 P.3d at 1003-04; *Messenger*, 727 N.E.2d at 552-54; *Howell*, 612 N.E.2d at 703; *Finger*, 566 N.E.2d at 144; *Leddy*, 843 A.2d at 490; *WJLA*, 564 S.E.2d at 387-88.

[109] *See, e.g.*, *Beverley*, 587 N.E.2d at 278-79; *Town & Country Props., Inc.*, 457 S.E.2d at 361-62.

[110] The court wrote in *Ozer v. Borquez*, "A person acts with reckless disregard if, at the time of the publicity, the person knew or should have known that the fact or facts disclosed were private in nature." 940 P.2d 371, 379 (Colo. 1997) (en banc).

[111] *See supra* notes 18-22, 65-69, 80-87 and accompanying text.

[112] Thomas Scanlon, *A Theory of Freedom of Expression*, 1 PHIL. & PUB. AFF. 204, 214 (1972).

[113] *Id.* at 1013 (quoting JOHN STUART MILL, ON LIBERTY 13 (1956)).

[114] *Id.* at 214.

[115] *See, e.g.*, *King*, 485 F.3d at 593; *Roe*, 638 So. 2d at 829-30.

[116] *King*, 485 F.3d at 593; *Brown*, 201 F.3d at 662; *Bowling*, No. 91-5920, 1992 U.S. App. LEXIS 18505, at *2; *Beverley*, 587 N.E.2d at 278-79; *Town & Country Props., Inc.*, 457 S.E.2d at 362-64.

[117] *Ozer*, 940 P.2d at 379.

[118] *See, e.g.*, *King*, 485 F.3d at 593; *Brown*, 201 F.3d at 662; *Bowling*, 1992 U.S. App. LEXIS at *2; *Beverley*, 587 N.E.2d at 279-80; *Town & Country Properties, Inc.*, 457 S.E.2d at 365.

[119] See *supra* notes 20-22,

[120] *See supra* notes 25-29, 65-66, 74, and accompanying text.

[121] *See supra* notes 25-29, 65-66, 74, and accompanying text.

[122] *See, e.g.*, *King*, 485 F.3d at 591-92; *Zaffuto*, 308 F.3d at 486-91; *Bowling*, No. 91-5920, 1992 U.S. App. LEXIS 18505, at * 12-13; *Felsher*, 755 N.E.2d at 600-01.

[123] *See* Scanlon, *supra* note 112, at 214.

[124] *See, e.g.*, *Rivell*, 520 F.3d at 1310; *Methodist Hosp.*, 690 N.E.2d at 693

[125] *S.B.*, 959 So. 2d at 81; Lake, 582 NW 2d at 232-33.

[126] *See, e.g.*, *Alvarado*, 492 F.3d at 1218-19; *Ozer*, 940 P.2d at 374; *Uranga*, No. 27118, at *26-27 (2001 LEXIS) (Idaho June 21, 2001) (unpublished),

superseded by Uranga v. Federated Publ'ns, Inc. v. Idaho Statesman, 67 P.3d 29, 35 (Idaho 2003).

[127] *See, e.g.*, *Rivell,* 520 F.3d at 1310; *Methodist Hosp.*, 690 N.E.2d at 693.

[128] Amy Gajda, *Judging Journalism: The Turn Toward Privacy and Judicial Regulation of the Press*, 97 CALIF. L. REV. 1039, 1104 (2009).

[129] Florida Star v. B.J.F., 491 U.S. 524, 530 (1989); Cox Broad. v. Cohn, 420 U.S. 469, 492 (1975).

[130] *See supra* notes 43-46; 73 and accompanying text.

[131] *King*, 485 F.3d at 593; *Zaffuto*, 308 F.3d at 491; *Brown*, 201 F.3d at 662; *Bowling*, No. 91-5920, 1992 U.S. App. LEXIS 18505, at *2; *Beverley*, 587 N.E.2d at 278-79; *Town & Country Props., Inc.*, 457 S.E.2d at 362-64.

[132] New York Times Co. v. Sullivan, 376 U.S. 254 (1964).

[133] *Zaffuto*, 308 F.3d at 491.

[134] *Town & Country Props., Inc.*, 457 S.E.2d at 362-64.

[135] *See, e.g.*, *Roe*, 638 So. 2d at 829-30.

[136] *See, e.g.*, *Taus*, 151 P.3d at 1208; *Shulman*, 955 P.2d at 474; *Ozer*, 940 P.2d at 378; *Howell*, 612 N.E.2d at 703-05; *Finger*, 566 N.E.2d at 143; *Town & Country Props., Inc.*, 457 S.E.2d at 363-64.

[137] *See supra* notes 42-47, 64-67 and accompanying text.

[138] *See, e.g.*, *Lowe*, 497 F.3d at 251-52; *Doe 2*, 331 F.3d at 421; Willan v. Columbia County, 280 F.3d 1160, 1163 (7th Cir. 2002); *Howell*, 106 F.3d at 220; *Coplin*, 111 F.3d at 1404; *Messenger*, 727 N.E. at 552-54; *Howell*, 612 N.E.2d 703; *Beverley*, 587 N.E.2d at 278-79; *Leddy*, 843 A.2d at 490; *WJLA*, 564 S.E.2d at 387-88.

[139] *See, e.g.*, *Groden*, 61 F.3d at 1051; *Dickerson & Assoc.*, 34 P.3d at 998-1001; *Howell,* 612 N.E.2d at 703; *Finger*, 566 N.E.2d at 143.

[140] *Haw*, No. CV-OC-0205441D, 2003 WL 21015134, at *6.

[141] *See supra* notes 25-29, 64-65, 73, and accompanying text.

[142] *See supra* notes 25-29, 64-65, 73, and accompanying text.

[143] *See, e.g.*, *King*, 485 F.3d at 591-92; *Zaffuto*, 308 F.3d at 486-91; *Bowling*, No. 91-5920, 1992 U.S. App. LEXIS 18505, at * 12-13; *Felsher*, 755 N.E.2d at 600-01.

[144] *King*, 485 F.3d at 593; *Zaffuto*, 308 F.3d at 491; *Brown*, 201 F.3d at 662; *Bowling*, No. 91-5920, 1992 U.S. App. LEXIS 18505, at *2; *Town & Country Props., Inc.*, 457 S.E.2d at 362-64.

References

Adams, Elbridge L. "The Right of Privacy, And Its Relation to the Law of Libel." *American Law Review* 39 (1905).

Allen, Anita. *Privacy Law and Society*. St. Paul: Thomson/West Publishing (2007).

Anderson, David A. "First Amendment Limitations on Tort Law." *Brooklyn Law Review* 69 (2004).

Ashdown, Gerald G. "Media Reporting and Privacy Claims—Decline in Constitutional Protection for the Press." *Kentucky Law Journal* 66 (1978).

Baker, C. Edwin. "Autonomy and Informational Privacy, or Gossip: The Central Meaning of The First Amendment." *Social Philosophy and Policy* 21 (2004).

____. "Scope of the First Amendment Freedom of Speech." *UCLA Law Review* 25 (1977).

Baldasty, Gerald J., and Roger A. Simpson, "The Deceptive 'Right to Know': How Pessimism Rewrote the First Amendment." *Washington Law Review* 56 (1981).

Barron, Jerome A. "Access to the Press—A New First Amendment Right." *Harvard Law Review* 80 (1966).

BeVier, Lillian. "An Informed Public, an Informing Press: The Search for a Constitutional Principle." *California Law Review* 68 (1980).

Bezanson, Randall P. "Means and Ends and Food Lion: The Tension between Exemption and Independence in Newsgathering by the Press." *Emory Law Journal* 47 (1998).

____. "Political Agnosticism, Editorial Freedom, and Government Neutrality Toward the Press." *Iowa Law Review* 72 (1987).

____. "The New Free Press Guarantee." *Virginia Law Review* 63 (1977).

____. "The Right to Privacy Revisited: Privacy, News, and Social Change, 1890-1990." *California Law Review* 80 (1992).

Blasi, Vincent. "The Checking Value in First Amendment Theory." *American Bar Foundation Research Journal* (1977).

Bloustein, Edward J. "Privacy as an Aspect of Human Dignity: An Answer to Dean Prosser." *New York University Law Review* 39 (1964).

____. "Privacy, Tort Law, and the Constitution: Is Warren and Brandeis' Tort Petty and Unconstitutional as Well?" *Texas Law Review* 46 (1968).

____. "The First Amendment and Privacy: The Supreme Court Justice and the Philosopher." *Rutgers Law Review* 28 (1974).

Boggess, Thomas Phillip. "Cause of Action for an Infringement of the Right of Publicity." *Causes of Action Guide*. St. Paul: Thomson/West Publishing (2d ed. 2008).

Bollinger, Lee C. "Free Speech and Intellectual Values." *Yale Law Journal* 92 (1983).

Boone, Keith. "Privacy and Community." *Social Theory & Practice* 9 (1983).

Bork, Robert H. "Neutral Principles and Some First Amendment Problems." *Indiana Law Journal* 47 (1971).

Campbell, W. Joseph. *Yellow Journalism: Puncturing the Myths, Defining the Legacies*. Westport, CT: Praeger Publishers (2003).

Cate, Fred, H. *Privacy in the Information Age*. Washington, DC: Brookings Institution (1997).

Citron, Danielle Keats. "Mainstreaming Privacy Torts." *California Law Review* 98 (2010).

Cohen, Julie. "Examined Lives: Informational Privacy and the Subject as Object." *Stanford Law Review* 52 (2000).

Cohen, Morris L. and Kent C. Olson. *Legal Research in a Nutshell* (2003).

Dendy, Geof. "The Newsworthiness Defense to the Public Disclosure Tort." *Kentucky Law Journal* 85 (1997).

Easton, Eric B. "Public Importance: Balancing Proprietary Interests and the Right to Know." *Cardozo Arts and Entertainment* 21 (2003).

Edelman, Peter B. "Free Press v. Privacy: Haunted by the Ghost of Justice Black." *Texas Law Review* 68 (1989).

Emerson, Thomas I. "Colonial Intentions and the Current Realities of the First Amendment." *University of Pennsylvania Law Review* 125 (1977).

____. The *System of Freedom of Expression* New York, NY: Vintage Books (1971).

____. "The First Amendment and the Right to Know." *Washington University Law Quarterly* (1976).

____. "The Right of Privacy and Freedom of The Press." *Harvard Civil Rights-Civil Liberties Law Review* 14 (1979).

Amitai Etzioni, *The Limits of Privacy* New York, NY: Basic Books (1999).

Fried, Charles. "Privacy [A Moral Analysis]." In *Philosophical Dimensions of Privacy: An Anthology*, edited by Ferdinand David Schoeman. New York: Cambridge University Press, 1984.

Fuson, John H. "Has The Promise Of The Free Press Failed?" *University of Pennsylvania Law Review* 148 (1999).

Gajda, Amy. "Judging Journalism: The Turn Toward Privacy and Judicial Regulation of the Press." *California Law Review* 97 (2009).

____. "What If Samuel D. Warren Hadn't Married a Senator's Daughter?: Uncovering the Press Coverage that Led to "The Right To Privacy." *Michigan State Law Review* (2008).

Gavison, Ruth. "Too Early for a Requiem." *South Carolina Law Review* 43 (1992).

Gerety, Tom. "Redefining Privacy." *Harvard Civil Rights-Civil Liberties Law Review* 12 (1977).

Gewirtz, Paul. "Privacy and Speech." *Supreme Court Review* (2001).

Glassman, Benjamin C. "Making State Law in Federal Court." *Gonzaga Law Review* 41 (2006).

Goffman, Erving. *The Presentation of Self in Everyday Life*. Garden City, NY: Doubleday Anchor Books (1959).

Goodale, James C. "Legal Pitfalls in the Right to Know." *Washington University Law Quarterly* (1976).

Goodenough, Oliver R. "Go Fish: Evaluating the Restatement's Formulation of the Law of Publicity." *South Carolina Law Review* 47 (1996).

Gormley, Ken. "One Hundred Years of Privacy." *Wisconsin Law Review* (1992).

Gross, Hyman. "The Concept of Privacy." *New York University Law Review* 42 (1967).

Hayes, Michael J. "What Ever Happened to 'the Right to Know'?: Access to Government-Controlled Information Since *Richmond Newspapers*." *Virginia Law Review* 73 (2007).

Hill, Alfred. "Defamation and Privacy Under the First Amendment." *Columbia Law Review* 76 (1976).

Ingber, Stanley. "The Marketplace of Ideas: A Legitimizing Myth." *Duke Law Journal* (1984).

Jourard, Sidney M. "Some Psychological Aspects of Privacy." *Law and Contemporary Problems* 31 (1966).

Kahn, Jonathan. "Privacy as a Legal Principle of Identity Maintenance." *Seton Hall Law Review* 33 (2003).

Kalven, Harry. "The New York Times Case: A Note on "The Central Meaning of The First Amendment." *Supreme Court Review* (1964).

Kateb, George. *The Inner Ocean: Individualism and Democratic Culture*. Ithaca, NY: Cornell University Press, 1992.

Kilkenny, Ryan. "Why *Bartnicki v. Vopper* Disserves the Right of Privacy and the First Amendment." *Ohio State Law Journal* 64 (2003).

Kirtley, Jane. "Freedom of the Press: The Most Serious Threat Is . . . The Cloak of Privacy." *Columbia Journalism Review* 30 (1991).

Kramer, Irwin R. "The Birth of Privacy Law: A Century Since Warren and Brandeis." *Catholic University Law Review* 39 (1990).

____. "The Full-Court Press: Sacrificing Vital Privacy Interests on the Altar of First Amendment Rhetoric." *Cardozo Arts and Entertainment Law Journal* 8 (1990).

Joseph H. Kupfer, *Autonomy and Social Interaction*. Albany: SUNY Press, 1900.

Lee, William E. "The Supreme Court and the Right to Receive Expression." *Supreme Court Review* (1987).

Mclean, Deckle. "Lower Courts Point the Way on Press and Privacy Rights." *Communication and the Law* 22 (2000).

McClurg, Andrew. "Bringing Privacy Law out of the Closet: A Tort Theory of Liability for Intrusions in Public Places." *North Carolina Law Review* 73 (1995).

____. "Kiss and Tell: Protecting Intimate Relationship Privacy Through Implied Contracts of Confidentiality." *University of Cincinnati Law Review* 74 (2006).

Media Law Resource Center. *Media Privacy & Related Law: MLRC 50-state survey*. New York: Oxford University Press, 2010.

Meiklejohn, Alexander. *Free Speech and Its Relation to Self-Government*. New York: Harper and Brother Publishers, 1948.

____. Political Freedom: The Constitutional Powers of the People. New York: Harper, 1969.

____. "The First Amendment Is an Absolute." *Supreme Court Review*. (1961).

Mill, John Stuart. *On Liberty*, edited by David Bromwich & George Kateb. Yale University Press, 2003.

Milton, John. *Areopagatica: A Speech to the Parliament of England, for the Liberty of Unlicensed Printing*. Cambridge: Chadwyck-Healey. (1999).

Mudd, Jesse A. "Right to Privacy v. Freedom of Speech: A Review and Analysis of *Bartnicki v. Vopper*." *Brandeis Law Journal* 41 (2002).

Murphy, Richard S. "Property Rights in Personal Information: An Economic Defense of Privacy." *Georgetown Law Journal* 84 (1995).

Nimmer, Melville B. "The Right to Speak from Times to Time: First Amendment Theory Applied to Libel and Misapplied to Privacy." *California Law Review* 56 (1968).

Nizer, Louis F. "The Right of Privacy: A Half Century's Developments." *Michigan Law Review* 39 (1941).

O'Brien, David M. "Reassessing the First Amendment and the Public's Right to Know in Constitutional Adjudication." *Village Law Review* 26 (1980).

____. "The First Amendment and the Public's 'Right to Know,'" *Hastings Constitutional Law Quarterly* 7 (1979).

Parent, W.A. "A New Definition of Privacy for the Law." *Law and Philosophy* 2 (1983).

Parks, Wallace. "The Open Government Principle: Applying the Right to Know Under the Constitution." *George Washington Law Review* 26 (1957).

Pember, Don R. *Privacy and the Press: The Law, The Mass Media, and The First Amendment*. Seattle: University of Washington Press (1972).

Post, Robert C. "Rereading Warren and Brandeis." *Case Western Reserve Law Review* 41 (1990).

____. "The Social Foundations of Privacy: Community and Self in the Common Law Tort." *California Law Review* 77 (1989).

____. "Three Concepts of Privacy." *Georgetown Law Journal* 89 (2001).

Prosser, William L. "Privacy." *California Law Review* 48 (1960).

"Primer on Invasion of Privacy." *News Media and the Law* 31 (2007).

Rachels, James. "Why Privacy Is Important." *Philosophy and Public Affairs* 4 (1975).

Redish, Martin H. "The Value of Free Speech." *University of Pennsylvania Law Review* 130 (1981).

Reiman, Jefrey H. "Privacy, Intimacy, and Personhood." *Philosophy and Public Affairs* 6 (1976).

____. "Privacy, Intimacy, and Personhood." In *Philosophical Dimensions of Privacy: An Anthology*, edited by Ferdinand David Schoeman. New York: Cambridge University Press, 1984.

Richards, Neil M. "Intellectual Privacy." *Texas Law Review* 87 (2008).

Richards, Neil M. and Daniel J. Solove, "Privacy's Other Path: Recovering the Law of Confidentiality." *Georgetown Law Journal* 96 (2007).

Richards, Neil M. and Daniel J. Solove. "Prosser's Privacy Law: A Mixed Legacy." *California Law Review* 98 (2010).

Richards, Neil M. "The Puzzle of Brandeis, Privacy, and Speech." *Vanderbilt Law Review* 63 (2010).

Rolfs, Jacquelin. "*Florida Star v. B.J.F.*: The Beginning of the End for the Tort of Public Disclosure." *Wisconsin Law Review* (1990).

Rosen, Jeffrey. "The Purposes of Privacy: A Response." *Georgetown Law Journal* 89 (2001).

Rubenfeld, Jed. "The Right of Privacy." *Harvard Law Review* 102 (1989).

Sanford, Bruce W. *Libel and Privacy 2004 Supplement*. Englewood Cliffs, NJ: Prentice Hall Law & Busines, 1999.

Scanlon, Thomas. "A Theory of Freedom of Expression," *Philosophy and Public Affairs* 1 (1972).

Schauer, Frederick. *Free Speech Principle: A Philosophical Enquiry*. New York: Cambridge University Press, 1982.

____. "Reflections on the Value of Truth," *Case Western Reserve Law Review* 41 (1991).

Schudson, Michael. *Discovering the News: A Social History of American Newspapers*. New York: Basic Books, 1978.

Schwartz, Paul M. "Privacy and Democracy in Cyberspace," *Vanderbilt Law Review* 52 (1999).

Shapiro, Fred R. "The Most Cited Law Review Articles,"*California Law Review* 73 (1985).

Smolla, Rodney A. "Accounting for the Slow Growth of American Privacy Law," *Nova Law Review* 27 (2002).

____. "Privacy and the First Amendment Right to Gather News," *George Washington Law Review* 67 (1999).

____. *Free Speech in an Open Society*. New York: Knopf, 1992.

Daniel J. Solove, *Nothing to Hide: The False Tradeoff Between Privacy and Security*. New Haven, CT: Yale University Press, 2011.

____. "Conceptualizing Privacy," *California Law Review* 90 (2002).

____. "Taxonomy of Privacy," *University of Pennsylvania Law Review* 154 (2006).

____. *The Future of Reputation: Gossip, Rumor, and Privacy on the Internet.* New Haven, CT: Yale University Press, 2007.

____. "The Virtues of Knowing Less: Justifying Privacy Protections Against Disclosure," *Duke Law Journal* 53 (2003).

Stewart, Potter. "Or of the Press," *Hastings Law Journal* 26 (1975).

Strossen, Nadine. "Protecting Privacy and Free Speech in Cyberspace," *Georgetown Law Journal* 89 (2000).

Thomson, Judith Jarvis. "The Right to Privacy." In *Philosophical Dimensions of Privacy: An Anthology*, edited by Ferdinand David Schoeman. New York: Cambridge University Press, 1984.

Warren, Samuel D. and Louis D. Brandeis, "The Right to Privacy," *Harvard Law Review* 4 (1890).

Westin, Alan. *Privacy and Freedom*. New York: Atheneum, 1967.

White, G. Edward. "The First Amendment Comes of Age: Emergence of Free Speech in Twentieth-Century America," *Michigan Law Review* 95 (1997).

Zimmerman, Diane L. "False Light Invasion of Privacy: The Light That Failed," *New York University Law Review* 64 (1989).

____. "Information as Speech, Information as Goods: Some Thoughts on Marketplaces and the Bill of Rights," *William and Mary Law Review* 33 (1992).

____. "Requiem For a Heavyweight: Farewell to Warren and Brandeis's Privacy Tort," *Cornell Law Review* 68 (1982).

Index